HOMESCHOOLING

The Teen Years

CAFI COHEN

Linda Dobson, Series Editor

HOMESCHOOLING
The Teen Years

YOUR COMPLETE GUIDE TO

SUCCESSFULLY HOMESCHOOLING

THE 13- TO 18-YEAR-OLD

THREE RIVERS PRESS

NEW YORK

Originally published in the United States by Prima Publishing, Roseville, California, a member of the Crown Publishing Group, New York, in 2000.

Front cover photos from left to right: copyright © Steve Prezant–The Stock Market; copyright © Photo Disc; copyright © Franz Pfluegl–Tony Stone; copyright © PhotoDisc.

Library of Congress Cataloging-in-Publication Data
Cohen, Cafi.
    Homeschooling, the teen years : your complete guide to successfully homeschooling the 13- to 18-year-old / Cafi Cohen.
        p.   cm.
    Includes index.
    1. Home schooling—United States. 2. Teenagers—Education—United States.
I. Title.
LC40.C645   2000
371.04'2—dc21   00-026151
                                                                                              CIP

ISBN 978-0-7615-2093-1

14

Printed in the United States of America

First Edition

To my first homeschool mentors,
Cathy Claus and Carol Cynova

CONTENTS

ACKNOWLEDGMENTS

*F*OR THIS BOOK, more than one hundred homeschooling families worldwide took time from their busy lives to respond to my long, detailed survey about educating teenagers. Thank you so much. You have joined a grand tradition in which homeschoolers learn not from education professionals, but instead from those with street smarts—other experienced parents and teens. Through this book, your ideas and anecdotes inform, teach, and entertain, making homeschooling teenagers seem not only possible but also desirable.

Although I used pseudonyms for the one-hundred-four survey respondents, I used the real names of two homeschool graduates who contributed long essays for the last chapter. Thanks to Breana Mock and Ariel Simmons—and to their mothers Kristen Mock and Cerelle Woods Simmons—for writing so eloquently and speaking so frankly about the results of homeschooling.

My agent, Ling Lucas, believes in my quest to inform the public about the possibilities offered by homeschooling. I owe her my continuing gratitude for trusting her gut instincts and common sense and taking on unknown quantities—both me and the cutting edge subject matter.

Linda Dobson and Prima Publishing both deserve kudos for expanding the inspirational and practical how-to-do-it literature available to would-be home educators. Linda, thank you for putting up with my trivial questions and doubts that I would ever complete this project. Thanks to Prima editors, Jamie Miller, Ruth Younger, and Libby Larson, for the professional review and editing of my work.

For encouraging my writing about homeschooling, I owe debts to Mark and Helen Hegener of *Home Education Magazine*, Maureen

McCaffrey and Craig Young of *Homeschooling Today*, Patrick Farenga of *Growing Without Schooling*, and Mary Leppert of *The LINK*. Home educators of all stripes and colors need to support each other. Together we *can*.

My homeschool "family" in Arroyo Grande, California, the parents and students in Shining Light Homeschool Co-op, keep me up-to-date *and* humble, as do the contributors to the Web-based Kaleidoscapes homeschool bulletin boards. My interaction with these two groups assures that homeschoolers' latest day-to-day concerns seldom escape my notice.

My family—my two grown homeschoolers, Jeffrey and Tamara —as well as my parents, John and Dolores Fischer, and my second mom, Bernice Cohen, have cheered me on. My husband, Terrell Cohen, patiently reviewed all my first drafts and provided invaluable editorial assistance when the text was least intelligible. I love you all. This volume would not exist without your emotional, practical, and financial support.

Finally, thanks to God, who makes all things possible.

INTRODUCTION: THE HOMESCHOOLING LEARNING JOURNEY

WHEN WE BEGAN homeschooling our twelve-year-old son and eleven-year-old daughter in the 1980s, I located every book written on the subject. There weren't many—perhaps fewer than ten. Most focused on homeschooling early- and middle-years children. Those that included information on teens only recounted a few brief anecdotes—certainly not enough information to see my teens through grade 12.

The omission did not concern me. After all, we would never try to teach difficult subjects, create teen social outlets, find team sports, negotiate college admissions, and deal with other challenges that confront all parents homeschooling teens. Surely by the time our children reached high school age, they would return to school.

Of course, just the opposite happened. By grade 9, our son and daughter found themselves committed to many community activities and academically ahead of their former classmates. Each year we discussed returning to school, and every year they chose to continue learning at home. Eventually, we homeschooled both children through high school, and they were admitted to their first-choice colleges. Our only regret was not beginning sooner.

At conferences around the nation and world, I have seen the number of families homeschooling teenagers swelling from a trickle to a flood. With today's growing concerns about safety, negative socialization, political correctness, and low academic standards, more and more parents are turning to home education. Technology also fuels growth. Unlike ten years ago, self-instructional computer software, video curricula, and the Internet now make homeschooling teenagers easier than you might think. Increasing cooperation with public and private schools encourages additional families to consider learning at home.

Many new homeschooling parents find statistics convincing. Numerous studies and a mountain of anecdotal evidence point to the academic superiority of home education—even through high school. Typically, homeschoolers average 20 percent higher on standardized tests than their schooled counterparts. Not surprisingly, every year homeschool graduates win National Merit Scholarships. Many are admitted to selective colleges like Stanford and Harvard, often at higher rates than graduates of public schools. Additional studies show homeschoolers thriving socially. Published accounts reveal that our two children—heavily involved in community activities like volunteering, youth groups, and sports—had a typical teenage homeschooling experience.

Embarking on home education no longer involves reinventing the wheel before starting your journey. Of course, you will need to think and prepare. The more you research, the more you will learn about the wide spectrum of approaches. At first, some parents are dismayed to learn that there is no One Right Way to educate. Instead, parents who have traveled this road tell us that success comes from learning about options and choosing the best way to homeschool from among unlimited possibilities.

With real-life stories from dozens of families, this volume reveals the rewards as well as the challenges of working with teenagers. We gleaned anecdotes and comments from the answers to 104 lengthy questionnaires from homeschooling parents worldwide and thirty-three shorter surveys from homeschooled teenagers. I located the volunteer survey respondents by posting messages on a wide range of Internet homeschooling bulletin boards and mailing lists.

As you will read in the first chapter, survey-respondent parents run the gamut from high school dropouts to those with multiple graduate degrees, from the working poor to the wealthy. These families homeschool for different reasons and use varied methods and resources. Some are heavily involved in causes within the homeschooling community; others focus primarily on their families. They share two traits: the desire to provide the best education for their children and the willingness to support that goal with their time.

Part One of this book, Preparing for Your Family's Learning Journey, introduces you to our survey respondents in more detail and demonstrates the many ways families homeschool their teenagers. Just as in the two earlier volumes in this series, you will read about movement along the homeschooling continuum in eight areas: motivation, financial expenditures, approach, assessment, technology utilized, physical accommodations, parental involvement, and outside assistance. Throughout the book, we expand on the survey results with comments and stories from the survey respondents.

Part One goes on to discuss learning assets of the teen years. These include facilitating self-directed learning, initiative, networking skills, independence, and values education. Here you will find a list of reasons to homeschool older children (great to show those doubting relatives!). To get you ready for homeschooling, we include sections on fears and doubts, record keeping, and legal issues. At the conclusion of Part One, we feature a beginner's checklist to help you either evaluate your current efforts or get ready to homeschool for the first time.

Part Two, A World of Resources, is the nitty-gritty of the book, the first place to look for answers to the questions, "What do we do tomorrow?" and "How can we accomplish it?" We cover writing, literature, math, science, history, geography, and other subjects essential to a well-rounded education. Our survey respondents provide ideas and insights to show you how to make seemingly daunting tasks easy and inexpensive. In addition, we address topics of special concern to teens, like driver's education. We conclude this part with discussions of special situations, such as homeschooling on a shoestring, single-parent home education, and approaches for both academically advanced teens and learning disabled and "below grade level" students.

Part Three, Keeping the Learning Journey Fun and Successful, helps you personalize this information and apply it to your family. We describe enticing home learning environments and include a revealing list of our survey respondents' top ten island resources—items they consider essential to their efforts. We relate how technology—computers and television—can enhance your journey. Our survey respondents, experienced home educators, tell us how they get the most out of their top three destinations: support groups, the library, and the community. In addition, they report on practical matters, such as accommodating younger learners and maintaining a sane, organized household.

This book is not just for full-time home educators. We also offer suggestions for part-time homeschooling and afterschooling. Home educators have discovered a world of helpful resources and approaches to help you remediate and enrich your schooled teenager's education, many of which we detail here.

Finally, we conclude with information for the end of the journey: graduating your homeschooler and moving on to careers, college, and other opportunities. The last chapter contains two outstanding college application essays written by teenage homeschoolers, accompanied by interviews with their parents. Several of our survey respondents, home educators looking back on their experiences, provide valuable advice to those beginning the journey.

Some home educators say, "Homeschooling is not for everyone, but it is the best approach for our family." While learning at home may not be for everyone, every parent, every teacher, and everyone interested in innovative approaches to learning with teenagers will find here helpful information drawn from the real experts—homeschooling parents worldwide. Both descriptive and prescriptive, this book offers ideas and suggestions from a wide range of perspectives.

Interested? Intrigued? By all means, learn more. Read here about the ins and outs of family learning contrasted with institutional education. Read how schooling choices affect lifestyles as well as educational outcomes. Learn how homeschooling benefits not only your children, but also you, the parent. Read about challenges and defeats and triumphs. Learn about diversity and the many roads to success. I firmly believe that anyone who wants to homeschool can find a way to succeed.

May the following chapters help prepare you for the trip of a lifetime.

HOMESCHOOLING

The Teen Years

Part One

PREPARING FOR YOUR FAMILY'S LEARNING JOURNEY

1

HOMESCHOOLING AND
TODAY'S FAMILY

In This Chapter

✦ Where are they going?

✦ The amazing homeschool continuum

✦ It doesn't matter where you begin, just begin!

✦ Simple starting points

✦ Resources

S NAPSHOTS OF HOMESCHOOLED teenagers flood my mind. Kendra, fifteen, reads Shakespeare for fun and operates a cake-decorating business. Maria, sixteen, uses self-instructional materials and meets weekly with a teacher from her public high school independent-study program. Jason, seventeen, builds a single-engine airplane with his father and takes creative writing at a local community college. Luke, fourteen, learns algebra and biology through an online high school homeschooling program.

All these scenes are possible, indeed common, because of a quiet revolution that has taken place in the last twenty years. In 1980, with fewer than 10,000 home educators nationwide, the word "home-school" drew blank stares at best. At worst, it elicited the wrong assumption—that you were a backwoods hippie or religious fanatic determined to shelter your child from the world. Twenty years ago, home education was illegal in many states.

Ten years later, by 1990, we had come a long way. Home education had been legalized in some form in all fifty states, and there were 200,000 to 400,000 homeschooled children nationwide. Even with the increased numbers, relatively few homeschooling families—perhaps less than 10 percent—educated teenagers at home. Many parents, concerned about teaching high school subjects or awarding unaccredited diplomas, gave up after grade 8.

> In a typical suburban neighborhood, more likely than not, you will find other homeschoolers living within a block or two.

Another ten years later, in the year 2000, the growth of home education continues, and families homeschooling teens are just as commonplace as families homeschooling first-graders. Current estimates of the number of homeschoolers in the United States range from one to three million. In a typical suburban neighborhood, more likely than not, you will find other homeschoolers living within a block or two.

Families considering home education for their teenagers in the year 2000 have new concerns directly related to our national social ills. Many parents worry about their children's safety. Events like the Columbine High School tragedy and shootings at other schools engender visceral fear. Parents also know that drugs and peer group pressure to engage in risky sexual behavior threaten their teenagers. For safety reasons alone, many families now see homeschooling as a legitimate—and necessary—educational alternative.

What else has changed? In the last twenty years, our access to information and educational resources has exploded. Just as television brought the world into our living rooms, the Internet now allows us to interact with that world without leaving home. Via their keyboards and computer monitors, students now research and communicate with people all over the globe—including instructors and other students. Whereas ten years ago fewer than ten independent-study high schools with multi-state enrollment were in operation, now more than one hundred exist, some of which operate completely online.

A year ago someone asked what surprised me most about homeschooling during our first year, more than ten years ago. Several things came to mind. First, homeschooling is not like a math problem with one right answer. The "Perfect Curriculum" has not been written. Successful home schools are messy, experimental enterprises—miniature learning laboratories, where families try various approaches, keep what works, and discard what does not.

Second, homeschooling is more than an educational choice—homeschooling is a lifestyle, positively impacting all family activities and relationships. Homeschooled teens have more free hours each day than their conventionally schooled peers. As a result, they spend more time with all members of the family, and this increased family connection builds strong relationships. My two homeschooled children became each other's best friend and remain so to this day, even though as adults they live in different states.

Third, homeschooling is a journey. Like any journey to an unknown place, travelers see both the expected and the unexpected. Amazingly, your homeschooled teenagers will try things you never considered and will even teach themselves. At other times, you will all take a detour while your teens sit outside and watch the clouds roll by for hours or days or weeks. You will cover some subjects well, others poorly. You will have fun, and you will be bored. Like democracy, homeschooling is not perfect. Nevertheless, many families choose home education because it offers the best mode of transportation for their destination.

WHERE ARE THEY GOING?

AS YOU WILL see when we explain the amazing homeschool continuum, each family defines the destination, the goals of homeschooling, differently.

Some families homeschool primarily for academic excellence. They challenge their teenagers with demanding classical curriculum, including Latin and Greek, or with advanced subjects such as calculus and physics. These families talk about several specific goals like a well-rounded, in-depth education, high SAT and ACT test scores, and winning substantial scholarships to competitive colleges.

Many families homeschool for religious and philosophical reasons. Some integrate Christian teaching into every aspect of daily life. In contrast, adherents of other faiths, members of minority groups, and secular humanists find public schools too narrowly focused on the Judeo-Christian tradition and Western civilization in general. They embrace home education so their children can absorb their beliefs and culture in a nonthreatening environment.

Some parents emphasize family time and relationships over institutional priorities. They seek relaxed lives for themselves and their teenagers. These families will often tell you that the process will eventually define the destination.

For a few families, home education solves a scheduling problem. Their teenager plays violin like Isaac Stern or golf like Tiger Woods. These teens know exactly where they are going, and their families homeschool to provide practice time, sometimes six to eight hours each day. Some would say they homeschool backwards, fitting education around dance or piano or gymnastics.

THE AMAZING HOMESCHOOL CONTINUUM OR WHY THERE ARE 1,000,001 WAYS TO HOMESCHOOL

IMAGINE A WORLD with no state-mandated curriculum. Imagine that you can change your mind instantly about what to learn and how to learn it. Imagine freedom.

If I were to query one hundred families that homeschool teenagers about how they educate their children, I would hear one hundred versions of How to Homeschool. Some families prefer the structure afforded by curriculum, textbooks, tests, and grades. Others give teens complete freedom to explore interests—from art and drama and music to auto mechanics and gardening and woodworking. Still others walk a middle line between traditional methods and student-directed learning.

> If I were to query one hundred families that homeschool teenagers about how they educate their children, I would hear one hundred versions of How to Homeschool.

With experience, many families change how they homeschool. We certainly did. Like many, we began with textbooks and tests and grades. After several years, though, our homeschool resembled a summer camp more than a classroom. We learned how to cover typical school subjects with self-selected reading, hands-on projects, work in the community, and recreational activities like movies and travel. As we learned about resources and observed our children, we moved along a continuum. We changed until we had a homeschool that fit us.

To illustrate this continuum of homeschooling practice, we conducted an e-mail survey and asked home educators across the nation about eight homeschooling variables:

- ✦ Motivation
- ✦ Financial expenditures
- ✦ Approach
- ✦ Assessment
- ✦ Use of technology
- ✦ Physical space in the home

✦   Parental involvement

✦   Outside assistance

We asked each respondent to assess (on a scale of 0 to 100) where they are now and where they were when they began—whether that was last month or many years ago. While not a scientifically constructed study, the data collected creates a fascinating cross-section of homeschooling today.

Meet the Families

A total of 104—101 mothers, two fathers, and one grown sister who homeschools her teenage brother—responded to our e-mail survey. They homeschool in Alabama, Alaska, Arizona, Arkansas, California, Colorado, Delaware, Florida, Georgia, Hawaii, Iowa, Idaho, Illinois, Indiana, Kentucky, Oklahoma, Oregon, Ohio, New Jersey, Maine, Maryland, Massachusetts, Michigan, Minnesota, Montana, Nevada, New York, Pennsylvania, Tennessee, Texas, Virginia, Washington, West Virginia, and Wyoming. Respondents also wrote from five foreign countries—Australia, Canada, Japan, New Zealand, and the United Kingdom.

These families have homeschooled from one to seventeen years. Twenty-one of the 104 families (20 percent) began within the last three years. Fifty-eight families (56 percent) have four to ten years of homeschooling experience. Twenty-five families (24 percent) qualify as old-timers—they began homeschooling before 1990 and have educated their children at home for more than ten years.

The respondents' families average 2.6 children per family, ranging from one child to seven children in each household. Family size is distributed as follows:

Number of children	Number of families
1	7
2	41
3	28
4	16
5	6
6	5
7	1

Family composition varies also. Of the 104 families, a majority (67 percent) are homeschooling teens and early- and middle-years children. Twenty-two percent are homeschooling teens only. Six percent have teens and adult children. And 2 percent have all three—younger, teen, and adult children. Three of the families had reached the end of their journey: All their children are grown.

What do our families see when they look out the window? Thirty-nine families (37 percent) live in suburbs, and 35 (34 percent) describe their location as rural. Others reside in small towns (15 percent) and cities (13 percent). Two families call a military base home, and one family lives on a large cattle ranch.

When asked to describe in one to three words their homeschooling approach, a majority of the families (55 percent) identify themselves as "eclectic," "mixed," or "multiple styles." A smaller number (23 percent) call themselves "traditional" or "curriculum-centered." The remainder (22 percent) fall into the "relaxed," "child-led," and "unschooling" categories.

Of our 104 respondents, four families omitted the continuum part of the questionnaire. Three other families show almost no movement on the continuum, indicating less than a 10 percent change in any variable since they began. Two of these families have homeschooled for five years, using traditional, curriculum-based methods. The third family, homeschooling for thirteen years, identifies themselves as unschoolers.

The remaining families, 97 out of 104, have altered their home-schooling significantly in one or more categories since beginning. We defined significant as a change of 30 points or more out of 100.

Motivation Continuum

0	100

| *Public school problems* | *Matter of principle—philosophical, religious, political, and so on* |

A majority of the families surveyed (65 percent) report minimal or no change in their reasons for homeschooling. The remainder (19 percent) say that they have moved to the right, putting more emphasis on philosophical reasons for homeschooling. At the same time, 16 percent report movement to the left, citing public school problems as an increasingly important reason to homeschool.

Those who moved to the right began homeschooling because of school problems. Yet they continue homeschooling for philosophical, political, or religious reasons. Yolanda in Reno, Nevada, says, "We began homeschooling because of problems at school. My son feared going to school so much that we finally brought him home on the advice of our family doctor. . . . After a few months, we had our happy, healthy son back, and he made more academic progress than he had in two years! Today we homeschool because it suits our son and our educational philosophy."

Those respondents who moved to the left on this continuum cite public school problems, rather than philosophical conviction, as their motivation for continuing to homeschool. Many of these parents of teenagers mention "dumbed-down" academics, drugs, and violence.

How are our respondents distributed along the motivation continuum today? A majority (59 percent) lie in the middle, assigning numbers between 25 and 75. The next largest group, 25 percent, report numbers from 76 to 100 on this continuum, indicating strong philosophical reasons as the primary impetus for home-schooling. The smallest group, 16 percent, assigned numbers from 0 to 25, saying the public school problems override philosophical considerations.

Financial Expenditures Continuum

0   100

Spend over $1,500 per year   *Spend nothing*

Only three of our respondent families report spending more money to homeschool now compared to when they started. Ten times as many respondents, thirty families, report significantly decreasing expenditures during their journey. With experience, many homeschooling families learn to shop wisely and take advantage of free community resources.

Some experienced home educators point out that you can homeschool successfully with nothing more than pencil, paper, and access to a good library. A majority of our survey respondents (56 percent) understand that statement. Reporting on their current expenses, they place themselves in the upper quarter of this continuum, spending less than $375 per year.

> With experience, many homeschooling families learn to shop wisely and take advantage of free community resources.

At the same time, 38 percent of those answering the survey put their expenses in the middle of the continuum, spending between $375 and $1,125 per year. A small minority (6 percent) report expenses of $1,125 per year or more.

Expenditures are tricky to evaluate, though. Dinah in Burlington, Massachusetts, writes, "If expenses like singing classes, theater, circus, art classes, and ice skating are included, we're off the left end of the scale. But are those homeschooling expenses? I see a lot of schooled children in most of these classes, and if my son and daughter attended school, they would still want to do those things."

Educational Approach Continuum

0   100

Structured   *Unstructured*

HOW WE HOMESCHOOL

Terminology used to describe homeschooling methods may sound foreign and is not always found in dictionaries. While definitions vary depending on the source, the following are basic descriptions of the most common homeschooling approaches.

✦ Traditional Approach:

Synonyms are school-at-home, curriculum-based homeschooling, and structured learning. Families adopting this approach use textbooks, grades, and schedules, much as schools do. Educational philosophy is, "I teach, you learn." A popular subset of traditional-approach home education is the classical approach, using a curriculum that concentrates on the basic subjects and also includes Greek and Latin and higher order thinking skills.

✦ Unit Studies:

Also called integrated or thematic studies. Pick a topic, and study it in depth. Eventually you will cover all school subjects. As an example, a unit study of birds

A majority of the homeschooling families who answered our survey (53 percent) have not significantly changed their approach to homeschooling over the years. Most of these respondents classify themselves as eclectic. These families mix traditional, unit study, and unschooling approaches.

Comparing their beginning and current homeschooling approaches, just over a third of our survey respondents (35 percent) report moving 30 points or more toward the right, from structured to unstructured. It is interesting that so many families homeschooling teens move in the direction of less structure even with college looming on the horizon.

might include reading about famous ornithologists (history, language arts), studying bird anatomy and life cycles (science), diagramming migration pathways (math, geography), and building bird houses (math, art). Educational philosophy: "Knowledge is not artificially segmented into school subjects. Students learn best from hands-on projects and real-world activities."

✦ Unschooling:

Also called interest-initiated, child-led, or natural learning. Unschooling families trust the student to determine what he needs to learn, when he needs to learn it. Parents facilitate, helping children pursue their interests and goals. Educational philosophy is, "Students learn best when their interests direct the learning." Unschooling families see all of life as school and view the world as their classroom.

✦ Eclectic Approach:

Eclectic homeschoolers use all of the above—traditional materials, unit studies, and unschooling—and anything else that encourages enthusiasm for learning. Educational philosophy? "There is no one way that all children learn best all the time. Use anything that encourages enthusiasm for learning."

A much smaller group, about 12 percent, are now more structured than when they began. One mother writes, "While we still give our son plenty of time to pursue his interests, we also think it's important that he learn to play the academic game—read textbooks, answer essay questions, and so on."

Overall, where are our respondents today on the educational approach spectrum? Almost one-third (29 percent) describe their homeschooling as unstructured, assigning a value of 75 or greater. Less than one in five (17 percent) consider themselves primarily structured, reporting a continuum value of 25 or less. The majority (54 percent) fall between the two extremes.

Assessment Continuum

0   100

Regular testing   *Don't worry about it*

Homeschooling laws vary. Some states require testing every year, some every other year. Some states require no testing at all. And, although some state statutes mandate standardized testing, others accept alternative assessments, like portfolio reviews.

According to our survey, 27 percent of our respondents have moved thirty or more points to the right on this continuum. These parents do not worry about testing nearly as much as they did initially. A much smaller group (about 5 percent) engages more frequently in regular testing now than they did in their first days homeschooling.

Currently, forty-seven families (47 percent) selected a number between 75 and 100, indicating a lack of concern with formal testing and assessment. A smaller group (36 percent) put themselves somewhere in the middle, between 25 and 75 on the continuum. And less than one in five selected a number between 0 and 25, indicating that regular testing is an important part of their homeschooling.

Several respondents say they test only to fulfill legal obligations, adding that the test results do not tell them anything new. Candy in

Oregon writes, "We assess by simply listening and talking with our son. How he sees the world around him, the connections he makes, his increasing ability to figure things out, all show how much he is learning. I don't really put a lot of stock in his annual test. I do have to admit I get a real charge when I see his test score go up each year, something that never happened when he was in public school."

Technology Utilized Continuum

0   100

None   *We do all our learning
on the computer*

Here we asked respondents about learning with and without the computer and how that had changed over time. A striking 43 percent of those surveyed say the amount their children learned with the computer had significantly increased since they began homeschooling. Only 4 percent report decreased computer use during their journey.

When assessing how much their teenagers used a computer for learning today, 73 percent report numbers between 25 and 75 on the continuum. The computer plays a significant part in learning for almost three-fourths of our survey respondents. Fifteen percent of those surveyed use numbers between 1 and 25, reflecting minimal computer use. And 7 percent say that their teens use the computer for most of their learning, assigning a number between 75 and 100. While all these families have a computer and Internet access, it appears that a large majority spend time learning with a variety activities, as opposed to sitting in front of the computer all day.

Do you need to set up a schoolroom in your home to succeed with home education? Not if you listen to the voice of experience. When it comes to creating workspaces in homes specifically for schooling, 25 percent of our families report making fewer physical accommodations for homeschooling now than when they began.

Physical Space Continuum

0   100

A specific schoolroom setup   *No special accommodations for schoolwork*

Talking about their current situation, 60 percent of our survey respondents assigned a number between 75 and 100 to this variable. More than half of our survey respondents make little or no special physical accommodation for home education.

Another 20 percent of our respondents describe their situation with a number between 25 and 75, indicating usually that their teenager had a desk, either in his room or in another part of the home. Marilyn in Sanger, California, says, "He has a desk, but he much prefers to work where the action is—the kitchen table."

Fewer than one in six respondents (15 percent) report numbers less than 25 on the physical space continuum. Special accommodations for home education in these homes ranged from desks and computer workspaces to full-fledged classrooms, which teens share with their siblings.

Parental Involvement Continuum

0   100

Mom is involved with homeschooling   *Dad is involved with homeschooling*

Experts have told us for years that parental involvement is directly related to educational success. Although no one can deny that homeschooling parents are closely involved with their children, it is interesting to see who does what.

Of the eight variables, our respondents report the least amount of change in their homeschooling when it came to parental involvement. Only eleven families report significant movement, more than 30 points, since they began homeschooling. Nine of these families moved toward more involvement from fathers. Two moved toward increased time with mothers.

So, where do our families lie on the continuum today? Fifty-eight percent place themselves on the left side of the line, using numbers from 1 to 25 to indicate that Mom is the parent most directly involved in home education. Encouragingly, 31 percent of the families report numbers from 25 to 75 for this variable—substantial, near-equal involvement by both parents. A few families (7 percent) report that the father is the principal homeschooling parent.

Outside Assistance Continuum

0   100

No help from others   *All learning occurs*
                                                              with outside
                                                                 assistance

Families homeschooling teenagers have a world of outside assistance available—from private tutors to independent-study schools to adult mentors in their communities. Eighteen of our respondents (18 percent) indicated a substantial increase in outside help. Six families (6 percent), report using less outside assistance now than when they began.

Today, 60 percent of those answering our surveys assign a number from 1 to 25 for this category. They say they get by with little or no outside assistance. Another 29 percent, almost one-third, place themselves between 25 and 75, indicating a balance of home sources and outside assistance to homeschool. Roughly 10 percent report a value of 75 to 100 for this variable, indicating the majority of learning occurs with outside assistance.

> Families homeschooling teenagers have a world of outside assistance available—from private tutors to independent-study schools to adult mentors in their communities.

According to Susan in Maryland, "It's so hard to put a number value on [outside assistance] since my son's learning is so informal. I consider him to be in school twenty-four hours a day, with the opportunity to learn any given moment from any person or thing. No one is hired to teach him, but that doesn't mean he doesn't learn from others." Although most homeschooling families currently do not hire individuals to teach their teenagers, many do take advantage of informal learning opportunities in their communities.

Continuum Conclusions

Homeschooling is idiosyncratic and infinitely customizable. Home educators succeed with different resources, different schedules, different approaches, and different goals. And they succeed whether they spend $1,000 each year or near nothing. That is why we can talk about a continuum of practice.

You may find yourself in the majority with respect to one continuum variable, in the minority on another. The point is not to join the majority. Instead, understand that for any variable, homeschooling works across the spectrum. That means you can succeed no matter where you begin on the continuum. In addition, realize that you, like most families, can and probably will change how you homeschool during your journey.

For our continuum variables, respondents report the greatest change in three areas—expenditures, testing, and computer use.

Most of those surveyed say they spend less with each succeeding year. They adjust as they realize that they can live without every glitzy new product at the statewide home education conference. Similarly, many respondents relaxed about testing, some moving away from all testing. Many report that one-on-one discussion usually provides all the feedback parents need.

Most noticeable was the move toward computer use for learning. The computer was the tool of the '90s and certainly will be the cornerstone of twenty-first century technology. Homeschoolers are lucky to be able to provide almost unlimited information access for their teenagers.

Overall, our survey results show individual home educators changing as they proceed on their journey. We see travelers increasing computer use and spending less money on instructional resources as their children move into their teens. A majority of families also move away from conventional school trappings, including testing, special school spaces, and traditional curriculum.

In addition to surveying homeschooling parents, we also received responses to a much shorter teen survey for homeschoolers aged thirteen to nineteen. Look for their comments throughout the remaining chapters.

IT DOESN'T MATTER WHERE YOU BEGIN, JUST BEGIN!

HOMESCHOOLING IS LIKE entering a lifeboat from a large cruise ship. The cruise ship—like some schools—is pleasant enough, but unfortunately travels in circles, seeming to go nowhere. Some passengers learn to handle or even enjoy the prescribed activities. Others openly rebel by acting out or spacing out.

One day, knowing there must be a better way, you and your family board a lifeboat to chart your own course. Your children look to you for direction, and you smile back, a little scared and definitely lost. Uncertain of your destination, you look around the great big ocean from your tiny lifeboat, wave good-bye to the cruise ship, and start rowing.

That is how most families begin homeschooling. They dip their oars into the water and shove off, using the equipment available— their experience, learning materials in their homes, and free community resources. Eventually, they reach an island where they find other homeschooling families and learn about a world of resources and opportunities. Their children begin to flourish, and they wonder why they ever had any doubts about leaving the ship.

You can begin with a text-based curriculum that closely resembles the curriculum offered at traditional schools. You can start with your teenager's existing interests and activities and build from there. Or you can just live life and see what learning opportunities appear. These are all valid beginnings. Just start. You will make mistakes. No big deal. The only people who don't make mistakes are those who don't do anything.

INTERIM HOMESCHOOLING

It is November, and you have just pulled your teenager out of school. You need ideas for tomorrow. While you read this book, legalize your teen's homeschooling, and sort through resources, here are some educational activities for the first month.

+ Visit the library frequently. Encourage your teen to select his own books and insist on daily reading (language arts). Get books on tape for reluctant readers.
+ Assign daily household tasks (home economics or independent-living skills). Include meal planning, pet care, laundry, auto maintenance.
+ Have your teen keep a daily journal (language arts).
+ Play board games like Monopoly (math) and computer games like Sim City (social studies).
+ Visit art exhibits (fine arts) and science museums.
+ Read the daily paper and discuss (current events, social studies).
+ Watch TV documentaries (science, history, art).
+ Encourage your teenager to pursue any of his interests.

SIMPLE STARTING POINTS

✦ *Visit your local library.* Search for books using the keywords "homeschool" and "home education." Read the first paragraph of any homeschooling books, and check out those that seem to speak to you. In addition, specifically search for titles listed at the end of this chapter. If your local system does not have the titles, ask your librarian about Inter-Library Loan.

✦ *Get sample issues of the national homeschool magazines.* Request samples from magazines listed in this chapter's resources. Read the articles and the advertisements, noting particularly those ads that seem intriguing.

✦ *Send away for catalogs from homeschooling suppliers.* Start with both those who placed the intriguing ads and those listed at the end of this chapter. Many homeschooling catalogs contain not only product descriptions but also ideas and teaching tips.

✦ *Surf the Internet.* Using "homeschool" or "home-school" or "home education" as search terms, surf the Internet. Currently hundreds of online articles relate to homeschooling teenagers. Some of the best sites are listed in the end-of-chapter Resources. You say you do not have a computer and Internet access? Ask a Web-enabled friend for help. Or check at your local library, where it will take them fifteen minutes to show you how to point and click.

✦ *Attend a local homeschool support meeting.* Get referrals to local groups from state groups (listed on many of the Web sites below and also in *The Homeschooling Book of Answers*).

RESOURCES

Books

Our survey respondents, all families with experience homeschooling teenagers, most frequently mentioned the following general homeschooling titles. Check the end of each chapter for titles specifically related to that chapter's content.

Bell, Debra. *The Ultimate Guide to Homeschooling.* Word Books, 1997.

Cohen, Cafi. *"And What About College?" How Homeschooling Leads to Admissions to the Best Colleges and Universities, Completely Revised Second Edition.* Holt Associates, 2000.

Colfax, David and Micki. *Homeschooling for Excellence.* Warner Books, 1988. Also, *Hard Times in Paradise.* Warner Books, 1992.

Dobson, Linda. *The Homeschooling Book of Answers.* Roseville, CA: Prima Publishing, 1998.

Gatto, John Taylor. *Dumbing Us Down: The Hidden Curriculum of Compulsory Schooling.* New Society Publishing, 1991.

Griffith, Mary. *The Homeschooling Handbook.* Roseville, CA: Prima Publishing, 1997. Also, *The Unschooling Handbook,* Prima Publishing, 1998.

Guterson, David. *Family Matters: Why Homeschooling Makes Sense.* Harvest Books, 1993.

Lande, Nancy. *Homeschooling: A Patchwork of Days: Share a Day with 30 Homeschooling Families.* Windy Creek Press, 1996.

Llewellyn, Grace. *The Teenage Liberation Handbook.* Lowry House, 1998. Also, *Real Lives: Eleven Teenagers Who Don't Go to School.* Lowry House, 1993.

Moore, Raymond and Dorothy. *The Successful Homeschool Family Handbook: A Creative and Stress-Free Approach to Homeschooling.* Thomas Nelson, 1994.

Swann, Alexandra. *No Regrets: How Homeschooling Earned Me a Master's Degree at Age 16.* Cygnet Press, 1989.

Waring, Diana and Cathy Duffy. *Beyond Survival: A Guide to Abundant-Life Homeschooling.* Emerald Books, 1996.

Periodicals

To follow find the most frequently mentioned periodicals from our survey respondents.

F.U.N. News, 888-FUN-7020,
    http://www.unschooling.org/funnews.htm
Growing Without Schooling, 617-864-3100,
    http://www. holtgws.com
Home Education Magazine, 800-236-3278,
    http://www.home-edmagazine.com
Homeschooling Today, 954-962-1930,
    http://www.homeschooltoday.com
The LINK: A Homeschool Newspaper,
    http://www.homeschoolnewslink.com
Practical Homeschooling, 314-343-7750,
    http://www.homeschool.com
The Teaching Home, 503-253-9633, http://www.teachinghome.com

Catalogs

The Elijah Company 888-2-ELIJAH, http://www.elijahco.com
Greenleaf Press, 800-311-1508, http://www.greenleafpress.com
Heart of Wisdom Publishing, 800-BOOKLOG,
    http://www.heartofwisdom.com
John Holt's Bookstore and Catalog, 617-864-3100,
    http://www.holtgws.com
Lifetime Books and Gifts, 941-676-6311,
    http://www.lifetimeonline.com

Web Sites

In addition to the resources mentioned above, check out these, for articles relating to homeschooling teenagers.

Clonlara School, http://www.clonlara.org
Eclectic Homeschool Online, http://www.eho.org
Homeschool-Teens-College, http://www.homeschoolteenscollege.net
School Is Dead, Learn in Freedom, http://learninfreedom.org

2

LEARNING ASSETS OF THE
TEEN YEARS

In This Chapter

✦ Exploring interests

✦ Initiative and networking

✦ Self-directed learning

✦ Negotiating education

✦ Developing values

✦ Independence for better or worse

✦ Simple starting points

✦ Resources

W HEN THEY BEGIN homeschooling teenagers, both new-comers and veteran home educators travel to a new, exciting land. In this new territory, our apprentice adults amaze us with their inde-pendence, self-confidence, stamina, enthusiasm, accomplishments, mental abilities, and integrity. Janice in Coeur d'Alene, Idaho, says, "When teens really want to learn a new skill, no outside help is required. They focus completely on their objective."

Adolescents race towards independence, exhibiting many adult capabilities, even as early as ages thirteen and fourteen. Unlike early- and middle-years youngsters, most teenagers manage adult house-hold tasks as well as their own personal needs. At ages nine and ten, our son and daughter could make breakfast, but I still needed to su-pervise—especially the cleanup. As teenagers, these same children not only made breakfast; they planned, shopped for, and prepared meals for an entire week. Independent living skills build self-reliance and define the area in which many teenagers first begin to function as adults.

Our children's drive toward independence accelerates during the teen years beyond living skills. Teens seek a personal identity. They want to function effectively outside the family and to find their place in the community and in the world. Our children, as they mature, think increasingly about their future occupations and lifestyles. This drive to establish personal and vocational identity brings goals into focus and spurs learning. As Arleta in California tells us, "Thomas, age six-teen, works hard. He envisions a career in med-ical research, and he's taking several college math and science classes concurrent with his high school homeschooling."

> This drive to establish personal and voca-tional identity brings goals into focus and spurs learning.

Physically, teenagers seem to have unlimited strength and stamina. Depending on their in-terests, they read, skateboard, practice violin, draw and paint, or program computers for hours and days and weeks on end. Jane in Collierville, Tennessee, says, "Our son learns in depth anything that interests him. Right now, it's guitar. He reads books and researches about different pick-ups. He practices so much that I marvel that his fingers aren't worn down!"

The energy and enthusiasm teenagers devote to activities amazes their parents. Leanne, who has been homeschooling since 1995, echoes many respondents' sentiments. "My son, seventeen, has a zest for learning, especially when he initiates it."

Just as everyday living skills build independence, energy and enthusiasm fuel self-confidence. Penny in New Jersey comments on her teenagers' belief in their own invincibility: "Many times I have seen [our son and daughter] tackle something that traditional wisdom says cannot be done. They come up with a superior solution that not only does the job, but also succeeds beyond everyone's dream. A favorite expression around here is, 'It's amazing how much you can accomplish when you don't know the task is impossible.'"

Teenagers' accomplishments reflect their more mature capabilities. Teenagers write articles and books, run businesses, invent labor-saving devices, earn college degrees, build boats, and raise funds for worthy causes. Our fifteen-year-old daughter was the sole props manager for an adult community theater production. Our sixteen-year-old son, with his years of musical training, taught piano to children and adults.

These accomplishments result from teenagers' more mature mental machinery. Teenagers' minds differ from those of their younger siblings in two ways. First, adolescents have a larger knowledge base than younger children. As an example, most teens know historical time lines and can find Texas or China on a map. When discussing current events with teenagers, you don't have to start at square one, recounting history and reviewing geography.

Second, adolescents exhibit abstract and critical thinking skills that most early- and middle-years children lack. Tess explains, "Teens can take information from various sources and pull it together into an organic whole. They question authority and sources of information."

Kay adds, "[Teenagers] understand abstract concepts and question premises and ideas. I love listening to my son discuss the concept of intelligence. This has led to discussions on how scientists study whether life exists elsewhere."

Using their critical and abstract thinking abilities, teenagers solidify their values. Adolescents enjoy exploring right and wrong in depth. This is a time for lengthy discussions of actions and consequences. As young adults, our teenagers experience the results of actions in real-world situations.

Home educators—as we shall see—are uniquely positioned to take advantage of the learning assets of the teenage years, most particularly in the following areas:

✦ Exploring interests

✦ Initiative and networking

✦ Self-directed learning

✦ Negotiating education

✦ Developing values

✦ Independence

> Setting aside time for chores, meals, and personal hygiene, homeschooled teenagers have from four to ten discretionary hours each day—a great deal more than their schooled peers.

EXPLORING INTERESTS

EVEN THE MOST structured home educators—families who use traditional methods—find their teens complete academics in two to four hours per day or less. Setting aside time for chores, meals, and personal hygiene, homeschooled teenagers have from four to ten discretionary hours each day—a great deal more than their schooled peers. Most homeschoolers put the time to good use the same way you and I do—by pursuing whatever interests them.

Teenage interests encompass every activity on the planet. I have known adolescent homeschoolers who developed expertise in all of the following areas:

- ✦ historical costume design
- ✦ reptiles
- ✦ recreational mathematics
- ✦ Scrabble
- ✦ ancient history
- ✦ archeology
- ✦ photography
- ✦ model rocketry
- ✦ chess
- ✦ horses
- ✦ family history
- ✦ Shakespeare
- ✦ vegetarian cooking
- ✦ landscape design
- ✦ pottery
- ✦ gardening
- ✦ Civil War reenactments

As this list makes clear, homeschoolers need not limit themselves to typical extracurricular activities, like sports, drama club, or cheerleading. Instead, they make their communities and the world their after-school resource room. These young adults look around them, find something interesting to do, and do it. "Homeschooled teens seem to know that it's okay to learn. They don't have to worry about being labeled geeky or weird. They learn what is important to them, in any way they see fit," according to Trudy.

Homeschooling families, taking their cue from unschoolers, learn to translate many of these activities into school subject categories. Gardening is science and physical education. Vegetarian cooking is math and science. Civil War reenactments are history and language arts. Janice, who is homeschooling two teens, says, "We count part-time jobs, volunteer work, travel, and daily Bible reading as school."

INITIATIVE AND NETWORKING

LIKE THEIR YOUNGER siblings, most teenagers demonstrate initiative by proposing activities related to their interests. Denise explains: "I see in my teens a willingness to try anything and to give

SPEAKING EDUCATIONESE

Reading the Daily Paper	=	Current Events, Social Studies
Drawing	=	Art
Playing Monopoly	=	Math
TV Documentaries	=	History, Science
Travel	=	Geography, Social Studies
E-Mailing Friends	=	Language Arts
Flute Lessons	=	Fine Arts
Pet Care	=	Science, Physical Education
Photography	=	Science, Art
Genealogy	=	History, Language Arts
Self-Selected Reading	=	Language Arts, History, Science
Talking with Grandpa About His Life	=	History
Cooking	=	Math, Science
Shoveling Snow	=	Physical Education
Keeping a Journal	=	Language Arts
Church Choir	=	Fine Arts
Sunday School	=	Religious Studies
Computer Games	=	Math, Geography, History, Science
Building a Web Page	=	Language Arts, Art, Computer Science
Tae Kwon Do	=	Physical Education

their all. They are almost completely unfazed by popular opinion. If they are interested, they ask questions, jump right in, and become involved."

Adolescent initiative differs from that of younger children, however. With teenagers, you get not only the initiative, but also the maturity to carry out plans. Older homeschoolers suggest projects. Then, with their more mature capabilities, teens network to realize their goals.

Kay tells us about her son, Matt, using his networking skills. "When he wanted to join a book discussion group, there wasn't one. So he called several friends, and they began the Teen Homeschoolers Book Group. Matt contacted a bookstore that was willing to sponsor them. They now have a reserved table for meeting days, and the store management has offered the members 20 percent off book discussion titles."

Homeschooling parents, just like individual teachers in schools, can never master every subject—especially at the high school level. And, believe it or not, that is a good thing. Adults face this situation—lack of expertise to effect a desired outcome—every day. Learning to wrest techniques and information from the world at large needs more emphasis everywhere, in our public schools and in our home schools.

> With teenagers, you get not only the initiative, but also the maturity to carry out plans.

So take advantage of the freedom homeschooling offers. Freely admit your ignorance. And then remember that you are surrounded by good teachers—your friends, neighbors, relatives, and other home educators. True, most of these people do not have teaching credentials. But you will find that their enthusiasm for subjects close to their hearts is contagious. Find mentors for your teens. Better yet, help your teenagers find their own mentors.

Our son discovered leaders at a local Civil Air Patrol Squadron to help him learn about aviation and aerospace. Our daughter's principal mentors were her piano and voice teachers. Dinah in Salem, Oregon, reports, "Tom's mentor is his grandfather, a civil engineer. This summer, Tom had the opportunity to job shadow with Grandpa in Oklahoma. He learned a lot and the boss offered him a summer job for next year."

Mentors not only communicate subject-matter expertise, they also provide feedback and evaluations, independent of parents. Most teenagers value and work hard for the approval of adults they respect. According to Anita in Freeport, Illinois, "Sometimes Mom and Dad can say that their teens are very talented, but they [the teens] don't believe it. However, when their mentor says it, they listen."

SELF-DIRECTED LEARNING

MANY HOMESCHOOLING PARENTS find that teenage initiative leads to self-directed learning. Our survey respondents report that

ENCOURAGING SELF-DIRECTED LEARNING

✦ *Encourage self-directed activity.* Self-directed activity, even nonacademic activity, like folding origami animals, builds confidence and leads to self-directed learning.

✦ *Restrict television and mindless video games.* Teens will only stare at the four walls for so long. Sooner or later (sooner in the absence of television) they initiate self-directed activity!

✦ *Facilitate rather than teach.* When subject matter exceeds your expertise, seek outside help. Network with your teens for outside teachers together.

✦ *Choose self-instructional academic resources.* Often the author or publisher says quite plainly that a given resource lends itself to self-instruction. If not, try it out, discovering for yourself if a given math or history text can be used without a teacher.

✦ *Model self-directed learning.* Teach yourself something and share the ups and downs with your teenagers. Your children may or may not share your interests, but they will usually absorb the self-directed-learner lifestyle.

their homeschoolers have taught themselves hundreds of subjects, including algebra, geometry, trigonometry, biology, chemistry, physics, Latin, computer programming and repair, American and world history, drawing, woodworking, small engine repair, Bible, government, nutrition, yoga, swing dancing, tennis, and Web-page design.

Contrary to conventional wisdom, teenagers can learn all typical high school subjects without a credentialed teacher. Some families use self-instructional materials provided by independent-study schools or supplied by homeschooling publishers. Others prefer eclectic approaches. Lauren in New York tells us, "Our teens taught themselves world history by reading memoirs, watching educational videos, and volunteering at an Anne Frank exhibit."

Teens who can learn on their own attain educational nirvana— they direct their own studies and teach themselves. Just as important, they learn to locate resources, materials, and people to help them with any subject. Among the many self-instructional modalities our respondents cited were using trial-and-error, self-teaching books, videos, and computer programs; asking friends, neighbors, and relatives for help; seeking advice from experts; and searching the Internet.

NEGOTIATING EDUCATION

IN MOST HIGH schools, teenagers are told what classes to take and when to take them. Every year, each student enrolls in language arts (English), math, social studies (history or geography), and science. To individualize—and also to fill a five- to six-hour day— schools also ask students to choose two or three "electives," such as art, music, foreign language, and physical education.

Homeschooling families—by definition—have freed themselves from bureaucratic mandates of who learns what when. The family, not the state or school district, chooses subjects and learning resources. With early- and middle-years children, parents find themselves making many, if not most, educational decisions. With adolescents, parents and teens can jointly decide on topics and resources. We welcomed the chance to form an educational partnership with our teenagers—to talk things through, discuss educational approaches, and select learning materials with our son and daughter.

> We welcomed the chance to form an educational partnership with our teenagers—to talk things through, discuss educational approaches, and select learning materials with our son and daughter.

After homeschooling for several years, we formalized this process. I sat down with my son and daughter individually every three to six months. We each wrote a "goals and priorities list"—the first reflecting the parents' goals and priorities for homeschooling, the second describing the teenager's aims. We then discussed our lists and generated joint objectives for home education for the next six months.

In the second part of the process, we compared our new objectives with current academic and nonacademic pursuits. We then discussed how activities—like 4-H or using a particular math text—related to the new objectives. We kept what we agreed was working, and we dropped from the teen's schedule those resources and activities that no longer seemed productive.

Should your homeschooling reflect parents' goals and priorities or those of their teenagers? More than 80 percent of our survey respondents reported that their programs reflected a blend of parental and teen objectives. Janice comments on how they decide what resources to use: "Our classical emphasis is my idea, not negotiable. In addition, I try to find the best way for them to attain their goals. We got our son admitted to a junior college at age fourteen to pursue his interest in music."

Cheryl says that home education melds both parental and teenage objectives. "We wanted to instill a godly direction while preparing them for their lifework. They choose their lifework and direction, but we guide in selection and help clarify their objectives."

Several of our respondents reported shifting more of the responsibility for choosing texts and related materials as their teenagers mature. Belinda, who has been homeschooling her thirteen-year-old son since 1994, writes, "Through the years I have set the goals and priorities for school, but as Kevin gets older and develops his own interests, he does more of the guiding. We select learning materials together, buying published math, science, and social studies programs, and supplementing with books he chooses."

DEVELOPING VALUES

REFLECTING THEIR INCREDIBLE diversity, homeschooling families teach different values. Some families promote behaviors and ideals rooted in a specific faith. Marta, mother of seven children in New Jersey, speaks for many when she writes, "Our values are based on our religion. As a homeschooling family, we can live our lives around religious precepts."

Other families derive their values from great philosophers and moral teachers. Still others root their values in common sense, family-centered living, and social justice. Kate in Downey, California, says, "We talk a great deal about the importance of being charitable toward others, looking at things from another's perspective, and being positive contributors to the community."

How do families homeschooling teenagers instill values? Role modeling and discussion top the list. The importance of role models is obvious when you consider the peer-group values too many conventionally schooled teens develop. In contrast, most homeschooled adolescents adopt their family's values simply because they spend more time with parents. Values are caught just as often as they are taught.

To reinforce values, homeschool families discuss family situations, books, movies, and current events. Trudy tells us, "The Columbine High School tragedy gave us a way to talk about parents who work several jobs to provide their children with material things, but miss the importance of an adult emotional presence. They have also seen reasonably normal public-schooled teens obsess over the 'right' clothes, the 'right' cool attitude, and so on."

> Values are caught just as often as they are taught.

In addition to role modeling and discussion, some homeschooling parents use special materials and activities to impart values. Our survey respondents most often cited the following resources and routines:

+ practicing faith, including church attendance
+ participating in religious youth groups and classes
+ participating in non-religious youth groups, such as 4-H, Scouts and Civil Air Patrol
+ using formal teaching materials

INDEPENDENCE FOR BETTER OR WORSE

AN APPALLING NUMBER of American high school graduates cannot balance a checkbook, handle minor home repairs, shop wisely, plan balanced meals, prepare budgets, maintain a car, tend young children, care for sick family members, or determine appropriate medication dosages. Why? Because parents and teachers do all these tasks for them while the teenagers "get an education."

Homeschooling far surpasses school in instilling adult independent-living skills. Homeschooled teens have so many opportunities to learn these skills, just in the course of everyday life. Fortunately, you need purchase no special curriculum or spend extra money to ensure that your children graduate ready for the world. Keep it simple. Teach your teenagers all adult household tasks, and increasingly involve them in discussions relating to major family decisions.

Fostering independence goes beyond teaching independent-living skills. It also includes learning to function in your community. Again, time—free time, discretionary time—gives homeschoolers an edge. If my children had attended school, they would have had time for perhaps one to three community-based activities each week. As homeschoolers, my teenagers participated in five to ten activities each week—without compromising academics or family time.

Check out homeschooled teenagers' outside activities, as listed by our survey respondents:

- running a business
- working at paying jobs
- all team sports
- baby-sitting
- music and dance lessons
- arts and crafts shows and competitions
- 4-H and Scouts
- paper route
- cultural events—concerts, plays
- junior naturalist program at state park
- ranch work
- missionary projects
- community welfare activities
- charity work
- camp counseling
- teaching at church and school
- tutoring
- newsletter editing

- ✦ church choir
- ✦ community orchestra
- ✦ travel

Community activities help teens develop the tools of adult independence. With volunteer and paying jobs, young people learn to adapt to the schedules and priorities of others. They take responsibility for adult tasks, like conducting tours of historic sites or teaching a 4-H class. They work to accomplish real-world objectives, like publishing a newsletter or raising farm animals.

TEN REASONS TO HOMESCHOOL THROUGH HIGH SCHOOL

1. *Efficiency:* Many homeschoolers complete standard high school academics in eighteen to twenty-four months, very quickly compared to the four years most high schools take. Using self-instructional materials they chose, and learning in ways that make sense to them, most teens can cut the time for traditional high school by half.

2. *Head Start on College:* Homeschooled teenagers often take college classes to supplement high school homeschooling.

3. *Self-Directed Learning:* The absence of experts in the home promotes autonomy and self-directed learning. Most homeschooled teenagers not only learn to teach themselves, they also become expert networkers.

4. *Travel:* Freedom from the scheduling constraints of school allows homeschoolers to take advantage of travel opportunities whenever they present themselves.

5. *Work Experience:* Teenage homeschoolers have time for volunteer and paying jobs. Often they get better jobs than those who attend school simply because they are available during school hours.

Many develop skills related to their eventual occupations. Marla in Wyoming tells us about her daughter who is a Girl Scout Junior Leader: "I see her finding happiness in her adult life working with children, so I look at her time at Girl Scouts as helping her develop this skill."

Just as important, homeschooled teens also begin to develop the tools of adult interdependence. In his book, *The 7 Habits of Highly Effective People,* Steven Covey talks about moving from independence to a higher plane of effectiveness that he calls interdependence. According to Covey, once they have learned the skills to be independent, individuals can choose a life of interdependence by

6. *Time:* Homeschoolers not only have more hours each day for creative endeavors and learning activities; they also have more time to be alone, to think, to daydream—to develop a private self and a personal identity.

7. *Family Closeness:* In contrast to many adolescents who pull away from their families, homeschooling parents almost universally report that their teenagers grow closer to all family members.

8. *Limited Peer Pressure:* Removed from the near-constant peer pressure in schools, most homeschooled teens develop mature manners and values.

9. *Saving Money:* Both parents and teenagers may earn money while homeschooling, making home education less expensive than attendance at a public school, where average yearly costs for extracurricular activities can exceed $500 per year.

10. *Fun:* Homeschooling teens is fun for parents, who—in the light of their life experience—enjoy learning all the math and history and foreign language they missed the first time around.

"building rich, enduring, highly productive relationships with other people."

Best of all, homeschoolers learn independence and interdependence in a non-graded environment. When they excel or make mistakes, instead of earning an A or F, they are rewarded and penalized in real-world currency. If they miss too many practices, the coach kicks them off the team. If they polish a performance, they win applause. Freedom from report cards is freedom to fail, and freedom to fail is freedom to learn. Albert Einstein, genius physicist, said: "I think and think for months, for years. Ninety-nine times the conclusion is false. The hundredth time I am right."

SIMPLE STARTING POINTS

✦ *Help your teen list his current projects and activities.* Include the things he does when nobody is telling him what to do. On this list might be movies, reading, drawing, sports, music, art, and gardening. Translate your teenager's current activities in educationese.

✦ *Dream!* Ask you teenager about his priorities and goals: "What have you always dreamed of doing but not been able to do yet?" Brainstorm ways to address those priorities and goals.

✦ *List tasks or subjects you have taught yourself.* Think back over the last ten years, and list tasks or subjects that you have taught yourself. How did you learn those subjects? Books, videos, friends, mentors, trial-and-error? Your teen can become a self-directed learner using the same techniques.

✦ *Read a character-building book.* Read together with your teenager one of the character-building titles listed in the Resource section.

✦ *Make a list of your teenager's current independent-living skills.* What should you add to this list in the coming year?

RESOURCES

Character Building for Teens

Bennett, William J. *The Book of Virtues for Young People.* Simon & Schuster, 1997.

Canfield, Jack, Ed. *Chicken Soup for the Teenage Soul: 101 Stories of Life, Love and Learning.* Health Communications, 1997.

Covey, Sean. *The 7 Habits of Highly Effective Teens: The Ultimate Teenage Success Guide.* Simon & Schuster, 1998.

Noebel, David. *Understanding the Times: The Religious Worldview of Our Day and the Search for Truth.* Harvest House Publishers, 1994.

Communication and Instilling Values

Campbell, Ross. *How to Really Love Your Teenager.* Chariot Victor Books, 1993.

Dobson, James. *Preparing for Adolescence.* Gospel Light Publications, 1999.

Faber, Adele and Elaine Mazlish. *How to Talk So Kids Will Listen and Listen So Kids Will Talk.* Avon Books, 1991.

Glenn, Stephen and Jane Nelson. *Self-Reliant Children in a Self-Indulgent World: Seven Building Blocks for Developing Capable Young People.* Prima Publishing, 1999.

Tripp, Paul. *Age of Opportunity: A Biblical Guide to Parenting Teens.* Presbyterian and Reformed Publishing Company, 1997.

Independent-Living Skills

The Reader's Digest New Complete Do-It-Yourself Manual. Reader's Digest Association, Inc., 1991.

McCullough, Bonnie Runyan. *401 Ways to Get Your Kids to Work at Home.* St. Martin's Press, 1982.

Self-Directed Learning

Hailey, Kendall. *The Day I Became an Autodidact: And the Advice, Adventures, and Acrimonies That Befell Me Thereafter.* Out of print, but well worth reading. Look for it in libraries and used bookstores.

Llewellyn, Grace. *The Teenage Liberation Handbook.* Lowry House, 1998.

Thinking Skills

Allen, Steve. *Dumbth: The Lost Art of Thinking with 101 Ways to Reason Better & Improve Your Mind.* Prometheus Books, 1998.

Black, Howard and Sandra Black. *Building Thinking Skills, Book 3, Verbal, and Book 3, Figural.* Critical Thinking Books and Software, 1987.

Healy, Jane. *Endangered Minds: Why Our Children Don't Think.* Touchstone Books, 1991.

3

THE JOY OF LEARNING WITH
THE HOMESCHOOLED TEEN

In This Chapter

+ Pathway to knowledge

+ Pathway to social opportunity

+ Pathway to strong families

+ Pathway to health and safety

+ Pathway from school to home: decompression

+ Simple starting points

+ Resources

$\mathcal{A}$LL HOME EDUCATORS sooner or later journey to The Land of the Awestruck. You make a new acquaintance, and, after some casual chitchat, she learns that you educate your children at home. Then comes the response: "You must be a saint," or "You must be really smart and super-human." Truth be told, homeschooling is challenging. Nevertheless, ordinary people travel this road and meet the challenges every day. Along the way, they experience joy and inspiration.

Our surveys contained wonderful accounts of experiences families could have had only because they were homeschooling. So many parents comment on observing "Aha" moments—times when they see their teenagers' faces light up as they learn something new. Trina, homeschooling since 1990, says, "I delight when my son, on many occasions, after spending hours on his chemistry or algebra, pounds down the stairway yelling, 'Mom, this is so great. Do you know what I just learned?'"

Serendipity multiplies "Aha" moments in a way that schools cannot duplicate. With the world for a classroom, it is easy—and educational—to let one thing lead to another. Denise describes how her teenagers studied science: "The first year we homeschooled, the children built a fort in the woods. It turned into an animal blind so they could observe the forest creatures, then into a photography blind so they could try to catch the animals on film. This led to building our own dark room, investigations into lenses, tree and plant identification, star gazing, and a debate about binoculars versus telescopes."

Homeschooling allows teens time to experience things that school attendance precludes. And our young adults—in contrast to early- and middle-years children—now have the skills to take advantage of opportunities. Jill, a relaxed eclectic homeschooler, relates, "When my daughter was fourteen, she was asked to 'sign' at the media opening of the Light Magic parade at Disneyland. Because she had taken sign language for several years, including two semesters of American Sign Language (ASL) at a community college (which she would not have done if she was in regular school), she went behind the scenes at the Magic Kingdom, meeting the president of Disneyland in his office above Main Street!"

Some parents experience the greatest joys when their teen's expertise surpasses that of most people in the community. Penny writes, "Mark's first word was 'puter,' and homeschooling has allowed him to pursue his love of computers. He has taught himself five languages and HTML coding. When the county library expanded their Internet access for patrons, they asked him—at age fourteen—to give a series of programs for teens because he knew more than any of the librarians did. They left all of the content up to him. He operates his own Web-design business and has constructed several Internet relay chat networks. He is also skilled at explaining computers to beginners."

Focusing on homeschooling joys illuminates the journey as well as specific pathways to knowledge, social opportunity, strong families, health and safety, and from school to home.

PATHWAY TO KNOWLEDGE

WE ALL ACQUIRE knowledge in different ways. Some learn best from reading and other visual input. Others remember what they hear rather than what they read and see. Still others retain knowledge principally with hands-on projects and physical exercises—playing, dissecting, experimenting, and building.

Numerous teachers, writers, and researchers have studied and defined hundreds of learning styles. One of the best known, Dr. Thomas Armstrong, cuts through the academic verbosity that too often characterizes these efforts in his book *Seven Kinds of Smart*. He talks about the following "intelligences," or ways in which people acquire knowledge:

- ✦ Linguistic (word smart)
- ✦ Logical-mathematical (good with numbers and reasoning)
- ✦ Spatial (thinks visually, in three dimensions)
- ✦ Body-kinesthetic (prefers physical and hands-on)
- ✦ Musical (learns best with music)
- ✦ Interpersonal (people smart)
- ✦ Intrapersonal (learns through personal reflection)

Dr. Armstrong's books offer concrete instructional strategies for each of his intelligences or learning styles. He suggests alternatives when you "hit the wall" and lack expertise to teach a given subject, or for when you seek creative approaches to subjects like biology or history.

Many home educators further simplify the learning styles vocabulary, using the following three categories:

✦   *Visual Learners* remember best what they *read and see*. They prefer books, videos, and observation over direct participation.

✦   *Auditory Learners* retain most of what they *hear*. Audiotapes, reading aloud, and discussion work well for this group.

✦   *Kinesthetic Learners* understand best with hands-on projects and physical activities. Nature walks, experiments, travel, and building projects work best.

Many homeschoolers recognize yet another category, a category that overshadows all the others:

✦   *School-Phobic Learners*. These children say, "If it looks like school, I can't do it." Avoid textbooks for this group. Try alternatives like computer games, videos, and discussion.

Do you need to understand everything about learning styles to homeschool successfully? Certainly not. Several of our survey respondents pointed out that their teenagers discover their preferred learning styles simply by experimenting with different resources. Nevertheless, learning styles experts may help you understand why a particular curriculum or approach does not work for your teenager. At the same time, these experts can suggest alternatives.

LEARNING STYLE POINTERS

✦   Research on learning styles constantly evolves and findings change.

✦   Your preferred learning style may not match that of your teenager.

✦   Most individuals exhibit mixed learning styles.

✦   One learning style may work best for math, another for English and history.

✦   Preferred learning styles may change over time.

Education That Fits Your Teen's Learning Style

More than 90 percent of our survey respondents said that they make accommodations for their teenagers' learning styles. According to Kate in Downey, California, "When we pursue a subject, we look around for the most interesting and effective way of learning it. This sometimes means changing textbooks or approaches. The most common clue that you need to seek an alternative method is the comment, 'This is boring.'"

Many parents, especially parents of teenage boys, provide alternatives to textbooks and worksheets. Belinda in Ohio lists several approaches: "Our son, age thirteen, is an auditory learner. Our accommodations include reading to him and doing spelling aloud. He remembers everything he hears, so he finds review and discussion much more effective than drills and worksheets." Some parents also report that written exams can be counterproductive. "We don't have tests as often as we used to because he seems to understand the material better if he is not pressured into remembering trivial details," reports Beth, who has homeschooled her fifteen-year-old son since 1995.

> We can individualize not only *what* subjects are studied, but also *how* subjects are approached.

Claudia in New Zealand relies on her teenagers' choices. "In general, we encourage learning wherever and however they want—lying on the floor, listening to music in the background, using audiotapes and videos, and writing with the computer." Carolyn has one hands-on learner and one visual learner. She writes, "We limit fill-in-the-blank curriculum for the hands-on learner and give the visual learner lots of good reading material."

In discussing learning styles, all home educators find themselves in a position that most professional teachers envy. We can individualize not only *what* the subjects are studied, but also *how* subjects are approached. We find hands-on projects for kinesthetic learners and avoid textbooks with school-phobic learners. This flexibility allows home educators to build on strengths and shore up weaknesses.

Building on Strengths

When asked how they support their teenagers' strengths, our survey respondents most frequently mention two words—praise and encouragement. Parents listen, discuss, point out options, and suggest progressive challenges. In addition, our experts (our parents-in-the-trenches) seek ways to support their children's interests. "I am always looking for books, field trips, museum exhibits, movies, videos, and adult advisers to supplement their strengths," says Denise.

Creating unit studies from a student strength area—academic or nonacademic—can supplement regular curriculum. Tess encourages her son to branch out from his martial arts training. "At first, Ted's greatest success was in kung fu [a martial art]. To expand on this interest we read books by Lawrence Yep about Chinese folk tales and the Chinese laborers who built the transcontinental railroad. Then we read about China. We read aloud *Iron and Silk* by Mark Salsman. We later watched the movie version."

Several of our respondents describe another intriguing way to build on strengths—finding an opportunity for their teenager to teach a sibling, friend, or even adult. "We encourage our son to teach other family members, even parents, how he does what," writes Dinah in Oregon. Leanne echoes this sentiment, saying, "We encourage our teenagers to help others learn what they [our teens] already know."

> Several of our respondents describe another intriguing way to build on strengths—finding an opportunity for their teenager to teach a sibling, friend, or even adult.

Shoring Up Weaknesses

All homeschooling parents notice "holes" in their children's education. Some worry about subject-specific deficits, like world history or math or writing or foreign language. Others see problems with more general skills. They comment on a lack of creativity or critical thinking ability.

Our survey respondents suggest many techniques to shore up weaknesses. The most frequently cited include:

- Taking advantage of interests and using them to work on weaknesses.

- Doing a task differently—seeing a Shakespeare play rather than reading it, for example.

- Sitting beside teenagers as they work on difficult subjects— just keeping them company while they tackle difficult math, for example.

- Encouraging a positive attitude.

- Teaching at an appropriate level.

- Working at a slower pace.

Some parents creatively shore up multiple weaknesses with a single stroke. Tess describes an interesting activity. "We really enjoy grabbing a *National Geographic Magazine* and reading an article aloud. In doing so, we cover history, geography, sociology, science, map reading, oral reading, and listening skills. An article is not too overwhelming, whereas a textbook can be intimidating. Pretty soon, the big holes are little holes that we can deal with."

Families report differing results with repetition and other typical school approaches to addressing weaknesses. Carrie in Florida writes, "Some of the traditional teaching techniques I have tried have failed miserably. Instead, it seems my daughter improves skills when they become important to something that she wants to do. For example, spelling has always been drudgery. However, when she began using chat rooms on the Internet, she was too impatient to look up words or wait for me to spell for her. Very quickly, she became a proficient speller!"

In contrast, Amy, who is the mother of three teenagers in Portland, Maine, explains how she uses two very traditional teaching strategies: repetition and persistence. "We plug away at anything that is weak, little by little. My motto is that anyone can do anything for fifteen minutes per day and make great improvements over time. You might call it the tortoise approach."

Some teenagers, like their early- and middle-years counterparts, simply need adult involvement and redirection to work on difficult subjects. Cheryl, who lives in rural Missouri, where she homeschools two teenagers, writes: "We remediate in a fun way, defined by both our teenage children with the words, 'Parent Participation.' We might put things to song or in rhyme, or try to explain something differently. If we feel the curriculum is not doing the job, we pitch it and find something that works better. In some cases we might join a co-op or hire a tutor, but not very often."

PATHWAY TO SOCIAL OPPORTUNITY

SOME PEOPLE EXPRESS worries about the socialization of home-schooled teens. They ask: What about the prom, football games, and graduation? Like many homeschoolers, our son and daughter had the opportunity to participate in all these activities. Friends invited them to high school basketball games, homecoming dances, and proms. Our statewide homeschool support group offered a graduation ceremony. That is my quick answer to the "S-word" question.

The more complete answer is that our children, like most homeschoolers and indeed like most adults, have full social lives without relying on school-sponsored events and activities. Our survey respondents list hundreds of social outlets for their teens, including the following:

✦ Boy Scouts and Girl Scouts
✦ County library teen advisory board

- ✦ Ballet lessons
- ✦ Children's ballet theater
- ✦ Electric car team
- ✦ Church youth group
- ✦ Homeschooling support group field trips
- ✦ Sea Cadets
- ✦ Homeschool yearbook
- ✦ Community orchestra
- ✦ High school gymnastics team
- ✦ Habitat for Humanity
- ✦ Sierra Club
- ✦ Awanas (Christian youth group)
- ✦ Movies with friends
- ✦ Volunteering at hospitals and museums
- ✦ Chess club
- ✦ Community running club
- ✦ Salvation Army basketball league
- ✦ Neighbors

Socialization is not absent in homeschooling; it is simply different. Instead of marching band, cheerleading, football team, and school government, teenage homeschoolers' social lives include volunteer and paid work, teen group events and activities, co-op classes, adult community activities, family events, and just hanging out with friends.

In addition, homeschooled teenagers have access to more activities than most conventionally schooled students, activities that often lead to diverse social contacts. As homeschoolers, teenagers are not restricted to friends within a one- to two-year age range, most of whom live in the same zip code. My son and daughter had friends of all ages from all over the community. The phone rang constantly, and our biggest problem with socialization was keeping a lid on it.

Jane in Tennessee recounts typical results of home- and community-based socialization: "At a recent gathering our fourteen-year-old son talked to a group of adult relatives and their friends so easily that they commented on it later. They thought he was remarkable for being so at ease with adults. My brother, who kept telling my son he could watch TV if he was bored, finally understood that he wasn't bored. He enjoyed the conversation."

> Instead of marching band, cheerleading, football team, and school government, teenage homeschoolers' social lives include volunteer and paid work, teen group events and activities, co-op classes, adult community activities, family events, and just hanging out with friends.

While most communities provide more social outlets than you and your teens can ever explore, some homeschooling families find they need to improvise. "I wish I could provide more time with their peers. We live in a rural area, so it's hard for the kids to make friends," confesses Trudy in Colorado. Telling us how she copes, she writes: "Basically, I do a lot of driving. I hooked up with some Denver area homeschoolers online. We have always done volunteer work, and now my sons are also involved in a volunteer group just for home-schooled teens. Denver is an hour away, though. In addition, our children use the Internet to keep in touch and play interactive games with friends in several states."

PATHWAY TO STRONG FAMILIES

Almost all our survey respondents report that home education has strengthened their immediate and extended family ties. Emma notes a pronounced difference: "Most of our friends who do not home-school their teenagers are amazed at the closeness of our teens and younger children."

Sarah shares the visible benefits in her family. "At age fifteen, my son is still very affectionate with both me and his father, even in public, in front of other teenage boys!"

Homeschooling families spend far more time together than families whose teenagers attend school. Molly, who has worn the home educator hat since 1990, explains the benefits: "We are all close. Had [our son] been in school, we would not have had the time to maintain that closeness. The sheer logistics—gone eight plus hours each day, the stress, the homework, the extracurricular activities—work against closeness."

Most of our survey respondents report better relationships with extended family—especially with teenagers who previously attended school. One mother writes, "Before we homeschooled, my son and his grandfather clashed so much that I had to limit their contact. What a change we have seen. In the last two years, my son's grandparents have been inviting my teenagers to visit for several days. They all have declared the visits unqualified successes which they cannot wait to repeat."

Three of our respondent families also report that their socially mature teenagers do not always fit in with other high-schoolers. Their young adults have finished with childish things and are ready

TEENS TALK

Adults compliment me all the time. They tell me that I am able to carry on a conversation without rolling my eyes, or using slang, or one-word answers. One adult told me I am the first teen she has ever been able to have a conversation with. She said that she did not even like talking to her own nieces and nephews, who are public schooled. She is now my beading mentor and good friend.

—KATIE, AGE FIFTEEN, NORTH BEND, WASHINGTON

HOW WE DID IT

In spite of many social activities, I felt that our daughter didn't have enough interaction with other girls her age. To remedy this, I started a mother-daughter book club. This has greatly increased her circle of friends.

—JANICE IN COEUR D'ALENE, IDAHO

for adult ways of interacting. Donna in St. Catherines, Ontario, Canada, describes her sixteen-year-old son's situation: "Finding other homeschooled teenagers has been difficult to impossible. Our son still sees many of his schooled friends, though. While he would like to hang around other teens more often, he finds most of them well below his level. Define that any way you please—education level, intelligence level, ambition level, ethics level, and so on."

Homeschooled teenagers—unconstrained by a school calendar and able to travel independently—can pick up and go. Like my two teenagers, many visit relatives in other states for days or weeks at a time. As Shari Henry points out in *Homeschooling: The Middle Years,* these visits provide unique opportunities to share family traditions and heritage. Encouraging grandparents to share family stories builds relationships and deepens roots. You will enjoy the family traditions your teens recount after these visits.

Unfortunately, homeschooling does not improve all family relationships. Three of the homeschooling parents who answered our survey describe strained relationships with aunts, uncles, and grandparents who did not agree with the decision to homeschool. Donna in Canada says that her son's paternal relatives are all anti-homeschool. She explains: "They continually pressure [my son] about going back to school. They don't approve of his chosen career and do not acknowledge his achievements."

Some people, including some relatives, find doing anything outside the mainstream threatening. Home educators in this situation say that *time* is the best medicine. Once relatives see the results of homeschooling, many "come around." A few families report success winning over doubting relatives with a steady stream of information about home education. Most statewide and national support groups provide helpful question-and-answer brochures for this purpose.

DO-IT-YOURSELF GROUP ACTIVITIES FOR TEENAGE HOMESCHOOLERS

While many home educators have access to many activities in their communities such as 4-H and church youth groups and sports, some find the pickings rather slim. To create your own group activities with other teenagers, consider these ideas.

+ *Game Days.* Get everyone together to play Monopoly or Scattergories or Trivial Pursuit (indoors) or volleyball or flag football (outdoors).

+ *Book Discussion Group.* Ask libraries or bookstores for meeting space and schedule a monthly or bimonthly title for discussion.

+ *Gourmet Club.* Pick a theme (budget, finger food, Chinese, vegetarian), make recipe assignments, and have lunch monthly at different members' homes.

+ *Newsletter.* Whether you opt for a hard copy, e-mail, or Web-page newsletter, you probably have several budding authors, artists, and computer whizzes who can put together an entertaining publication.

+ *Investment Club.* Use fake money, divide up into teams, take weekly buy and sell orders, subtract reasonable commission, and leave the company research up to them!

+ *Hiking, Bowling, Skating.* These are all popular with teens. Set a date and go!

PATHWAY TO HEALTH AND SAFETY

Most of the parents answering our survey note a direct correlation between improved health and home education. Ron, homeschooling since 1991, reports: "We are not exposed to so many bugs, so the girls pick up fewer colds. They get the sleep appropriate to their ages, unlike my friends' children who constantly burn the candle at both ends and are often ill as a result."

Nutrition and exercise are the foundation of good health. Certainly all homeschooling families can provide healthier snacks and meals than most schools. Referring to her son, Kay in California notes, "Matt gets more exercise because he is not sitting behind a desk five hours a day."

Our survey respondents also report that teenagers with chronic conditions like asthma, diabetes, and depression achieve better health outside of school. Several parents say that they had considerably reduced the need for asthma medication and many families discontinued Ritalin, used primarily for attention deficit disorder.

Molly cites yet another health benefit of homeschooling when she says, "I see so many girls this age obsessed with their weight, and we have been able to deal with it before it became a problem." In a similar manner, many survey respondents report that reduced opportunity to use drugs and engage in risky sexual behavior positively impacts their teenagers' health.

> While no place, including our homes, boasts complete physical safety, home educators certainly reduce their chances of falling victim to school violence.

We often think of health and safety together, and the relative safety of home education is obvious to anyone who follows the news. Unlike thirty years ago, most high school parking lots now have a reserved spot for one or more police cars. In addition, many schools now operate with metal detectors and allow only see-through backpacks to catch students toting knives and guns.

While no place, including our homes, boasts complete physical safety, home educators certainly reduce their chances of falling victim to school violence.

PATHWAY FROM SCHOOL TO HOME: DECOMPRESSION

MORE AND MORE parents begin home education during their children's adolescence, after years of formal schooling. The first months, indeed the first year or two at home, most families with teens experience a period of adjustment called decompression, when they refocus their lives from enforced institutional imperatives to family and individual concerns.

During decompression both teenagers and their parents detoxify from the deleterious effects of institutional learning. To understand decompression, think about the opposite—the compression (or stress) created by full-time school attendance. Unfortunately, school too often imparts negative behaviors and expectations. Students are conditioned to:

+ Do only what they are told,
+ Work within a schedule of bells,
+ Ignore interests and talents,
+ Attend to meaningless subjects,
+ Earn passing grades with no effort, and
+ Work for grades rather than excellence.

When previously schooled children begin homeschooling, everything changes, and the entire family decompresses. Overnight your teenagers' lives transform from competitive, coercive, and peer-group-oriented to collaborative, self-directed, and family-oriented. Suddenly, there is time for privacy and time to be alone.

What can you expect during those first weeks and months? Our survey respondents report they observed all of the following during decompression:

+ Physical relaxation

+ Changes in sleeping habits

+ More affectionate behavior

+ Improved health

+ Dropping long-standing interests and activities

+ Increased time alone

What is the principal complaint of decompressing parents? Many relate that their teenagers exhibit little or no interest in carefully selected curriculum and academic materials. Emma in Atlanta, Georgia, says it most succinctly: "I spent hours choosing his curriculum at the statewide homeschooling conference, and now he just won't do anything." Parents need to remember that decompression—like adjustments to all major life changes—takes time.

How much time? Anywhere from six months to two years or more. One rule of thumb says that children need a month of decompression time—time with minimal academic expectations—for every year they attended school.

It is difficult to relax about this. Some parents, concerned by "all they are accomplishing at the school down the street," panic and assign enough academic work to discourage a Ph.D. candidate. No need. Studies have shown that all of typical grade K to 8 academic content can be mastered in eighteen to twenty-four months, as can all subjects taught in grades 9 to 12. Every year American School, an Illinois independent-study high school, has several students that complete four years of high school academics in less than eighteen months.

In addition to allowing time and space, several parents report that decompressing teenagers respond well to clearly stated expectations. Kristin in Texas, who began homeschooling in 1995, describes her family's decompression: "First we had to become more consistent with our discipline. I did not let them get around doing what they were required to do, which at first was hard. On the plus side, they had more free time and seemed less stressed."

Joan in Oklahoma tells us about her son, who had requested homeschooling: "At first, the biggest change was Zach's desire to learn. In school, he would not do any assignments or try in any way. I told him if he wanted to home-school, he would have to exert as much effort as I did. Within the first month, I could see improvement in his communication skills, both verbal and especially written. We also saw an attitude improvement. By attitude, I mean what he thought of himself, how he approached problems, his response to guidance, and his interaction with others, especially younger siblings."

> Parents need to remember that decompression—like adjustments to all major life changes—takes time.

Individualizing learning, taking advantage of opportunities for positive socialization, building close families, providing a healthy, safe environment—these are the advantages you will realize when you homeschool your teens.

SIMPLE STARTING POINTS

✦ *Read at least one book on learning style.* Start with one by Thomas Armstrong and one by Cynthia Tobias (see Resources section to follow) to find out how learning style information can positively impact your homeschooling.

✦ *List your teenager's strengths.* Then list ways to build on those strengths.

✦ *Ask about socialization opportunities.* Get ideas from others within and outside your local homeschooling support group. Make a list of the current activities of local teenage homeschoolers. Get contact information (names, phone numbers) of those that sound interesting.

✦ *Plan get-togethers for your extended family.* Encourage your teenagers to learn more about grandparents, cousins, aunts, and uncles. Interviewing grandparents and writing their biographies is a great place to begin.

✦ *Give your teenager time to decompress.* If you are taking a teenager out of school, give him or her time and space to decompress. Make the transition into academics slowly, perhaps one subject per month.

✦ *Educate homeschooling doubters.* If you have doubting relatives, give them some question-and-answer homeschooling literature from a national or statewide support group.

RESOURCES

Learning Styles

Armstrong, Thomas. *Seven Kinds of Smart: Identifying and Developing Your Multiple Intelligences.* Plume, 1999. Also *Awakening Your Child's Natural Genius.* J. P. Tarcher, 1991 and *In Their Own Way: Discovering and Encouraging Your Child's Personal Learning Style.* J. P. Tarcher, 1988.

Tobias, Cynthia. *The Way They Learn: How to Discover and Teach to Your Child's Strengths.* Focus on the Family, 1996. Also *Bringing Out the Best in Your Child: 80 Ways to Focus on Every Kid's Strengths.* Servant Publications, 1997 and *I Like Your Style: Strategies to Bring Out the Best in Each Child.* Focus on the Family, 1996.

Family Heritage

Cardwell, Tammy Marshall. *Front Porch History.* Greenleaf Press, 1999.

Crichton, Jennifer. *Family Reunion: Everything You Need to Know to Plan Unforgettable Get-Togethers.* Workman, 1998.

Croom, Emily Anne. *Unpuzzling Your Past: A Basic Guide to Genealogy.* Betterway Books, 1989.

Spence, Linda. *Legacy: A Step-by-Step Guide to Writing Personal History.* Ohio University Press, 1997.

Health and Safety

Brody, Jane. *The New York Times Book of Health.* Times Books, 1998.

Harris-Johnson, Deborah. *The Pre-Teen and Teenagers Guide to Personal Growth, Health, Safety, Sex, and Survival: Living and Learning in the 21st Century.* Amber Books, 1999.

Partow, Cameron and Donna. *Families That Play Together Stay Together.* Bethany House, 1996.

Strength and Shape: A Teenage Workout Video. Earth Smart, Inc., P.O. Box 115, Lincroft, NJ 07738, 800-EXERCI4.

Whitney, Bruce. *Homeschool Family Fitness: A Practical Curriculum Guide.* Homeschool Family Fitness Institute, 159 Oakwood Drive, Brighton, MN 55112, e-mail whitn003@maroon.tc.umn.edu

Decompression

Llewellyn, Grace. *The Teenage Liberation Handbook: How to Quit School and Get a Real Life and Education.* Lowry House, 1998.

For the Relatives

Cuthbert, Cathy, Editor. *When Your Grandchildren Homeschool: A Guide for Interested Relatives.* California Homeschool Network, 1999, 800-327-5339.

4

GETTING YOU READY FOR

HOMESCHOOLING

In This Chapter

✦ Are you already homeschooling?

✦ Fear, doubt, and other internal stumbling blocks

✦ Life as your teen's primary role model

✦ Legal issues—nothing you can't handle

✦ Putting together curriculum

✦ Using an independent-study program

✦ Record keeping

✦ Beginner's checklist

✦ Simple starting points

✦ Resources

*A*s THEIR CHILDREN reach adolescence, experienced home-schooling parents begin again. They join newcomers, asking questions about methods, legal issues, and record keeping. Fortunately, both new and veteran homeschooling families have more experience than they think. Read on to learn about addressing fears and doubts, role modeling, legal issues, curriculum planning, and independent-study programs.

ARE YOU ALREADY HOMESCHOOLING?

HOME EDUCATION SOUNDS like a big responsibility. And it is. Fortunately, you know more about it than you think. In some respects, every good parent provides educational opportunities for their children. Think about it. If your child attends school now, do you:

+ Help with homework?
+ Take trips to zoos, museums, and national parks?
+ Read with your teenager?
+ Watch science or history documentaries as a family?
+ Provide educational computer games?
+ Encourage your teens to use your computer word processor?
+ Visit the library and check out books?
+ Provide music or dance or art lessons?
+ Discuss current events?
+ Teach your teenager to cook? To budget or maintain a car?
+ Encourage sports participation?

If you answered yes to any of the above, experienced home educators say that you are already homeschooling your teenager to some extent. Lauren, an unschooling mother of four in Ithaca, New York, tells us, "Everything is school." And she is right. Those zoo and museum visits are science. Music lessons are fine arts. Budgeting is math.

By the time their schooled children reach adolescence, many parents complain about homework marathons—two to four hours each evening. Home education looks easy by comparison. Homeschooling families spend the same two to four hours on formal academics and finish before noon. In addition, if you currently help with homework, you already have experience. You know you can work one on one with your teen.

FEAR, DOUBT, AND OTHER INTERNAL STUMBLING BLOCKS

OF OUR 104 survey respondents, 100 doubted their ability to successfully homeschool. Claudia, mother of four boys ages nine to eighteen, covers the gamut: "Would I know enough? Would I be able to find out? Would I ruin them socially? Would I ruin them emotionally? Would they hate me for having made them different?"

Just about everyone fears new ventures, especially journeys off the beaten track. "It is a huge responsibility to take on the education of your child," writes Kate in Downey, California. "And, as a parent, you want the very best for them. It is natural to fuss over your ability to homeschool, just as you worry about your ability to parent adequately. I still have moments of gripping panic when things are out of harmony in our home. Other homeschool moms and my husband are my sounding boards. Developing patience to let things work out on their own has also been a tremendous asset."

Lydia, mother of a fourteen-year-old and an eleven-year-old, says, "Doubts . . . . Big time!! I was scared to death. I didn't know where to turn. How in the world could I teach my children when I barely made it through high school myself? I found the president of the homeschool association here in Montana. She gave me the encouragement I needed to get started. Without her help and guidance, I wouldn't have made the choice. I am learning how to 'do it' every day. No regrets."

Kate and Lydia have discovered several secrets of successful home educators. First, experienced parents can provide outstanding advice and support. Second, problems often solve themselves, in their own time. Third—and best of all—you can learn on the job.

Many of our respondents cite the cold hard fact that while homeschooling may be frightening, the alternative—school—is even more frightening. Amy, homeschooling since 1984, writes, "I was terrified by the awesome responsibility of actually educating a child. I overcame my fears by considering the alternative—school—which was even scarier."

Jane in Tennessee, homeschooling a fourteen-year-old son since 1996, agrees: "I was afraid if we didn't do this right, our son would suffer long-term consequences. Then my husband reminded me that I could improve on school with one hand tied behind my back, that no other people knew our son the way we did or cared more about his success, and that we had more formal education than most school teachers."

Viewing school realistically is the first step for many in gaining the confidence to teach. Several of our respondents, credentialed teachers who now homeschool their children, give the best testimony.

Gina, mother of three who has been homeschooling since 1998, writes, "I am a former teacher. At home, I can tailor education to my children individually. Also, in a home-based setting, our children learn unhindered by group constraints." Trisha in Camden, New York, says, "I was a teacher. We homeschool now because I did not want to see my children lose their thirst for learning."

Carrie cites other school negatives that fuel her confidence to homeschool: "I have a degree in education, in both mental retardation and elementary education and in adolescent education, and I taught in public school for five years. . . . With homeschooling, we have far less pressure to teach 'key skills.' Public school administrations put far too much emphasis on validation. That pressure interferes with learning. In a classroom, you are limited to activities that take into consideration behavior and 'control factor.'"

In addition to general doubts all home educators experience, parents of teens face another hurdle. Teaching a first-grader to read or a fourth-grader his math facts seems easy compared to covering chemistry and trigonometry and French at the high school level.

How do families handle subjects never taken or at best dimly recalled?

Annette in Arkansas reports, "When I first started teaching Jack, I feared that I would not be able to handle high school material. Math, particularly, was not my strong suit. However, after looking over the curriculum, I saw that it would be easy to stay one step ahead. I actually enjoyed learning with him!"

"I was only going to homeschool for a short time," writes Deanna, who has been homeschooling more than five years. "Certainly, I was not smart enough to teach high school. Over the years, reading and experience have taught me that I am capable even though I do not know algebra and chemistry! Every year we have prayed about our decision and have never been led to do anything else."

ADDRESSING DIFFICULT SUBJECTS

✦ Ask friends, neighbors, and relatives for help.

✦ Buy a self-instructional course, intended for use without an expert teacher. These come in book or computer form.

✦ Enroll in an independent-study course or program.

✦ Trade expertise with other homeschooling parents.

✦ Take a class with the local junior college or adult-education program.

✦ Find expertise through community youth groups like 4-H or Scouts.

✦ Volunteer with a local group. Consider community productions to learn drama, political campaigns for social studies, hospitals for science, and television and radio stations for language arts.

✦ Take private lessons or hire a tutor. Local colleges will often make tutor referrals from among their undergraduates who will work for a reasonable fee.

Many parents enjoy the challenge of learning right along with their teenagers. However, you need not review advanced algebra or biology to homeschool successfully. Instead you and your teens can network to locate helpful resources in your community and, indeed, in the larger world. See "Addressing Difficult Subjects" for a list of suggestions for tackling difficult high school subjects.

LIFE AS YOUR TEEN'S PRIMARY ROLE MODEL

AS A NEW homeschooling parent, you will add quantity time to quality time. Increased hours together each day makes you your child's primary role model. Approximately half of our survey respondents worry about this aspect of homeschooling. Most, like Marla, are philosophical about the implications. She writes, "I don't like when my children see my worst side, but I like that they see that adults are not perfect. I am glad they know adults have challenges as well."

Karleen, who homeschools two children, says, "I find being a role model a little intimidating, especially when my teen gives me the 'you are screwing up' look. I regularly remind them that I am a work in progress, just like them."

Ron tells us, "I think parents should be the primary role model for their children. I also think that parents should show their children that they are human. By that I mean that we make mistakes, say things we shouldn't say, and so forth. It is how we handle these mistakes that provides the real learning for the child."

Teenagers know immediately when parents err. Several of our respondents see this as an opportunity for personal growth. Joan, mother of five, writes, "I want each of my children to be the kind of person I see myself as. I have instilled my values deeply enough in my children so that if I slip, they point it out to me. I like this atmosphere of setting the pattern for my children to follow. It makes us parents better people."

LEGAL ISSUES—NOTHING YOU CAN'T HANDLE

LEGALITIES OF HOMESCHOOLING in the United States vary markedly from state to state, and sometimes from district to district within a state. The more heavy-handed state statutes mandate attendance and immunization records, curriculum plans, reports, and standardized test results. On the other end of the spectrum, some states exercise no oversight. They require no reporting, record keeping, or testing.

In addition, in many states you may choose between homeschooling within the confines of a homeschooling law or outside it. For example, in Colorado you can legally homeschool by (1) filing cursory paperwork required by the state homeschooling statute or (2) enrolling your teen in a private homeschooling umbrella school.

> As a parent, you are responsible for learning the legalities of homeschooling in your state.

As a parent, you are responsible for learning the legalities of homeschooling in your state. Many families investigating home education contact their school district or state department of education for legal information. That is not the wise choice. Too often, personnel at these government agencies either do not know the law or cannot interpret it.

For a complete picture of your state legal situation and climate, contact the organizations listed at the end of this chapter as well as your statewide home education support groups. Most can explain your options on the telephone and refer you to applicable printed matter. Always read laws and regulations for yourself. Ask questions of other homeschoolers until you fully understand your rights and responsibilities.

Twenty percent of our survey respondents are members of the Home School Legal Defense Association (HSLDA), a national organization that offers legal advice and support to member home-

HOW WE DID IT

Our neighbors never knew it was possible to educate a child outside of the school system. So three times in two years, they reported us to the state Department of Child Protective Services. Each time we were investigated, the claim was deemed "unfounded." During the third "investigation," the social worker said, "Look . . . you know who's reporting you. I cannot tell you, but I can tell you to tell a mutual friend that if they (the neighbors) do not cease and desist, you will sue them for harassment and defamation of character." We did just that, and never had another problem.

—TRUDY IN COLORADO

schooling families. The remaining 80 percent see no need to join HSLDA.

Only a handful of our survey respondents say they have had legal hassles related to home education. Those who encountered problems (usually with their local school districts) responded either by calling HSLDA or by citing the terms of the law to those who questioned them.

Trina in Pennsylvania, who has educated her children at home since 1990, writes, "[When we began homeschooling,] we met with the superintendent and tried to show him why we were in the right. Finally we had to have HSLDA send a threatening letter to him informing him that we were in compliance with our homeschooling law."

Joan, who started homeschooling in 1997 in Oklahoma, relates her experience: "The public school system tried to convince me I was not qualified and threatened to turn my children in as truant. I simply sent them a letter of good faith outlining the homeschooling laws in the state and ignored them. They went away."

Donna in Canada, like Joan, found strength in her knowledge of applicable laws, saying, "My local school board tried to harass me about taking Ted out of school. I panicked. Then I phoned my sister [a more experienced homeschooling mom] and had her help me draft a letter to the school board. We set out exactly what our rights were according to the Education Act. Knowing the law and being confident of your rights are of paramount importance."

PUTTING TOGETHER CURRICULUM

ABOUT 80 PERCENT of our survey respondents use a mixture of materials to teach high school subjects. They put together their own curriculum using books, computer programs, videos, texts, and community resources. Unschoolers—that subset of homeschoolers who educate by responding to their children's interests—determine the curriculum after the fact. The remaining 20 percent rely heavily on independent-study programs, which are discussed in the next section.

Chapters 5 through 7 will cover specific approaches to language arts, math, science, and social studies—the four major subject areas for high school. Chapter 8 describes how homeschoolers handle extras like foreign language and physical education. Think of that information in the larger scope of an entire homeschool program.

As an overview, college requirements dictate most high school programs. Mid-range competitive colleges—like many state colleges—will require that applicants demonstrate educational equivalents to the following:

- ✦ Four years of language arts (English)

- ✦ Three years of math (usually through geometry or algebra II)

- ✦ Two to three years of science

+ Three to four years of social studies (history and geography)

+ Two years of foreign language

+ Two years of electives (music and drama, for example)

Requirements of very selective colleges will exceed these. For example, they may require four years of science and three years of foreign language.

If you intend to put together your own program and you are concerned about college admissions, begin with the four basic subject areas: language arts, math, social studies, and science. Read about approaches to these subjects in the chapters that follow, and enjoy researching your teenager's learning itinerary.

> If you intend to put together your own program and you are concerned about college admissions, begin with the four basic subject areas: language arts, math, social studies, and science.

USING AN INDEPENDENT-STUDY PROGRAM

SOME FAMILIES CHOOSE independent-study programs (ISPs) to help them "cover all the bases," as well as for keeping records, assisting with transcripts, and granting a diploma. Others enroll their teenagers in ISPs because they prefer the ISP requirements to those of state homeschooling statutes.

Homeschoolers cite other reasons to consider independent-study programs. Some teenagers prefer working with adults other than their parents for academics. They like the independent assessment and validation ISPs provide. With most programs providing high school–level courses, the student communicates directly with the school and instructors. The parents' responsibilities include signing checks and perhaps providing motivation to complete the assigned work.

ISPs are also the principal suppliers of online high school courses. Some adolescents who abhor textbooks find themselves enthusiastically studying geometry or American history—when it's online.

The most popular independent-study programs with our survey respondents include Clonlara, American School, and A Beka. See the end-of-chapter Resources for a longer list.

RECORD KEEPING

TRAVELERS SPEND ANYWHERE between five minutes to five hours each month keeping records. Families keep records to:

- ✦ Comply with state statutes
- ✦ Meet requirements of independent-study programs
- ✦ Motivate parents and students
- ✦ Document work completed for high-school reentry or college admissions

Annette explains why she keeps records: "I kept grades and samples of his work. I knew he would most likely reenter public school and wanted to have the information for them if they required it."

Karen in Belfair, Washington, says record keeping acts as a reality check. "Keeping records reminds me that we have done more than I remember. It keeps me from overloading my teens and helps me see how we have grown in our homeschooling."

Ron began keeping records for the same reason but eventually found it too time-consuming. He writes, "At one point I tried to keep a journal 'just in case,' and also to show myself the learning that had taken place that day. I was brought up in the old school way. I found it helpful to review the day as reassurance that learning was occurring. I dropped it because it took far too much time that I didn't have."

Although record keeping varies according to the needs and preferences of each family, you may find that you need more detailed records for teen homeschoolers than for early- and middle-years children.

Why? Unless your child is enrolled in an independent-study program, you will eventually use the your records to create transcripts or portfolios for college admissions and job applications.

> Although record keeping varies according to the needs and preferences of each family, you may find that you need more detailed records for teen homeschoolers than for early- and middle-years children.

Carrie, who has been homeschooling since 1989, details her record keeping: "I keep a Daytimer book in which we record all activities outside of home. At the end of the year, I transfer this to a listing of hours spent on various activities. Most of the time, I write curriculum notes in a spiral notebook, keeping lists of books, references, ideas, addresses, and so on. We make schedules of activities that last one or two weeks. These serve as daily check sheets of requirements, deadlines, and so on. Our teens keep the check sheets in folders with their books. On completion, each check sheet goes into their portfolio folder."

One simple record-keeping, credit-assignment method involves listing all academic and nonacademic activities on a calendar. Most teens do the daily listing themselves, taking about five minutes each morning to detail the previous day. Each line is coded with a time and subject-area designation (IL=Independent-Living Skills, SS=Social Studies, FA=Fine Arts, LA=Language Arts, M=Math, S=Science). Here is a typical listing:

Made breakfast (½ hr) IL

Watched and discussed news (½ hr) SS

Practiced piano (½ hr) FA

Read *Wuthering Heights* (1 hr) LA

Walked dog (½ hr) PE

Lunch

Wrote report for 4-H newsletter (1 hr) LA

Saxon Algebra 1 lesson (1 hr) M

TV science documentary (1 hr) S

4-H meeting (2 hrs) SS and LA

At the end of each month, the parent or teen totals each subject area. Eventually (for the transcript) they assign one credit for 120 to 180 hours of work. In regular schools, one credit equals one year of high school work in a single subject.

BEGINNER'S CHECKLIST

IN CHAPTER 1, we described where our survey respondents fall on the homeschool continuum. Some of the continuum descriptions probably fit you. Others undoubtedly sound foreign. Now it is

RECORD-KEEPING METHODS

- ✦ Lesson plan books (available at teacher supply stores)
- ✦ Attendance pages (on calendar)
- ✦ Diaries and journals (narratives of daily work completed)
- ✦ Calendars (listing tasks each day)
- ✦ Files with portfolio material: photos, programs, awards, letters of recommendation
- ✦ Files of work samples and test results
- ✦ Reading lists

time to decide how you see yourself in each of these categories. Remember that prepared travelers begin with maps. Here, we turn the eight continuum categories into a kind of map, a beginner's checklist. Completing this checklist prepares your family for a successful journey.

Motivation

Why are you homeschooling? You will be asked this question many times. Jot down some quick answers now and brainstorm other responses with your family.

Other useful questions to help you explore your family's motivation include:

✦ What will home education offer your teenager?

✦ What does homeschooling offer your family?

✦ What will your days be like?

✦ How do people learn best?

Discuss these questions with your teenagers, and keep the resulting comments handy for future reference.

Budget

Homeschoolers spend anywhere from almost nothing up to $2,000 per child each year. On the low end, families spend less than $100 annually. Medium costs run $250 to $750 per year. High costs top $1,000 or more.

How much can you allocate each month? Plan to spend what you can afford and no more. Families from all economic levels successfully homeschool. They prove that cost does not necessarily correlate with quality. You can have a good program for $50 per year, just as you can have a good program for $1,000 per year. In addition, keep in mind the following three points:

✦ *First, you can find free or very inexpensive resources for any subject.* Generally, locating low-cost materials for home education resembles finding anything for less money. It takes time and ingenuity. Are you willing to devote extra time to shop smart? Can you research, talk to other home educators, and generate creative, money-saving solutions to educational challenges?

✦ *Second, homeschooled teens have hours more each day than traditionally schooled students for outside activities.* Pursuits like 4-H, softball, karate lessons, church camps, music competitions, co-op field trips, and community college classes can seriously impact your budget. How many of these activities will you count as school?

✦ *Third, teenagers can earn money for many of their expenses.* Even with minimum-wage jobs, many homeschoolers finance their own lessons, projects, and travel. What are your expectations about your teenager's financial contributions to his education?

MONEY SAVER

We use the library catalog together with the *World Book Encyclopedia Typical Course of Study.* We borrow most of our material from the library.

—MOLLY IN OLMSTEAD FALLS, OHIO

Approach

As we saw in chapter 1, some home educators run structured programs. They enroll their children in independent-study programs or carefully plan individualized curriculum around scope and sequence information. Others relax and allow their teenagers to follow their interests. Some families pursue a middle road, planning some subjects, practicing unschooling for others.

Be realistic about your personality and your teenager's goals and priorities. Together with your teenager, discuss the following questions. "Which approach feels most comfortable?" "How will we structure our days?" "What subjects are most important?"

Assessment

How will you determine how much your teenager is learning? Popular assessment tools include discussion, written work reviews, grades, and standardized tests. Many home educators use a combination of all four.

In addition, state laws and independent-study programs may dictate certain assessments, like quarterly reports and yearly standardized tests. Make a list of specific requirements that apply to your situation before you begin.

Anita, who lives in Illinois, which has no state requirements for assessment, emphasizes the importance of communication to determine how much her children are learning. "We use grades, standardized tests, and discussion to assess, but rely on discussion the most. Standardized tests are fine if you want to show schools something, but are useless otherwise."

In addition, families with teens may need to generate grades for transcript, college applications, special summer educational programs, internships, or even just automobile insurance. For these purposes, you may assign letter grades based on percentages or based on more subjective measures. We simply gave our children A's for any task or subject that they mastered. How you assign grades does not matter. Simply be consistent and honest about your approach.

Ask yourself if you will be comfortable relying on discussion for assessment, or will you need occasional or frequent test scores?

Technology

Arguments rage about the effectiveness of television and computers as educational tools. Certainly Benjamin Franklin, C. S. Lewis, and

Margaret Mead—famous homeschoolers all—received outstanding educations without access to electronic devices. Hundreds of thousands of families homeschool successfully without them.

That said, technology plays a major role in many homeschools, which we will expand upon in chapter 11. Do you want to bring the world into your home with science and history videos? Should your teenagers research on the Web? Will you use educational computer games, or televised and online high school and college courses?

If you answered "yes" to any of these questions, think now about how technology will fit into your homeschool. Will your teenagers have unlimited access to these easily abused conveniences? What kinds of limits will you place on their use? How will you allocate time among competing siblings? Discuss these issues and iron out problems ahead of time.

Physical Space

Where will your teenagers work? And where will you store educational supplies? What changes should you make to ensure a rich home-learning environment?

While some homeschooling families create a separate classroom in the family room or basement, homeschooled teenagers often prefer the kitchen table. Before you make drastic changes to your floor plan, discuss with your children where they would feel most comfortable.

A separate desk in a quiet room may help alleviate distractions from other family activities. On the other hand, if your teenager's education consists largely of hands-on activities throughout your home and in the community, he may never use a desk.

In either case, you will probably need to allocate some shelf space for records and books. We use a large closet for project supplies, texts, paper, and pencils, and so on. Having everything in one place simplifies life and keeps us from buying items we already have. Involve your teenager in deciding how and where to organize.

Parental Involvement

All two-parent homes have one characteristic. Mom has some talents, and Dad has others. Mom may feel comfortable addressing writing and history. Dad's strength may be science and computers. In an ideal world, each parent would assist and teach in his or her strong areas.

But the world is not ideal. One parent, usually the father, spends most of his time earning a living. For this reason, parents need to realistically assess how much time each can contribute to homeschooling. While some fathers cover science and French in evenings and on weekends, others understandably find themselves too exhausted to commit to teaching.

Have a frank discussion with your spouse. Who will determine your homeschool approach? Who will select materials? Who will make assignments and check work? Who will keep records? If you decide to divide the subjects, who gets what? How will each parent fit the commitment into his or her schedule?

Outside Assistance

What about those subjects in which neither parent has expertise? Probably all families homeschooling teenagers seek outside assistance more often than families with younger children. List areas in which you think you will need help. Examples might be advanced math, laboratory science, or foreign language. Next, talk with other homeschooling families in your community, and learn how they meet these needs.

Never forget that you have a world of experts at your fingertips. Begin with this book, and proceed to your community and the Internet. Networking for resources and expertise teaches your teenagers creative problem-solving.

SIMPLE STARTING POINTS

✦ *Make a list of the ways in which you are already homeschooling.* Can these activities become part of your learning journey?

✦ *List your fears and doubts.* Discuss them with other home-schooling families online or in local support groups.

✦ *Study all laws pertaining to home education in your state.* Make a list of questions and discuss them with local and state homeschooling leaders.

✦ *Decide what record-keeping system makes sense for your situation.* Create files to keep copies of awards, programs, photos, and work samples.

RESOURCES

Encouragement/Support

Books

Pride, Mary. *Schoolproof: How to Help Your Family Beat the System and Learn to Love Learning the Natural Easy Way.* Crossway Books, 1988.

Reed, Donn and Jean. *Homeschool Source Book.* Brook Farm Books, 1999.

Waring, Diana and Cathy Duffy. *Beyond Survival: A Guide to Abundant-Life Homeschooling.* Emerald Books, 1996.

Popular Online Message Boards

Biblical Impressions Homeschool Support Bulletin Board, http://www.biblical.com/html/homeschool.html

High School Homeschooling Board, http://www.vegsource.com/wwwboard/hischool/wwwboard.html

Home Education Magazine's Networking and Discussion Boards, http://www.home-ed-magazine.com/wlcm_brds.html

Homeschoolers' Curriculum Swap Forums, http://www.theswap.com/dcforum/dcboard.cgi

Independent-Study High School Message Board, http://www.paradise-web.com/plus/plus.mirage?who=jlg

Kaleidoscapes, http://www.kaleidoscapes.com

SonLight Curriculum Forums, http://www.sonlight-curriculum.com/www.board/index.html

Legal Issues

Home Education Magazine Homeschooling Information and Resource Pages, http://www.home-ed-magazine.com

Home School Legal Defense Association, P.O. Box 3000, Purcellville, VA 20134, 540-338-5600, http://www.hslda.org

National Home Education Network, P.O. Box 41067, Long Beach, CA 90853, http://www.nhen.org

Curriculum Guides

Bauer, Susan Wise and Jesse Wise. *The Well-Trained Mind: A Guide to Classical Education at Home.* W. W. Norton, 1999.

Duffy, Cathy. *The Christian Home Educators' Curriculum Manual,* Volume 2. Grove Publishing, 1997.

Pride, Mary. *The Big Book of Home Learning,* 4th Edition, Volume 3: Junior High Through College. Alpha Omega Publications, 1999.

Shelton, Barbara Edtl. *Senior High: A Home-Designed Form-U-La.*

Web Sites

High School Subject Reviews,
http://www.learningshortcuts.com/new1ReviewsC.html

Record Keeping

Home School Organizer, 334-634-1849,
    http://www.homeschoolorganizer.com/HSOWelcome.htm

HomeSchool Easy Records, 888-328-7587,
    http://home.earthlink.net /~vdugar/index.html

HomeSchool Organize! 703-791-2794,
    http://members.aol.com/hfsoftware /hspress.html

Homeschool Record Keeper, 908-638-8667,
    http://fp97.inet-images .com/salem/

Selected Diploma-Granting Independent-Study Programs

Bob Jones University Academy of Home Education,
    864-242-5100, ext. 2047,
    http://www.bju.edu/ministries/acad_home_ed/index.html

American School, 708-418-2800 or 800-531-9268,
    http://www.iit.edu/~american/

Brigham Young University Independent Study High School;
    801-378-2868, http://www.coned.byu.edu/is/

Cambridge Academy, 800-252-3777, http://www.home-
    school.com /Mall/Cambridge/CambridgeAcad.html

Christian Liberty Academy Satellite Schools (CLASS),
    800-348-0899, http://www.homeschools.org

Clonlara Home-Based Education Program and Clonlara
    CompuHigh, 313-769-4515, http://www.clonlara.org

Hewitt Homeschooling Resources, 800-348-1750,
   http://www.homeeducation.org

ICS Newport/Pacific High School, 800-238-9525 ext. 7496,
   http://www.icslearn.com/ICS/courses.htm

Keystone National High School, 800-255-4937,
   http://www.keystonehighschool.com

Laurel Springs High School, 800-377-5890,
   http://www.laurelsprings.com

NorthStar Academy, 888-464-6280,
   http://www.northstaracademy.org

Oak Meadow School, 802-387-2021, http://www.oakmeadow.com

School of Tomorrow, 800-925-7777,
   http://www.schooloftomorrow.com

Seton Home Study School, 540-636-9990,
   http://www.setonhome.org/new.htm

Summit Christian Academy, 800-362-9180, 972-602-8050,
   http://scahomeschool.com

Texas Tech University Division of Continuing Education;
   800-692-6877, ext. 320, http://www.dce.ttu.edu/

University of Nebraska, Lincoln Independent Study High School,
   402-472-4321, http://www.unl.edu/conted/disted/ishs.html

Westbridge Academy, 773-743-3312,
   http://www.flash.net/~wx3o/westbridge/

Part Two

A WORLD OF

RESOURCES

5

READING AND
WRITING TO LEARN

OUR COMMUNICATION SKILLS influence every part of our lives, whether researching an automobile purchase, writing a college application essay, enjoying a play, or persuading a community group to install a crosswalk. Good readers and listeners benefit by their ability to efficiently acquire new information. Good writers and speakers have even more power. They synthesize new ideas, ignite imaginations, and change minds about important issues.

For these reasons, a well-rounded education begins with language arts: reading, writing, speaking, and listening. Try teaching history or even math to a nonreader or a poor listener, and you will quickly see that communication skills create a path to all other subjects. Underscoring the importance of English, many educators say, "Teach language arts, and everything else is easy."

In addition, reading—perhaps more than any other factor—determines our children's ability to direct their learning and education. By age thirteen, our son's aviation and aerospace knowledge surpassed ours because he devoured every aircraft and rocketry book he could find. Similarly, many teenage homeschoolers can outpace adults in history, science, or geography. Simply by reading, they teach themselves.

To instill adult-level language arts skills, our fellow homeschool travelers use a variety of traditional and creative methods. Read on for information on favorite books and classic literature, research skills, reluctant writers, and speaking and listening.

SO MANY BOOKS

LESS THAN 10 percent of our survey respondents rely exclusively on reading or literature programs. Instead most parents say that their teenagers read, read, read—one to ten books per month or more. Some families pillage their local library every week, just to satiate their children's interests and demands. The question for most is not "Which program? or "Which literature text?" Instead they ask, "Which book next?"

> The question for most is not "Which program?" or "Which literature text?" Instead they ask, "Which book next?"

Just over half of our survey respondents say that it is important for their teenagers to read "the classics." They point out that exposure to serious literature increases vocabulary and introduces students to important archetypes and ideas in our culture. Reading about famous fictional characters, say Shakespeare's King Lear or Sidney Carton in *A Tale of Two Cities,* invites adolescents to The Great Conversation, the 4,000-year-old heritage of the written word.

PARENTS' TOP TEN AUTHORS/TITLES FOR TEENS

✦ Jane Austen (*Pride and Prejudice, Sense and Sensibility*)

✦ The Bible

✦ Charles Dickens (*Great Expectations, A Tale of Two Cities*)

✦ Emily Dickinson (Poems)

✦ Robert Frost (Poems)

✦ C. S. Lewis (*Chronicles of Narnia, Mere Christianity*)

✦ William Shakespeare (Plays and Sonnets)

✦ John Steinbeck (*Travels with Charley, Grapes of Wrath*)

✦ Leo Tolstoy (*War and Peace*)

✦ Mark Twain (*Huckleberry Finn, A Connecticut Yankee*)

When we queried parents about titles they thought were important for their teens to read, we got author recommendations just as often as specific titles. Check the sidebar for the top ten authors and titles mentioned by parents responding to our survey.

While no definitive list of classical literature for teenagers exists, you can obtain outlines of recommended reading from various sources—colleges, high schools, book catalogs, and the Internet, among others. One of my favorite sets of book recommendations for teenagers appears in The Elijah Company catalog. A chat with your local reference librarian can also produce recommended reading lists for teens.

Marla, who homeschools four children (two of them teenagers), tells how she uses book lists: "I gave each of my older children literature suggestions for college-bound students. They choose what they want to read, using it as a guide. When they ask, I get them Cliff Notes for specific works." Cliff Notes and similar publications

> Although many of our survey respondents put the classics at the forefront of what to read, others question the validity of a solid diet of Great Books titles.

(to enlighten those who did their high school and college work the hard way) contain easy-to-understand synopses and explanations of classic literature.

Although many of our survey respondents put the classics at the forefront of what to read, others question the validity of a solid diet of Great Books titles. "I would like to see my son read some of the classics, but I really didn't read and enjoy them until I was in my late twenties. I had to overcome my forced introduction to them in high school. Although I suggest some of these books to my son and explain that most colleges expect some of these authors' works have been read, I am unwilling to push him into reading them," explains Kate.

Lauren adds, "I think it is important that [our children] are exposed to a variety of materials—from modern fiction to classics." Karleen considers her own educational background. "I would like to say it is important to read the classics, but I have never read many of them myself—and I have a master's degree! We are going to try many of them, however, as we study American and world history these next two years."

Close to one-third of our respondents give their teenagers free rein with respect to reading materials. Sharon, who has been unschooling since 1985, encourages her teenage son to read "anything he considers useful, entertaining, relevant, or important." Donna reports, "I allow our son to choose his own books to read—currently mostly on war, philosophy, magic, and religion."

Karen, mother of two teenagers who have homeschooled since 1997, says, "Since our children did not like to read when they were in school, I am more interested in them reading for pleasure than I am in insisting that they read a certain classic." Homeschooling father Ron agrees: "I think it is more important to develop a taste for good writing than to force any particular titles on teens."

What types of materials do teens choose when left to their own devices? In addition to classics, parents report the following eclectic mix:

- Nonfiction instructional books
- Books of lists and records (*The Top Ten of Everything*)
- Technical computer books and manuals
- Books about sports
- Titles dealing with cars
- Comic books
- *Reader's Digest*
- Hardy Boys books
- Fishing books
- Books on combustion engines and how to build them

The Trip Factor

Of course, not all homeschoolers read voraciously all the time. Ron says, "[My daughter] goes in fits and starts. For months, she reads two or three books a week. Then she will claim she cannot find any more good ones and will not read much for weeks or longer. I still read aloud to her during the cooler months, when we choose more 'adult' books."

Reading need not always come in book form. Lauren relates, "My fifteen-year-old prefers periodicals and articles to books."

Tess, who has been dealing with a late, reluctant reader, tells us, "Mostly we read library books, *National Geographic,* and so on. I try to guide some of the selections, but at this point, it is more important that our son read a lot and read often. Some literature is very hard. We read it as a family, or I read it to him so that he can appreciate the literature even if the reading difficulty is beyond his skills.

He also listens to books on tape and watches videos of classics that have been made into movies."

One way to sneak in good fiction and nonfiction is to simply let teenagers trip over it in your home. "I assign some reading and make lots of book suggestions. My daughter chooses the rest of her reading materials. We often leave enticing books lying around for her to 'discover.'"

We got our teens to try some of the classics simply by urging them to give everything a 10 percent chance. What does that mean? Try the first 10 percent of any book. For a 170-page book, that would be 17 pages; for a 300-page book, 30 pages. At that point, the book has either captured you or not. If not, urge your teen to copy adults. Discard it and move on.

> One way to sneak in good fiction and non-fiction is to simply let teenagers trip over it in your home.

WRITING

ALTHOUGH MOST HOMESCHOOLED teens read enthusiastically, less than 20 percent say they enjoy writing. We asked our survey respondents about teaching specific writing skills, researching, and dealing with reluctant writers. We learned that families attack the challenges of creating good writers with wonderful, creative, diverse approaches.

Nuts and Bolts

Writing skills include handwriting, spelling, grammar and usage, and vocabulary development. Some homeschoolers have near-adult skills in these areas by age thirteen. Others are just beginning to refine them.

Asked first about cursive handwriting, a startling 90 percent of those responding to our survey agree with Dinah in Colorado,

TEENS' TOP TWENTY AUTHOR AND BOOK PICKS

- James Herriot (*All Creatures Great and Small* and other titles)
- George Orwell (*Animal Farm* and *1984*)
- L. M. Montgomery (*Anne of Green Gables*)
- The Bible
- C. S. Lewis (Chronicles of Narnia series)
- Anne Frank (*Diary of a Young Girl*)
- Anne McCaffrey (*Dragon Riders of Pern* and other Pern series titles)
- Margaret Mitchell (*Gone with the Wind*)
- J. R. R. Tolkien (*The Hobbitt* and *Lord of the Rings* Trilogy)
- Homer (*The Iliad* and *The Odyssey*)
- Laura Ingalls Wilder (*Little House on the Prairie* and other titles)
- M. M. Kaye (*The Ordinary Princess* and *Trade Wind*)
- Jane Austen (*Pride and Prejudice* and other titles)
- Brian Jacques (Redwall Series)
- Frances Hodgson Burnett (*The Secret Garden*)
- Sir Arthur Conan Doyle (Sherlock Holmes titles)
- Michael Crichton (*Sphere*)
- Terry Brooks (*Stars Wars Episode One: The Phantom Menace*) and other Star Wars titles
- Harper Lee (*To Kill a Mockingbird*)
- Harriet Beecher Stowe (*Uncle Tom's Cabin*)

who states: "Cursive writing is not very important except when writing letters to non-sympathetic-toward-homeschooling relatives!" Karleen in West Virginia agrees: "Cursive handwriting has zero importance. Legible printing is preferable." Several parents say they prioritize typing and word processing over cursive handwriting.

HOW WE DID IT

I used to worry about my son's handwriting. He writes with a southpaw approach using his right hand. However, I found myself more at ease when I relaxed (the public school teacher in me) and allowed him to work out his own handwriting skills. He does italic handwriting with a slight loop cursive touch to it. After I taught him italic, he had told me he could not read regular cursive. So I had him do Smith Hand (a type of cursive) afterwards. He has developed his own style.

—SUSANNA IN BELLEVILLE, ILLINOIS

Other parents say handwriting matters. Ron explains, "People judge you by your handwriting, even in these days of computer everything." Marta also makes a good point: "Cursive is quicker than printing, and it is important for note-taking, a skill I want my girls to have for college."

In contrast to their approaches with early- and middle-years children, less than 10 percent of our hundred-plus survey respondents use formal spelling programs with their teenagers. Again, computer technology causes parents to rethink the importance of spelling. Some echo Tess's sentiments: "Spelling is not important when you use a word processor with spell check."

Most homeschool travelers work on spelling informally, without a curriculum. Belinda, an eclectic homeschooler since 1994, writes, "[Our son] has a problem with spelling, which we fix in his writing and by spelling aloud."

Experts say that good spellers have the ability to recognize misspelled words. Most families take note, and work on spelling simply by reading and writing. Why does this work? Students who read a great deal are more likely to identify misspellings. And writers who find their misspellings, either with an editor or with spell check, learn to spell better, just to expedite their writing. Several parents say their teens' spelling improved overnight when they began to e-mail friends.

Grammar is another area where many families prefer critiquing student writing to using curriculum. Marta comments, "We use grammar texts and formal English books only for reference."

Many on the homeschool journey say that exposure to quality literature forms the cornerstone of grammar and writing instruction. Teens use good grammar if they read and hear correct usage. Sharon explores another aspect of reading to teach grammar: "We read to him from an early age and always pointed out any grammatical awkwardness when we came across it. He has learned a great deal by reading *Fractured English*—funny examples of poor usage."

MONEY SAVER

Making word lists from misspelled words in your teenager's writing creates free, personalized spelling lists.

Candace, homeschooling for eight years in Texas, describes how her teens refine their grammar skills. "We covered grammar when they were younger. Now they learn by my (and their own) editing of their written work." Darla in Idaho, a picky, proofreading mother, follows a similar path, saying, "They did grammar curriculum several years ago. I do not see any point in doing it over every year. They write letters and e-mail and ask questions when they need help. Sometimes I have them write essays, and then I point out errors in them."

Of course, vocabulary development continues during the teen years. With college admissions tests staring them in the face, many families devote time every day to increasing knowledge of word meanings. Popular techniques to build vocabulary include completing courses in Greek and Latin roots, studying vocabulary lists, studying other subjects, and—probably the most effective approach of all—being exposed to wide-ranging reading.

Writing from Home

As Shari Henry points out in *Homeschooling: The Middle Years,* the best way to become a writer is to write. Teenagers continue to practice the writing skills they have learned in their pre-teen years. In addition, most teens are ready to address three tasks adult writers face:

> Several parents say their teens' spelling improved overnight when they began to e-mail friends.

✦ Editing their own work and that of others

✦ Rewriting and rewriting and rewriting

✦ Deciding when a piece is complete

Aside from the mechanics of spelling and grammar, how do homeschooled teenagers learn these advanced tasks? Travelers rely primarily on these five techniques (which they use singly or in combination):

✦ Reading good writing

✦ Journaling

✦ Practicing parent-assigned or curriculum-assigned writing

✦ Completing student-selected writing projects

✦ Writing for real-world purposes

Over and over again, our survey respondents mention exposure to good literature as an essential component of developing capable writers. This reading plus daily writing form the foundation of many homeschool language arts programs.

Journaling is a popular form of daily writing. My two teenagers kept public, as opposed to private, journals. Each morning they would write for about ten to fifteen minutes about one or more events of the previous day. The idea is not to create a polished piece, simply to routinely, comfortably generate descriptions and put them into either handwritten or typed form.

Some families prefer formal writing courses. Our survey respondents most frequently recommended *Writing Strands* and *Wordsmith* (see Resources at the end of this chapter). Others, like Carrie, create their own curriculum. "I give our teens a writing assignment at least four times a week. The assignment can be a report, a list, a graph or chart, a poster, a letter, a poem or play, or a job application."

> Popular techniques to build vocabulary include completing courses in Greek and Latin roots, studying vocabulary lists, studying other subjects, and—probably the most effective approach of all—being exposed to wide-ranging reading.

Fortunately, real-world reasons for writing increase as our children move into their adolescence. Teenagers write television scripts, advertisements, poems, letters to the editor, plays, movie reviews, short stories, jokes and riddles, captions, and much more. Cheryl in Missouri reports, "Our teens are learning to write by entering contests."

Molly in Colorado tells us, "My daughter has a small magazine that she produces quarterly. There is an entire network of these magazines being produced by homeschooled girls, and they all write for each other's publications."

From Trisha in New York: "Our teens are learning to write without a curriculum. They write comics all the time and are in the process of writing a book."

Finally, Sharon in British Columbia relates, "Our son was part of a teen writer's circle. He's working on a screenplay. Generally he is learning to write by writing."

Research Skills

Research precedes most writing; hence research skills are usually taught in conjunction with writing. Those who responded to our survey differ on the value of assigning research papers.

Monica has been using Seton Home Study materials since 1990. She briefly describes the benefits of the program: "Our curriculum begins requiring research papers, with footnotes, bibliography, and so on, in grade eight. This is no picnic, but it is a wonderful learning tool."

Johanna, an eclectic homeschooling mother since 1992, disagrees: "Personally, I cannot stomach the idea of forcing children to write reports and fake research papers. They are unnecessary in a homeschool setting, unless they serve a particular, real-world purpose. I think it is more important that my daughter learn how to write well."

> Many of the survey respondents say that helping teens follow their interests led to the most productive research efforts—and the biggest increase in skills.

Almost all families encourage their teenagers to practice research skills, whether or not connected to a writing project. They begin simply, with a question: "What are you wondering about?" Many of the survey respondents say that helping teens follow their interests led to the most productive research efforts—and the biggest increase in skills.

The most popular research venues? Try encyclopedias, libraries, and the Internet.

Jane in Tennessee describes her son's experiences: "He learns by doing. We go to the college libraries, regular libraries, and Internet. At the State Archives, we researched our ancestors. We found a Canadian ancestor who had been in a Civil War battle near here, as part of the Confederate Cavalry. Our research was included in a genealogy book and the author thanked my 'junior sleuth' son."

Teenage Writer's Block

"But I hate writing!" Homeschool parents hear that refrain all too often. What can you do about teens who would rather jump off a cliff than write a paragraph?

Separating description from transcription helps in some cases. Have your teenager dictate his thoughts either directly to you or onto an audiocassette. Then transcribe—put in handwritten or typed form—the description. Belinda in Toledo, Ohio, reports, "Writing is very difficult for [our son], but I think it is important. Some remedial things we have done include speaking into a tape recorder and then transcribing the contents. Or he tells me what he wants to say, and I write it word for word. Then he types it up and edits it."

Empowering teenagers with choices about what to write often provides motivation. Jeannette describes her situation: "My daughter is a reluctant writer if we make a 'writing assignment.' She enjoys writing when she chooses the topic."

Carol simply backs off. "We leave writing alone until outside situations require it. One child's music teacher required him to write neatly and spell better. Another child took a couple of correspondence courses."

Carrie advocates a relaxed approach. "At different times my daughter has been a reluctant writer, but I have found if I don't push it, it resolves itself. I usually try to find something that would give her an intrinsic need to write, such as a diary, a new notebook, a fill-in-the-blank book, or some kind of form."

HOW WE DID IT

Our daughter would much rather draw or describe an explanation than write it. I have let her explore writing in ways that interest her. For example, she created a dragon encyclopedia this past year in which she researched different dragons, taking notes and then compiling them into drawings, descriptions, and stories of each dragon. This became a 4-H project for which she won Best-of-Fair and Grand Champion ribbons.

—KARLEEN IN RIPLEY, WEST VIRGINIA

Group approaches work for some teenagers. Consider forming a writing cooperative within your homeschool support group where teens can share their writing. Or ask at your local libraries and bookstores for information about writing groups. Many teenagers enjoy participating in adult groups.

Johanna, mother of two, tells us about using a group approach within the family. "We have had success with a strategy called tandem writing. After agreeing on a specific topic, we each compose a paragraph or so and then read what the other person has written and compare perspectives (we do not correct each other's work). My children have also enjoyed cooperative stories, where one family member begins the story, passes it to the next person, and so on."

> Consider forming a writing cooperative within your home-school support group where teens can share their writing.

Anita, an eclectic homeschooler and mother of two teenage girls, takes a proactive stance. With her reluctant writer, she says, "I gently ease her into it. Short assignments made frequently work best."

Janice, homeschooling a teenage son and daughter, states, "I started assigning a one-page essay on the topic of my daughter's choice for at least three days per week during the school year. At first this was like pulling teeth, but she gradually became comfortable putting her thoughts down on paper. So comfortable, in fact, that she entered the writing contest sponsored by our library this year, and is already planning next year's entry."

SPEAKING

JUDGING FROM RESPONSES to our survey, teenage homeschoolers have a wide variety of opportunities to develop public speaking skills.

Molly in Colorado tells us, "My daughter has raised a Guide Dog puppy. That involves meeting with people in the community and giving talks. She has also taken advantage of 4-H public speaking opportunities."

Kay in suburban San Diego homeschools a fourteen-year-old son. She says, "He has been required to give presentations in several of the groups he belongs to. In 4-H they do speeches, and in drama he practices speaking also. He has done several demonstrations, and assists teaching karate, so these help develop public speaking skills."

Speech contests, often held within homeschool support groups or in churches, are popular. Kate says, "Our church sponsors a speech contest every two years. [Our son] also has the opportunity to teach his peers in church once in a while."

> Listening, also, is key to learning—poor listeners never hear great speeches.

Trisha, in New York, works on speaking skills more informally, at home. Her children read and memorize poems and then present them out loud to the family.

LISTENING

FAMILIES TOO OFTEN neglect listening in favor of more urgent concerns like writing and math. Or they may agree with Darla, who wryly says, "Our teens are naturally good listeners except when I assign chores."

Listening is an important skill, though, and excellent reasons exist to work on it. Listening forms the basis of all social relationships. Certainly you can win more friends with your ears than your mouth. Listening, also, is key to learning—poor listeners never hear great speeches. There is a lot to be said for paying attention.

On a practical level, since so many college classes are taught in a lecture format, many teenagers will need the ability to listen effectively—and to take notes. Our survey respondents report a host of techniques to enhance listening abilities.

Simple discussion tops the list. Jane, who homeschools her fourteen-year-old son in North Dakota, says, "We talk about videos that we watch together, and I get an idea about what he picks up."

Kristin, who homeschools two teenagers in Texas, describes her approach, "I read them an article out of the paper and have them summarize it."

In previous sections, we discuss reading aloud as an effective tool to encourage reading and writing. Marla tells us that reading aloud also enhances listening skills. "I read to my children often, even into and through the teen years."

Because most homeschoolers are not exposed to school lectures daily, some parents make an extra effort to provide note-taking experience in conjunction with listening opportunities. Several respondents report having their teens take notes whenever they hear a speaker, for instance during the weekly sermon in church. Still others make a yearly project out of interviewing elderly family members about their lives and taking notes.

Reading, writing, speaking, listening—each of the language arts builds on the others. Parents of teenage homeschoolers have a wealth of resources to enhance their communication skills.

QUICK & EASY

Cover listening with books on tape from the library.

SIMPLE STARTING POINTS

✦ *Ask your reference librarian for recommended reading lists for teenagers.* Or access one of these lists on the Internet (see chapter 11 Resources). Try one or more titles—and urge your teenagers to give each one a 10 percent chance.

✦ *Initiate a family read-aloud time or try some books on tape.* You will be addressing both reading and listening skills.

+ *Give your teenagers opportunities to trip over a variety of good reading material.* Have plenty available in your home. Let friends and neighbors know you want their magazine discards. Hit garage sales and library book sales to stock up.

+ *Think about how you will create daily writing experiences for your teenager.* For one week each, try journaling, tandem writing, and writing assignments—and any other techniques that sound interesting. What does your teenager think about each approach?

+ *List possible community speaking opportunities for your home-schooled teen.* If none exist, talk to local support group members about sponsoring a speech contest.

+ *Enjoy homeschooling's relaxed pace.* Listen to your teenagers, and they will listen to you!

RESOURCES

Language Arts

Atwell, Nancie. *In the Middle: New Understandings About Writing, Reading, and Learning.* Greenwood-Heinemann, 1998.

Reading

Cowan, Louise and O. S. Guiness, Editors. *Invitation to the Classics.* Baker Book House, 1998.

Estell, Doug. *Reading Lists for College-Bound Students.* IDG Books, 1993.

Fadiman, Clifton and John S. Major. *The New Lifetime Reading Plan.* HarperCollins, 1999.

Hampton, Barbara and Gladys M. Hunt. *Read for Your Life: Turning Teens into Readers.* Zondervan Publishing, 1992.

Pearlman, Mickey. *What to Read: The Essential Guide for Reading Group Members and Other Book Lovers.* Harperperennial Library, 1999.

Sherman, Gail W. and Bette D. Ammon. *Rip-Roaring Reads for Reluctant Teen Readers.* Libraries Unlimited, 1993. See also *More Rip-Roaring Reads for Reluctant Teen Readers.*

Spelling, Grammar, Vocabulary, and Writing

Bond, Jill. *Writing to God's Glory: A Comprehensive Writing Course from Crayon to Quill.* Holly Hall Publishing, 1997.

Goddin, Nell and Eric Palma. *Grammar Smart: A Guide to Perfect Usage.* Villard Books, 1993.

Lederer, Richard and Dave Morice. *Fractured English: A Pleasury of Bloopers and Blunders, Fluffs and Flubs, Gaffes and Goofs.* Pocket Books, 1996.

Lundquist, Joegil K. *English from the Roots Up: Help for Reading, Writing, Spelling, and SAT Scores.* Cune, 1996.

Robinson, Adam. *Word Smart: Building an Educated Vocabulary (The Princeton Review).* Villard Books, 1993. See also *Word Smart II: How to Build a More Educated Vocabulary.*

Sebranek, Patrick, Verne Meyer, and Dave Kemper. *Writers Inc: A Student Handbook for Writing and Learning.* Write Source, 1995. Also *The Write Source 2000: A Guide to Thinking, Writing, and Learning.*

Sheffer, Susannah. *Writing Because We Love To: Homeschoolers at Work.* Heinemann, 1992.

Stillman, Peter. *Write Away: A Friendly Guide for Teenage Writers.* Heinemann, 1995.

Strunk, William and E. B. White. *The Elements of Style.* Allyn & Bacon, 1999.

Zinsser, William. *On Writing Well. The Classic Guide to Writing Non-Fiction.* Harperreference, 1998.

Speaking and Listening

Aslett, Don. *Speak Up: A Step-by-Step Guide to Presenting Powerful Public Speeches.* Marsh Creek Press, 1996.

Van Fleet, James K. *Lifetime Conversation Guide.* Prentice-Hall, 1984.

Weiss, Jim. *King Arthur and His Knights.* Greathall Productions, 1997. See many other classic audiotapes by same storyteller.

Wilder, Lilyan. *7 Steps to Fearless Speaking.* John Wiley & Sons, 1999.

Learning Resources

Literature

A Beka Literature Curriculum, 800-874-2352, http://www.abeka.com

Alpha-Omega Language Arts Lifepacs, 800-622-3070, http://www.home-schooling.com

Cliffs Notes on Mythology, Greek Classics, Roman Classics, and other topics, 800-826-6831, http://www.cliffs.com

Handwriting

Getty, Barbara and Inga Dubay. *Write Now: A Complete Self-Teaching Program for Better Handwriting.* Continuing Education Press. Also Italic Handwriting series, books A–G.

Spelling

Spelling Power by Beverly Adams-Gordon. Castlemoyle Books, 888-773-5586, http://www.castlemoyle.com

Grammar and Writing

A Beka's Handbook of Grammar and Composition, 800-874-3590, http://www.abeka.com

BJUP Basics of Systematic Grammar, Bob Jones University Press, 800-845-5731, http://www.bjup.com

Easy Grammar Plus by Wanda Phillips. Isha Enterprises.

Exciting World of Creative Writing. Christian Liberty Press, 847-259-4444, http://www.homeschools.org

Jensen's Grammar, Wordsmiths, 541-476-3080, http://www.jsgrammar.com

Winston Grammar, Hewitt Homeschooling Resources, 800-348-1750, e-mail hewitths@aol.com

Wordsmith, Common Sense Press, 352-475-5757, http://www.cspress.com

Writing Strands: Creating Fiction, National Writing Institute, 800-688-5375

Web Reading Lists and Great Books

Buckner Homeschool Reading List, http://home.att.net/~j-buckner/hsreading.html

Farmington High School High School Reading List, http://www.infoway.lib.nm.us/kids/reading/readinglist.html

Great Books Foundation, http://greatbooks.org

Hillsdale College High School Reading List, http://www.hillsdale.edu/dept/English/EngHSList.html

Internet Classics Archive, http://classics.mit.edu/

North American Home Learners' Shakespeare Group,
   http://mypage.direct.ca/s/skeane/shakespr.html

Project Gutenberg, http://www.promo.net/pg/

The Western Canon,
   http://www.geocities.com/Athens/Acropolis/6681/index.html

6

MATH, SCIENCE,
AND COMPUTER LITERACY

In This Chapter

+ Math for everyone

+ Science

+ Computer skills

+ Simple starting points

+ Resources

$\mathcal{M}$ATH, SCIENCE, AND computer skills form the economic backbone of our society. Consider the growing list of technical occupations, many of which were not part of our vocabulary fifty years ago—systems analyst, industrial engineer, aerospace scientist, marine biologist, biostatistician, and software developer, to name a few. No doubt, a majority of jobs in the twenty-first century will be filled with math, science, and computer experts.

The importance of math, science, and computer literacy goes beyond finding a job. Some ask if we should encourage technological literacy for teens who resist, for teens who plan careers in the arts and humanities? Many answer yes, pointing out that citizens should be able to interpret global warming statistics, evaluate reports on nuclear waste disposal, and in general recognize when government figures and assertions do not make sense. In a few short years, our teenagers will vote on important issues that affect us all.

In their personal lives, our children's technology skills will enable them to solve everyday problems and enjoy the natural world. Researching different medical treatments, evaluating large consumer purchases, projecting the effects of an approaching hurricane, adding a room to the house, and even explaining the appearance of the sky on a clear, starry night—all these capabilities will empower them and enrich their lives.

MATH FOR EVERYONE

BASIC MATH IS an easy sell. Most agree that a good grasp of arithmetic, including fractions, decimals, and percentages, ranks right up there with learning to read. All adults need to be able to balance checkbooks, understand interest rates, comparison shop, and calculate materials needed for home-improvement projects. At a minimum, we never want to see our adult children in the poorhouse, simply because they could not understand the mathematical implications of compound interest.

> At a minimum, we never want to see our adult children in the poorhouse, simply because they could not understand the mathematical implications of compound interest.

But what about algebra, geometry, and trigonometry? Just how much advanced math do our teenagers need? Obviously, future physicians, aeronautical engineers, and computer specialists will need all the math we can cover. Others— budding lawyers, musicians, and journalists—ask a logical question: "When will I ever use all this?" Many parents, never needing boat-in-the-river problems or geometry proofs in real life themselves, have no good answer. They wonder, "How much is enough?"

What to Cover

Most middle and high schools answer the question "How much is enough?" with the typical school math sequence:

+ General math: includes advanced arithmetic, fractions, decimals, and percentages, grades 7 to 12, usually completed by grade 7 or 8

+ Pre-algebra, grades 7 to 11, usually in grade 8 or 9

+ Algebra I, grades 8 to 12, usually in grade 9 or 10

+ Geometry, grades 9 to 12, usually in grade 10 or 11

+ Algebra II, grades 10 to 12, usually grades 11 and 12

+ Trigonometry and analytic geometry, grades 11 and 12

+ Calculus, grade 12

Most high schools require three years of math for a diploma, and they recommend four years for college-prep students. Many home educators use the typical high school math sequence as a guide. Why am I describing school math programs in so much detail? Because one-third of our survey respondents say that they base their math curriculum on that of nearby high schools. An equal number (an additional third) use formal curriculum similar to what you find at a local high school. For many, the typical math sequence works fine.

Others find the emphasis on little-used skills taught in algebra and geometry courses overkill, especially for a homeschooler who plans work in the arts and humanities or in trades requiring no technical skills. They argue that their teenagers, like many schooled students, can satisfy three-year math requirements with a combination of general math, pre-algebra, and consumer math.

> Others find the emphasis on little-used skills taught in algebra and geometry courses overkill, especially for a homeschooler who plans work in the arts and humanities or in trades requiring no technical skills.

MOST POPULAR MATH PROGRAMS

The most popular math programs, as listed by our survey respondents, are:

+ Saxon Math (Math 7/6 through Calculus)
+ Key To series (*Key to Algebra* and *Key to Geometry*)
+ Harold Jacobs (Elementary Algebra and Geometry)
+ Chalk Dust Videos (Pre-Algebra through Calculus)
+ Bob Jones University (BJU) Math (Algebra through Calculus)
+ Bittinger-Keedy (Introductory Algebra, Intermediate Algebra)
+ UCSMP (University of Chicago School Mathematics Project) Algebra and Geometry
+ Barron's The Easy Way series (*Algebra The Easy Way, Geometry the Easy Way*)

We asked our survey respondents about an appropriate math level to complete. Six out of ten say algebra II or second-year algebra. Approximately two out of ten aim for a higher level, either trigonometry or calculus. The remainder, about 20 percent, say their teens simply need good arithmetic and consumer math skills plus basic algebra and geometry. Several unschooling parents, without apology, leave it up to their teenagers. They say their young adults will study math when they see a need, and no sooner.

Home educators also cover math topics too often overlooked in the typical school math sequence. These include consumer math, gaming and probability, statistics, recreational math, mental math, calculator math, math history, and bookkeeping. Future entrepreneurs—everyone from piano teachers to booksellers to Web-page designers—will use accounting skills. Beyond the practical, there is another excellent reason to pursue overlooked math topics. Emma in Atlanta, Georgia, explains: "Spending time learning mental math and playing math games makes the regular math program easy." See end-of-chapter Resources, where we list materials recommended by our survey respondents.

Doing Math: How They Learn

All but five of the families responding to our survey use a structured math program. One mother says that math is the only subject for which they use a textbook.

Fortunately, teenagers can instruct themselves with many math programs, precluding the need for Mom or Dad to relearn trigonometry. In cases where parents feel they need help, they trade expertise with other homeschooling parents, hire tutors, or simply enroll their teenage homeschoolers in college algebra or geometry or calculus.

In many homeschools, the formal math program is just the beginning. Most of our respondents say that their teenagers use math every day for projects, shopping, personal finance, home business, and travel.

Bill, a homeschooling father in British Columbia, tells us, "Rick, seventeen, works at a grocery store. He gets a regular paycheck deposited to his account. He keeps track of his account, putting some into term deposits and saving some for a car, and taking some out for spending."

"Our teens use math in their daily life primarily for consumer price and quality comparisons. Both girls love to read *Zillions* and *Consumer Reports*," reports Karleen, an eclectic homeschooler from West Virginia.

Fortunately, teenagers can instruct themselves with many math programs, precluding the need for Mom or Dad to relearn trigonometry.

QUICK & EASY

Use "math problem" and "math games" as search terms, and visit math-related Web sites for entertaining math contests and problems of the week.

HOW WE DID IT

Our survey respondents incorporated real-life math into their math programs in these ways:

+ Dividing up paper route checks
+ Planning purchases, budgeting
+ Making consumer comparisons
+ Computing distances and time for travel
+ Estimating miles per gallon
+ Measuring and planning for woodworking
+ Measuring and planning a garden
+ Measuring and planning for cooking and baking
+ Planning home improvement projects
+ Investing in a small amount of stock
+ Keeping track of savings account
+ Designing a future home
+ Calculating sports statistics
+ Acting as treasurer for 4-H club or other youth group
+ Keeping personal finance records and checkbooks
+ Maintaining books for home business

Travel provides an opportunity for real-life math. Karla says, "[Our thirteen-year-old son] planned the budget for our last vacation, a ski trip to Colorado." Jane adds that her fourteen-year-old son recently participated in some family math while traveling. "We checked money conversions on our trip to Canada and refigured the speed limits."

Projects provide other opportunities for hands-on math. Denise explains, "It looks like they will need math for their electric-car project." Kay says that her teen uses math for rocketry, doing many calculations to find the best fin or parachute size.

Catching Up

Of course, math does not come easily to every homeschooler.

"This year, at age fourteen, our son finally learned math facts well (addition, subtraction, multiplication, division). He used a basic college mathematics textbook," according to Sarah, who has

COUNTERINTUITIVE MATH TEACHING TIPS

These pointers sound like they shouldn't work—but do!

✦ *Use the text.* Don't let the text use you. Math programs contain review, much of it only appropriate for classroom situations. Just do selected problems—those the student needs to hone his skills or increase his understanding.

✦ *Use the text nonsequentially.* Do the easy chapters first, harder chapters later.

✦ *Do subjects nonsequentially.* Start algebra before you master your math facts. Or include geometry with your advanced arithmetic.

✦ *Choose math instructional materials with your teenagers.* If they dislike a certain format, nothing you do will make it work.

✦ *Try manipulatives.* Hands-on materials are not just for early- and middle-years children. Use M&Ms, pennies, toothpicks, egg cartons, and construction paper cutouts to make difficult problems concrete.

✦ *Accept alternate approaches to problems* if they consistently yield valid results.

✦ *Don't insist that everything be written out.* Do some math assignments orally.

✦ *If you are having difficulties, take a break of three to six months from formal math.* Sometimes roadblocks miraculously disappear with time.

✦ *Ask your math-phobic student to teach math to a younger child.*

homeschooled since 1992. For some, the teen years are a time when math finally clicks.

If your teenager is behind or math-phobic, do not panic. As a homeschooling parent, you can copy resource teachers all over the nation. Just work at his level, at his pace. Joan reports success remedying math deficiencies with lots and lots of practice.

Some homeschooling families never succeed with math, yet their children go to college and live full lives. Lauren confesses, "My daughter and I did not mesh when it came to math. I should have found a tutor for her. She has always had math challenges and has noisily resisted help. She now knows some very basic math—from slow and simple explanations and practice. She is enrolled in a remedial math class at college. Note: Her college art and theater classmates are also almost uniformly lousy at math!"

SCIENCE

SCIENCE DEFINES OUR times. The scientific method—a unique way of investigating and understanding the world—has led to everything from the lightbulb to landing a man on the moon. Scientists explore and describe nature, and they solve problems. Science, like other disciplines, has its own vocabulary and language. It is a rich body of knowledge—so rich that most professional scientists specialize and only study a small fraction of it.

Beyond the Big Three

Traditionally, students study general science, life science, and physical science during their junior high years and the big three—biology, chemistry, and physics—in high school. Some homeschoolers copy this sequence. They work their way through high school textbooks or follow the curriculum prescribed by an independent-study school.

Others branch out. Our son studied electronics with a local amateur radio club and rocketry and aviation with the Civil Air Patrol Cadet Program. We counted all of it as high school science. Kim, homeschooling three children (the oldest fourteen), tells us that her family is building a solar oven.

Denise combines language arts and science. "We enjoy reading popular science books like James Gleick's *Chaos Theory*, Lewis Thomas's *The Lives of a Cell*, *The Chemical History of a Candle* by Michael Faraday, and *The Physics of Star Trek*. Even certain Michael Crichton novels are valuable . . . because they lead to science discussions and more reading."

Claudia, homeschooling since 1986 in New Zealand, tells us about community-based science. "Our son belonged to the Hamilton Junior Naturalist Club, which had talks every Friday night. They also provided camps and field trips, where they learned biology, botany, and some astronomy."

> Our son studied electronics with a local amateur radio club and rocketry and aviation with the Civil Air Patrol Cadet Program. We counted all of it as high school science.

More than half of our survey respondents combine traditional science instruction with enrichment activities. Leanne explains: "We follow A Beka's texts for a basic outline. We add individual projects and library books to enhance the program. Aaron learned horticulture by designing and creating our front landscaping. He also studied agriculture, working for a goat farmer." Jane takes a similar approach. "We use a text and add to it other reading, field trips, and videos."

Many parents of teens worry about providing laboratory experiences in conjunction with formal science study. Fortunately, you can do science labs without a laboratory! Remember how real scientists work. They investigate natural phenomena and solve problems. Their laboratories include rivers, volcanoes, hospitals, and work places. Any hands-on science location—including your kitchen, garage, or yard—is a lab.

That is one answer to laboratory science dilemma. If you still think you would rather keep chemistry lab out of your kitchen, consider the many science lab kits now available. Heathkit and Radio Shack market electronics courses, complete with hands-on materials. Science-Labs-in-a-Box sells laboratory courses for biology, chemistry, and physics for ages fourteen and up.

Approximately one-third of our survey respondents describe science courses their teenagers take either through local homeschool support groups or at junior colleges. Sarah in Virginia explains, "We cover biology, chemistry, and physics by enrolling in courses at local homeschooling 'academies.' This year [our son] took high school biology in a homeschool 'academy.'" Sharon in Canada describes an

NATURE STUDIES

Naturalist studies are (dare I say it?) a natural for home educators. You begin in your backyard with a single question: "What's the name of every plant, every animal, every insect, and every rock?" To answer the question, use field guides, books set up like catalogs with descriptions and pictures of insects, birds, trees, flowers, and rocks. Most libraries and used bookstores have excellent selections of field guides. *The Amateur Naturalist* by Gerald Durrell (see Resources) offers an outstanding introduction to cataloguing your immediate environment.

With backyard identifications under their belts, teens branch out to nearby parks, rivers, and mountains. And they do what real scientists do: They specialize. They focus on a particular animal or plant or habitat or rock formation or problem to be solved. For specific project ideas, consult the nature titles at the end of this chapter. Amateur naturalists have lots of fun. Their topics and activities include plant and wildlife ecology, outdoor photography, bird-watching, geology, nature hikes, environmental issues, endangered species, and habitat studies.

alternative: "[Our son] has completed a lab course in entomology taught to home learners by graduate students at Simon Fraser University."

Lauren in New York, who has always homeschooled, also relies on community activities and her teenagers' natural curiosity. "We followed our interests in deciding what science topics to cover. One controversial plan here really got our children's attention. Cornell wants to use the water from our lake to cool its labs. We had numerous experts speak to us, all of whom covered various fields of science."

Still other families tie science to sports. Patty, in Anchorage, Alaska, says they study the anatomy and physiology of figure skaters.

These families demonstrate that homeschoolers need not restrict themselves to biology, chemistry, and physics—even for college-bound students.

Although colleges require two to four years of science, most do not specify which science. So feel free to branch out. Instead of, or in addition to, the overview courses—biology, chemistry, and physics—consider astronomy, microscopy, geology, physiology, nature studies, engineering, botany, nutrition, equine science, paleontology, herpetology, and meteorology. Students can learn just as much or more by copying professional scientists, by specializing.

Homeschooling families should also query local colleges and universities about special summer science programs—especially for students whose principal interest is science. One summer, at age sixteen, our son earned three college credits in a two-week course called "The Making of an Engineer" at the University of Denver. Something must have clicked because today he has a degree in aeronautical engineering.

MONEY SAVER

Check out science project books from the library by Janice Van Cleave and others (see Resources). Focus on projects that use materials you have at home to create free science laboratory experiences.

HOW WE DID IT
TEEN ROCKETRY PROJECT

I worked with a group of five teen homeschoolers to build a large model rocket, over five feet tall. They designed and built scientific payloads, and we discussed the scientific principles involved in rocket flight, as well as the history of the space program. Our teens did a wonderful job. They collected and interpreted all the data from their payloads. The resulting presentation was outstanding.

—KAY, IN SAN DIEGO, CALIFORNIA

Future scientists should also investigate science fairs and state and national science competitions. Intel offers an annual Science Talent Search, as does Siemens-Westinghouse (see Resources). To locate competitions, talk to counselors in local public and private high schools.

Clearly, there is no one best way to learn science. If you have teens who dislike formal science instruction, remind them of Thomas Edison and Albert Einstein. Both of these scientific geniuses were classroom failures. They demonstrate that scientific competence in the real world does not always correlate with classroom competence—or vice versa. Fortunately, home educators can cover science in any way they find appealing.

COMPUTER SKILLS

OVER AND OVER again, our survey respondents reiterate two points regarding computers. First, most teenagers know more than their parents about computers. Second, many teens teach themselves the necessary skills.

Claudia is typical. She says, "Whatever computer problems I have, my teens fix for me. They use the Internet, modem, e-mail, and chat rooms. They manage, zip, and unzip files; format disks; and do lots more that I don't even have the words for."

HOW WE DID IT

HOW TEENAGE HOMESCHOOLERS LEARN SCIENCE

Here are ways teens learn science, as reported by our survey respondents:

+ Weekly co-op classes
+ Nature field trips
+ Reading and discussion
+ Correspondence classes
+ College classes
+ Independent-study programs
+ High school texts
+ Individual projects
+ Computer programs
+ Summer programs, such as Space Academy
+ Internet
+ Lab kits
+ TV science specials and documentaries
+ Museum visits
+ Volunteering in hospitals, at universities
+ Experimentation and solving problems
+ Activities such as 4-H

How do teens become so proficient in the absence of experts and teachers? Denise simply creates the opportunity: "My teens learned keyboarding just with computer access coupled with plenty of online friends to write to." Laura talks about readily available self-instructional resources: "Our teens mastered Corel Printhouse, Excel, and Powerpoint on their own using program and Internet tutorials."

MONEY SAVER

No computer? Use one at the library or ask a friend, neighbor, or relative for weekly computer time.

Sharon reveals the importance of trial-and-error. "Our son writes Web pages and uses search engines. He is also hardware literate—he built a computer from used parts. He mastered the necessary skills by doing, reading manuals, and asking questions."

Austin, a lifelong homeschooler, now age fifteen, builds his education around computers. "Computers are my main interest. I sometimes spend as much as eight hours a day programming, communicating with friends, and playing games." He sees computers as fun, challenging, and the wave of the future.

Katherine, also age fifteen, agrees: "I love to spend time on the computer. I go online, look up stuff, and play computer games. I also enjoy our digital encyclopedia and another program we have containing everything you could possibly want to know about World War II."

No doubt, computers present a self-instructional opportunity many teenagers enthusiastically embrace. The most important skills include keyboarding (learning to type), word processing, creating databases and spreadsheets, and designing Web pages.

Although some teenagers learn keyboarding just by practicing, an equal or greater number use a tutorial. By far the most popular keyboarding program, mentioned by more than thirty of our survey respondents, is Mavis Beacon Teaches Typing. Many parents point to e-mail correspondence as a major motivator for their children to learn to type.

HOW WE DID IT

The local college, Howard Payne University, has been very good about letting us offer homeschool science labs in their facilities.

—CANDACE, MOTHER HOMESCHOOLING TWO TEENAGERS IN CENTRAL TEXAS

With typing skills in place, students usually move on to word processing. Although most programs today come with helpful tutorials, many teenagers prefer learning by trial-and-error. Encourage both types of learning.

High school record keeping presents opportunities to use databases and spreadsheets. Karleen describes an application with her fifteen-year-old daughter. "Jane is learning to use a database to keep track of her activities for high school credits."

If we have sidled into geek-speak territory, I apologize. A database is simply a large collection of data—in this case educational activities and hours and credits—organized to facilitate retrieval. Spreadsheets are specialized kinds of databases, which display numbers in cells, arranged in rows and columns. Values of numbers in cells depend on numbers in other cells. Computerized spreadsheets automatically recalculate all cells when you make new numerical entries. For example, a transcript spreadsheet might recalculate a grade point average every time you enter new grades.

No doubt, computers present a self-instructional opportunity many teenagers enthusiastically embrace.

If all this sounds foreign and too difficult to contemplate, keep in mind that many occupations utilize computer skills, word processing, and database manipulation. Many educational journeys will depend on computer skills. Still too difficult? Consider the thoughts of John Taylor Gatto, homeschooling advocate and New York State Teacher of the Year. He says that most of the computer literate in our country got that way not through school, but through trial-and-error and self-instruction. Jump right in with your teenagers, and get a head start at home.

SIMPLE STARTING POINTS

✦   *List your priorities for math.* How important are everyday math skills like measuring, budgeting, comparison-shopping, and deciphering pay stubs? How important are algebra, geometry, and advanced math? Discuss these questions with your teenagers.

✦   *Check out library books on mental math, math games, and recreational math.* Try some of the activities with your entire family.

✦   *Inquire about science offerings for your teenagers in your community.* Ask about special summer classes at local colleges and universities. Look for volunteer opportunities at zoos, museums, parks, and hospitals.

✦   *To determine what interests your teenager, check out science videos from the library.* Watch as many as are practical and discuss those your teen finds the most interesting.

✦   *If your teen lacks keyboarding and word-processing skills, plan to teach these.* If your home hasn't been computerized, learn at the local library or at a friend's home.

RESOURCES

Math and Science Titles

Burkett, Larry. *Money Matters for Teens Workbook.* Moody Press, 1998.

Durrell, Gerald. *The Amateur Naturalist* (out of print, but worth finding—check at your library).

Epstein, Lewis Carroll. *Thinking Physics: Practical Lessons in Critical Thinking.* Insight Press, 1989.

Gonick, Larry and Art Huffman. *The Cartoon Guide to Physics.* Harperperennial, 1992.

Jacobs, Harold R. *Elementary Algebra.* W. H. Freeman, 1995. Also *Geometry.*

Hope, Jack A. and R. Reys. *Mental Math in the Middle Grades.* Dale Seymour, 1997.

Keedy, Mervin and Marvin Bittinger. *Algebra and Trigonometry.* Addison-Wesley, 1993. Also *Introductory Algebra* and *Intermediate Algebra.*

McGowan, Christopher. *Make Your Own Dinosaur Out of Chicken Bones: Foolproof Instructions for Budding Paleontologists.* HarperCollins, 1997.

Parratore, Phil. *Investigation in Science: Chemistry.* Creative Teaching Press, 1995.

Stwertka, Albert and Eve Stwertka. *A Guide to The Elements.* Oxford University Press, 1999.

Tocci, Salvatore. *Biology Projects for Young Scientists.* Franklin Watts, 2000.

Van Cleave, Janice. *A+ Projects in Biology.* Wiley, 1993. Also many other titles by same author, including *A+ Projects in Chemistry* and *A+ Projects in Earth Science.*

Periodicals

Astronomy, P.O. Box 1612, Waukesha, WI 53187,
   http://www.kalmbach.com/astro/astronomy.html
Consumer Reports, http://www.consumerreports.com
Creation, 916-637-5568

National Geographic, 800-647-5463,
  http://www.nationalgeographic.com
Science News, 800-552-4412, http://www.sciencenews.org
Zillions, 800-388-5626,
  http://www.consumerreports.com/Services/kids.html

Catalog and Curriculum Companies

A Beka's Lab Science Materials, 877-ABEKABOOK,
  http://www.abeka.com
American Science and Surplus, 847-982-0874,
  http://www.sciplus .com
Apologia Education Ministries High School Science Curriculum,
  888-524-4724, http://www.highschoolscience.com
Bob Jones University Press, 800-845-5731, http://www.bjup.com
Castle Heights Press, 770-218-7998,
  http://www.flash.net/~wx3o/chp
Chalk Dust Math Videos, 281-265-2495,
  http://www.chalkdust.com
Dale Seymour Publications, 800-237-3142,
  http://www.cuisenaire-dsp.com
Edmund Scientific, 609-573-6250, http://www.edsci.com
Heathkit Electronics Courses, 800-253-0570,
  http://www.heathkit.com
Institute for Math Mania, 800-NUMERAL,
  http://www.members.aol.com/rmathmania/index.html
Key Curriculum Press, 800-995-MATH, http://www.keypress.com
Project Wild, 301-527-8900, http://www.projectwild.org
Saxon Math and Physics, 800-284-7019, http://www.saxonpub.com
Science Labs-in-a-Box, 800-687-5227, http://www.sciencelabs.com
UCSMP Math Texts published by Addison-Wesley, available at
  http://www.amazon.com

Science Competitions

There are many competitions at the national, state, and local levels. Use "science fair" as a search term to find them on the Web.

Intel Science Talent Search, Science Service, 1719 N Street, NW, Washington, DC, 20036, http://www.sciserv.org/sts/

Siemens Westinghouse Science Technology Competition, 877-822-5233, http://www.siemensfoundation.org/comp/comp.htm

Computer Programs

Mavis Beacon Teaches Typing

Math Blaster and Algeblaster (computer programs)

Math Workshop (computer program)

Stars & Stories, CD-ROM, Wildridge Software, 888-BIGGER-WORLD, http://www.wildridge.com

Science and Math Web Sites

Chemical Elements, http://www.chemicalelements.com

Exploratorium, http://www.exploratorium.com

Human Anatomy Online, http://www.innerbody.com/htm/body.html

Mad Scientist Network, http://www.madsci.org

Physics 2000, http://www.colorado.edu/physics/2000/index.pl

Quick Math, http://www.quickmath.com

Scientific American Ask the Experts, http://www.sciam.com/askexpert

7

UNDERSTANDING OUR LIFE AND TIMES: HISTORY, GEOGRAPHY, GOVERNMENT, AND ECONOMICS

In This Chapter

+ Social studies

+ Simple starting points

+ Resources

© Corbis

Wᴵᴛʜ ᴇᴀʀʟʏ- ᴀɴᴅ middle-years children, learning history and geography involves who, what, when, where, and why. Examples? Thomas Edison invented the lightbulb in the late 1800s. The Alps is a mountain range in Europe, primarily in Switzerland. Columbus sailed the ocean blue in 1492.

By the time they reach their teens, we expect our children to remember important dates and place them on a time line. They should also be able to locate major countries, oceans, rivers, and mountain ranges on a blank world map; name important historical figures; use atlases and other reference books; describe major forms of government; and perhaps even identify principal reasons for major conflicts like World War II.

Of course, our children, as teens, continue expanding their history-geography database. At the same time, they add a new dimension—namely the critical thinking capabilities that early- and middle-years children lack. Adolescents enjoy discussions of multiple causes and effects. They debate issues and events. Teens, unlike most younger children, read challenging first-person accounts and original source material.

In addition, adolescents can handle information you would never think of presenting to their younger siblings. As they make the physical transition from child to adult, teenagers learn about adult topics, like presidential scandals and the Holocaust. They also learn the facts behind the facts, perhaps that Europeans too often brought disease and terror to native American populations or that some United States founding fathers owned slaves.

SOCIAL STUDIES

JUST AS WITH science, high school social studies recommendations almost always include the big three. In this case, the big three are American history (unless you live outside the United States),

COLLEGE PREPARATORY SOCIAL STUDIES

This listing is an amalgam of the recommendations of several competitive colleges.

Grade 9: World geography

Grade 10: Government and economics

Grade 11: American history and the U.S. Constitution

Grade 12: World history and cultures

world history, and government. Other high school social studies topics include geography, economics, and the United States Constitution. Schools often teach economics with government, and the United States Constitution with American history or government.

> Homeschooled teens pursue other social studies subjects, such as anthropology, archeology, ancient history, Bible history, modern history, and sociology.

While our survey respondents say they include all of the above topics in their homeschooling, they do not stop there. They branch out. Homeschooled teens pursue other social studies subjects, such as anthropology, archeology, ancient history, Bible history, modern history, and sociology.

Some families combine history, government, and economics with English, art, and music into courses called "humanities." In unit-study fashion, they integrate literature, writing, history, economics, geography, and art and music appreciation. Often teenagers study American humanities followed by world humanities.

Others, like Marla, keep it more informal. "I think the above topics intermingle. I encourage my teens to follow their interests in history outside of their correspondence program. In doing so they study various governments, economic systems, geography, and so on."

History

Approximately one-third of our teenage survey respondents identify history as their best subject. Another third call it their worst subject, using terms like "boring," and citing difficulty memorizing names, dates, and places.

Comments on Textbooks

Families who have tried both textbooks and more creative approaches to history shed light on teenagers' reactions. Carrie describes her situation: "We have used some textbooks for history, but generally prefer reference books and trade books. We use local museums and government resources as much as possible. We read historical novels, diaries, and biographies. My teenagers prefer this eclectic approach to a steady diet of history textbooks."

Molly has similar experience: "We used a history textbook for the first time, and it was not a success. Computer games, maps, books of missionaries, and pretend trips were far more useful."

HOW WE DID IT
APPROACHES TO HISTORY

These approaches were among those cited by our survey respondents:

✦ Historical literature/fiction

✦ Travel

✦ Texts

✦ Real books as opposed to texts

✦ Books on period clothing, weapons, inventions

✦ Magazines

✦ The Internet

✦ Time lines

✦ Videos

✦ Museums

✦ Grandparents and friends

✦ Meals

✦ Audiotapes

✦ Family history

✦ Newspapers

✦ Visits to historic places/field trips

✦ Historical reenactments

Tess has found a way to get mileage out of textbooks. "At first [our son] hated history because of answering the questions after each section. So we told him to just read the text as though it was a novel. Then he loved history."

Marla echoes several other homeschooling parents when she says, "History is interesting. It is the textbooks that make it boring. I tell my children that textbooks provide an outline, a framework for history. Texts give ideas for further research, but they rarely cover any topic in a satisfying manner."

Making History Interesting

Most parents agree that history texts make better reference books than learning materials. For real learning, our survey respondents rely on one or more creative approaches.

First, they use real books rather than textbooks. Why? Consider how real books differ from texts. Real books usually have a well-defined point of view. In contrast, committees write most textbooks, targeting them for the widest possible audience. This not only dumbs textbooks down, but it dulls them down, making for desultory reading that induces yawns better than a sleeping pill. Distinct viewpoints provided by individual writers of real books create more interesting reading.

In addition, real books sport more attractive formats than texts. Compare the magazine format of Joy Hakim's *History of Us* to a typical double-column text with outdated photos, and you will see what I mean. Real books seldom contain irritating didactic devices, like review questions and enrichment activities. Finally, real books generally weigh less and seem less threatening than corresponding texts.

Of course, most teens know all this, even if they cannot articulate it. As a result, many prefer popular history like *How the Irish Saved Civilization* by Thomas Cahill or *The Illustrated Longitude* by Dava Sobel. Accounts of true events, such as Corrie ten Boom's story of her family's experience during World War II in *The Hiding Place*,

Many of our survey respondents say that historical fiction brings past events to life in a way perhaps only equaled by video productions.

also rate high. Autobiographies and biographies allow teens to focus on one individual in historical context—and, in the process, learn the history.

Many of our survey respondents say that historical fiction brings past events to life in a way perhaps only equaled by video productions. For example, *Gone with the Wind,* unlike dry textbooks, goes beyond telling us the southern perspective of the War Between the States. It shows us that perspective. In a similar manner, *The Robe* provides an indelible portrait of Christian life in the Roman Empire during the first century A.D. Historical fiction, entertaining and informative, whets the appetite for more serious history study. Marta, a curriculum-centered homeschooling parent, explains, "My daughters and I enjoy historical novels, which sometimes read faster than 'real' history books, and give us a flavor for the era."

Magazines and maps ignite interest, just like real books. Claudia says, "We have never covered history as a sit-down-and-learn subject. We read novels and biographies that have shot us off in all sorts of directions, but we have not covered individual historic topics. We love *National Geographic Atlas, Encyclopedia Britannica,* and wall maps of New Zealand [their home] and the world."

Using teenage interests, enthusiasms, and creativity sometimes sparks history study. Annette in Arkansas explains, "We focused only on medieval history since this is what our son finds interesting." Karleen takes a similar approach. When asked, "How do you make history interesting," she answers, "I don't. The girls do this for themselves. For instance this past year, Melinda decided to compare the clothing of the different classes of ancient Egyptian society by using her Barbie dolls. She learned an incredible amount of material to prepare for this."

Remember also that everything has a history—aircraft, astronomy, math, card games, gardening, horses, films, computers, everything. Many homeschoolers who otherwise find history unappealing enjoy exploring the history of a hobby or special interest. Math whizzes study ancient numbering systems. Karate practitioners read about the development of martial arts. Musicians trace music history back to ancient Egypt.

Parental enthusiasm also sparks interest in history. Marta says, "My husband and I are history buffs. We take frequent field trips to historical sites, and dinnertime conversation often centers on historical subjects. In our discussions, I try to focus on the people involved. How did they feel? Can you imagine what they must have thought? How did the poor live in comparison to the rich? What difference did a particular historical event have on the lives of people, whether they were involved or not?"

> Many homeschoolers who otherwise find history unappealing enjoy exploring the history of a hobby or special interest.

Personalizing history works for some families. Bill, who lives in a small town in Canada, says, "We study how our family came to North America in 1643 and include all the generations since then. We correlate historic events with family birth, marriage, and death dates." Kim has also used family history. "My daughter played the part of a historical figure in a musical this summer. She learned a lot about the character and she has an avid interest in her own ancestors. One time she made a doll depicting one of her ancestors, and she learned all she could about her."

Hands-on, interactive history often proves irresistible. Janice in Idaho says that her children enjoy doing living history in a co-op setting. Tess in Pennsylvania takes advantage of local Renaissance fairs and other historical reenactments. Carolyn in Oklahoma makes history interesting by "adding biographies and creative activities such as cooking, art, music, writing, and so on."

DO HISTORY

As family historians, teenagers not only *study* history, they *do* history. Family historians interview eyewitnesses (usually your relatives), take notes, read primary sources, organize research material, and write—all those tasks we worry about homeschoolers accomplishing when they go to college. Interview Grandma and Grandpa, create biographies of elderly relatives, and branch out from there.

If all else fails, see the movie. Historical films mirror real books and serve the same purpose—igniting interest. Consider the wealth of historical films and videos, like *The Longest Day,* which recount true events. Or choose videos with fictionalized characters in historic settings, such as *Fiddler on the Roof.* Anita writes, "Our children will get more from watching an hour video than reading a book they really don't care for. And seeing the movie often leads them to read the book!"

Geography

The geographic illiteracy of Americans receives much attention. Yet geography goes far beyond identifying names and places. Alan Backler and Joseph Stoltman, in "The Nature of Geographic Literacy," ERIC Digests No. 35, list the following fundamental themes of geography:

+ Location, position on the Earth's surface

+ Natural and cultural characteristics of place

+ Relationships of humans and environments with places

+ Movement, humans interacting on the Earth

+ How regions form and change

Clearly our teenagers need to learn more than the capital of France or the location of the Appalachians. At this age, finding, evaluating, and presenting geographic data become important. Knowing the location of the Appalachians is of little value if we cannot describe how this mountain range affected history or how it impacts climate and culture today.

Geography, like history, is poorly served by most textbooks. Instead more than 90 percent of our survey respondents use a host of terrific tools to communicate geography themes.

JOIN THE REENACTORS

Civil War reenactment groups all over the nation welcome teenagers. And why should they not? Except for live ammunition, reenactors strive for realism. Certainly teenagers fought in Civil War battles. Generally, participants assume the identity of someone in a particular regiment. They research, dress for the part, and join the battle. It's hands-on history. For more information, check out the Civil War Reenactment site at www.cwreenactors.com.

Or try the Society for Creative Anachronism (SCA), an international organization dedicated to (according to their Web site) "The study and recreation of the European Middle Ages, its crafts, sciences, arts, traditions, literature, and so on. The SCA historic period includes Western civilization before 1600 A.D., focusing on the western European High Middle Ages. Under the aegis of the SCA we study dance, calligraphy, martial arts, cooking, metalwork, stained glass, costuming, and literature . . . if they did it, somebody in the SCA does it (except die of the plague!)." What separates the SCA from a humanities 101 class is hands-on learning. Events include feasts, archery tourneys, dance balls, and meetings. Find the Society for Creative Anachronism at http://www.sca.org or 800 780-7486.

FAVORITE HISTORICAL VIDEOS OF HOMESCHOOL FAMILIES

Our survey respondents most frequently recommended the following video productions as useful for social studies. Caution: Some of these films carry PG and R ratings. If you have concerns about content, either preview them or watch them with your teenagers.

The Agony and the Ecstasy	How The West Was Won
Amadeus	I Claudius
"American Experience" (PBS Series)	The Last Days of Pompeii
Amistad	The Longest Day
Apollo 13	A Man for All Seasons
Becket	Masada
Ben Hur	The Miracle Worker
Braveheart	Patton
"The Civil War" (Ken Burns series)	Pride and Prejudice
"Civil War Journal" (TV series)	Red Badge of Courage
The Diary of Anne Frank	Rob Roy
Dr. Zhivago	Robin Hood
Empire of the Sun	Roots
Eyes on the Prize	Saving Private Ryan
Fiddler on the Roof	Schindler's List
Gettysburg	St. Joan of Arc
The Great Escape	The Ten Commandments
Great Expectations	Titanic
Henry V	Tora, Tora, Tora

Expanding Horizons

Games top the list. Many families enjoy geography board games, like National Geographic's Global Pursuit. Others, like Karleen (who homeschools twelve- and fifteen-year-old daughters), invent their own. She writes, "Their father plays geography games with them during supper using map place mats." Belinda takes it on the road. "When we travel we make up games for remembering states and capitals, state motto, nickname, bird, and so on."

Geography lends itself to informal study. Cheryl in Missouri says, "Foreign stamps spark much discussion and curiosity." Lauren in New York writes, "My husband's shortwave radio is perhaps the best. He picks up countries from around the world that we then identify and learn about." Marla comments, "We don't use anything special for geography. We find places in the news and in the books we are reading on the map and globe. Sometimes we discuss what geographic features played a role in a particular event."

Sharon, in Canada, merges real journeys with the homeschool learning journey: "Our sons like to map our routes for holiday road trips. We also enjoy noting geographical facts as we travel—climate, terrain, proximity to water masses, and so on." Belinda says, "We explore the areas where we travel, looking for historical sites, like a confederate cemetery or Lincoln's father's house."

Many homeschooled teenagers travel independently for the first time in their lives. Perusing national homeschool publications, you will find opportunities every year for sightseeing trips, educational sojourns, and service or missionary journeys. Our son and daughter spent two weeks one summer fixing up houses with a church group in an inner-city neighborhood across the country. They combined service with sightseeing. Student exchanges create additional possibilities. Emma in Atlanta, Georgia, describes her daughter, age sixteen, taking a student exchange trip to France.

Back home, personalizing geography makes a difference. Denise says her teens communicate with and follow the travels of their

MONEY SAVER

Obtain historic videos free at your local library. Or tape them from PBS, The Learning Channel, The History Channel, and Arts & Entertainment. If you do not get cable, ask a friend or relative to tape shows for you.

HOW WE DID IT

I think basic geography is crucial, so I talk about it whenever I drive some-where. I make it relevant so it is interesting. Since we move a lot and we also love to explore, we have plenty of practice using geography skills. I often get lost, so the child sitting in the front seat has to be good at map reading, looking for ad-dresses and roads, tracking which block we are in and which side of the street we should be looking at.

—DENISE IN EWA BEACH, HAWAII

military dad as he goes out to sea. Beth's children study different areas of the world where friends live. Kristin in Texas describes her teens' geography learning. "We pray for different areas of the world, read about them in current events. We also have exchange students from different parts of the world live with us." Interpersonal learners explore geography with pen pals.

For several years, our teenage daughter corresponded with a young man in Russia. She could have read in a textbook that Siberia was cold, but hearing from her correspondent that Siberians go ice fishing not when it freezes, but instead "when it warms up," made an indelible impression. *Home Education Magazine* publishes pen pal lists in every issue.

Look It Up

Families responding to our survey talk enthusiastically about essen-tial geography references in their home libraries. Janice says that they have maps and travelogues plus a huge world map that covers an entire wall in their den. Other popular geographic references include atlases, almanacs, globes, and magazines, like *National Geographic*.

Government and U.S. Constitution

In the 1980s and early 1990s, as home-education statutes were proposed, written, and passed, many homeschoolers experienced government firsthand. They attended legislative sessions and heard pro and con arguments about home education. Parents read bills and legislative proposals and discussed them with their teens. Some teenage homeschoolers even testified before legislative committees.

Homeschooled teens of the 1990s continued the hands-on tradition. Today the rallying cry remains: "Get involved!" And it is easier than you might think.

> Interpersonal learners explore geography with pen pals.

Hands-On Civics

Lauren writes, "Our eighteen-year-old has volunteered at a congressman's office, worked with the Peace Corps, and attended workshops on participatory democracy." Sharon says, "We have always included the children in our discussions of election issues, taken them with us to vote, watched parliamentary debate on important issues on TV, and worked on election campaigns." Working with candidates and elected representatives—most of whom use all the volunteer help they can get—provides civics experience for teenagers. It also allows elected representatives to put faces with the term "home education," something that can only help homeschoolers in the long run.

There are so many ways to see the nuts and bolts of government. Both Terrie and Karleen's teens have spent time as pages at the State Capitol. Bill's children attend town council meetings. Carrie reports, "Because we live near the capital of Florida,

MONEY SAVER

Growing Without Schooling, a national publication, lists subscribers who are willing to host traveling homeschooling families.

we have easy access to government. We visit the state Senate and House of Representatives while in session. We also have a local teen court and tours of the Capitol and other government buildings, state archives, the state museum, and so on."

Hands-Off Civics

Of course, some families prefer formal instruction for government. They use courses provided by major curriculum suppliers, like A Beka or Christian Liberty Academy or American School. Beyond in-dependent-study courses, Kate points out that the Boy Scouts offer three government-related badges: Community, Nation, and World. 4-H has similar citizenship and leadership projects, every bit as demanding as formal coursework. College presents yet another option. Candace in Texas describes her teenager's experience: "My daughter took a gifted and talented summer program (three weeks) at Southern Methodist University this summer and received three units of college credit in government."

> Working with candidates and elected representatives—most of whom use all the volunteer help they can get—provides civics experience for teenagers. It also allows elected representatives to put faces with the term "home education," something that can only help homeschoolers in the long run.

Is That Constitutional?

The United States has the oldest national constitution currently in effect. This document sets forth the three branches of government, their jurisdictions, and the rights of citizens. As the law of the land, the U.S. Constitution enters into the study of government. Most homeschooling families in the United States cover the Constitution at one time or another during the teen years.

We asked survey respondents how they address the U.S. Constitution, and more than one-third say they read it. That's it—

just read it and discuss it. As an adult, I found re-reading this historic document an excellent review of material I only dimly understood the first time around, in high school.

Beyond that, current events provide ongoing grist for the U.S. Constitution discussion mill. Think of the issues that the Supreme Court tackles. These include abortion, censorship, the death penalty, gun control, impeachment, and privacy rights. Add to these the right to privately educate one's own children and the right to homeschool. Researching constitutional interpretations for any topic creates in-depth unit studies ideal for teenagers. Tess makes a year-round effort, writing, "We bring up issues from the news . . . that have constitutional implications and discuss them in terms of what the Constitution says. It is an ongoing study."

> Current events provide ongoing grist for the U.S. Constitution discussion mill.

Economics

Thirty years ago, economics was a college subject. No more. Economics constantly enters into history and current events, making it essential to learn how individuals, private companies, and political entities allocate money and resources.

Topics covered in high school economics courses include kinds of economic systems, free enterprise, role of the consumer in the economy, consumer credit and federal regulations, prices, supply and demand, major business organizations, Federal Reserve system, and measuring the economy—GNP and business cycles. You may feel on shaky ground in this area. If so, begin with the book by Richard Maybury, *What Ever Happened to Penny Candy?*—a favorite with home educators nationwide.

MONEY SAVER

Write to local, state, and national governments for tourist materials and maps. Most will send you fascinating photos, brochures, and maps for free.

History, geography, government, and economics—the study of one leads to the study of all. Take advantage of the many fine resources available.

SIMPLE STARTING POINTS

✦   *Make your home social studies friendly.* Subscribe to the local newspaper and a weekly or monthly news magazine. Make time each day to discuss current events. Acquire at least one world atlas, one almanac, and one globe.

✦   *Decide what historical subjects make sense for your teens.* As an introduction to the first subject, watch one or two related videos.

✦   *Assess your teenager's geography knowledge with discussions, games, or tests.* Decide how you want to pursue geography during the high school years.

✦   *Help your teenager find a pen pal on another continent.* Peruse the *Growing Without Schooling* subscriber lists and the *Home Education Magazine* pen pal column for contacts.

✦   *Plan one or two field trips to local or state government sites.* Visit the Capitol, legislature in session, courtrooms, and county boards of supervisors.

✦   *If you are an American citizen, read the Constitution with your teenagers.* Note any issues in which your teens seem particularly interested.

RESOURCES

Books

Adams, Scott. *The Dilbert Principle.* HarperBusiness, 1996.
Bennett, William J., Editor. *The Spirit of America: Words of Advice from the Founders in Stories, Letters, Poems and Speeches.* Touchstone Books, 1998.

Bowen, Catherine. *The Miracle at Philadelphia: The Story of the Constitutional Convention.* Little Brown, 1986.

Bundy-Smith, George. *You Decide: Applying the Bill of Rights to Real Cases.* Critical Thinking Books and Software, 1992.

Cahill, Thomas. *How the Irish Saved Civilization.* Doubleday, 1996.

Davison, Michael and Neal Martin. *Reader's Digest Everyday Life Through the Ages.* Reader's Digest, 1993.

Eggleston, Edward. *A History of the United States and Its People.* Lost Classics Book Company, 1998.

Hakim, Joy. *History of Us,* 2nd Edition. Oxford University Press, 1999.

Hansen, Fay R. *The American History Teacher's Book of Lists.* Center for Applied Research in Education, 1999.

Hart, Michael A. *The 100: Ranking the Most Influential People of All Time.* Carol Publishing Group, 1993.

Hazlitt, Henry. *Economics in One Lesson.* Fox and Wilkes, 1996.

Henty, G. A. *In the Heart of the Rockies.* Lost Classics Book Co., 1998. Also other titles by G. A. Henty.

Hopkinson, Christina and others. *The Usborne History of the Twentieth Century.* EDC Publications, 1994. See also many other Usborne products including *Tales of Real Escape, Tales of Real Heroism,* and the *Usborne Book of Europe.*

Kapit, Wynn. *Geography Coloring Book.* Addison-Wesley, 1999.

Loewen, James. *Lies My Teacher Told Me: Everything Your American History Textbook Got Wrong.* Touchstone Books, 1996.

Maybury, Richard. *What Ever Happened to Justice?* Bluestocking Press, 1992. Also *Ancient Rome, How It Affects You Today; What Ever Happened to Penny Candy?;* and *Are You a Liberal? Conservative? Or Confused?*

Menzel, Peter et al. *Material World: A Global Family Portrait.* Sierra Club Books, 1994.

Moes, Garry. *Streams of Civilization.* Answers and Genesis, 1980.

Scarre, Carrie. *Smithsonian Timelines of the Ancient World.* DK Publishing, 1993. See also many other excellent DK titles, including *Pompeii: The Day a City Was Buried, DK in the*

Beginning. . . A Nearly Complete History of Almost Everything, The DK History of the World, and *The DK Panoramic Atlas.*

Sparks, John B. *The Rand-McNally Histomap of World History.* Rand-McNally, 1990.

Urdang, Laurence. *The Timetables of American History.* Touchstone Books, 1996.

Periodicals

Christian History Magazine,
http://www.Christianity.net/christian history
Family Chronicle, 888-326-2476, http://www.familychronicle.com
History Magazine, 416-491-3699,
http://www.history-magazine.com
National Geographic, 800-NGS-LINE,
http://www.nationalgeographic.com
Smithsonian, http://www.smithsonianmag.si.edu
The World and I, published by the *Washington Times,*
http://www.worldandi.com

Games and Hands-On Activities

Aristoplay Educational Games (Where in the World and Hail to the Chief), 888-GR8-GAME, http://www.artistoplay.com
Mapping the World by Heart, 800-342-0236,
http://www.mapping.com
Read A Mat (educational place mats) and U.S. and World Mark-It Laminated Maps, 626-821-0025,
http://www.excellenceineducation.com

Homeschool Teen Travel Opportunities

American Student Travel, 800-231-1731, http://www.astravel.com
Citadel Summer Camp, 843-953-6704
North Carolina Outward Bound, 828-299-3366,
http://www.ncobx.org

Not Back-to-School Camp, 541-686-2315, http://www.nbtsc.org

Solid Rock Wilderness Adventures, 888-721-9110,
  http://www.srom.org

Teen Missions International, 407-453-0350,
  http://www.teenmissions.org

Curricula and Catalogs

American Textbook Committee, 205-674-3548 (titles include
  Clarence Carson's Basic Economics and *A Basic History of the
  United States)*

Beautiful Feet Books (*History Through Literature, Geography Through
  Literature,* and more), 800-889-1978, http://www.bfbooks.com

BJU PRESS History Books, 800-845-5731, http://www.bjup.com

Bluestocking Press, 800-959-8586, http://www.bluestocking.com

Greenleaf Press, 800-311-1508, http://www.greenleafpress.com

History Alive! 605-642-7583, http://www.dianawaring.com

Jackdaw Publications (reproductions of primary sources)
  800-311-1508, http://www.jackdaw.com

Runkle Geography, 877-436-8398, http://www.runklepub.com

Web Sites

The American Civil War Worldwide Information Archive,
  http://www.users.iamdigex.net/bdboyle/cw.html

Ben's Guide to U.S. Government, http://www.bensguide.gpo.gov/

History of Money from Ancient Times to the Present Day by Glyn
  Davies, http://www.ex.ac.uk/~RDavies/arian/llyfr.html

The History Net, http://www.thehistorynet.com

HyperHistory Online,
  http://www.hyperhistory.com/online_n2 /History_n2/a.html

8

EVERYTHING ELSE: FOREIGN LANGUAGES, ARTS, DRIVER EDUCATION, PHYSICAL EDUCATION, AND RELIGION

In This Chapter

+ Foreign languages

+ The arts

+ Living well

+ Religious education

+ Driver education

+ Simple starting points

+ Resources

$\mathcal{Y}$OU HAVE CONSIDERED approaches to the traditional high school subjects, namely reading, writing, math, science, history, and geography. Now it is time to think about all those topics that schools call elective or "extra"—foreign language, music, art, drama, driver education, health, physical education, and religious studies.

Regarding the extras, our fellow homeschooling travelers make three points—loud and clear. First, many teenagers consider one or more of these subjects the best reason to get up in the morning. Because they live for music, drama, art, or sports, these teens see these subjects as essential, not as extra. Many say that music, in particular, provides motivation to complete more mundane subjects.

Second, the agenda of a majority of home educators differs markedly from that of public schools. More than 80 percent of our survey respondents incorporate religious education into their home-schooling every day. Many families build studies around religious teachings. Others buy curriculum fully integrated with material designed to instill and reinforce religious beliefs. Even more than music and art, these families say religion is essential, not an extra subject tacked on after the fact.

Third, many homeschooling parents worry less about how to cover extras like foreign language, music, or team sports than English or math. With less pressure (are we doing it right? are we covering everything?), families explore creative approaches to these subjects more often than with the three R's. Read on to learn what they are.

> Homeschoolers study foreign languages for many reasons, and preparation for college admissions is number one. Competitive colleges usually require the equivalent of at least two years foreign language study.

FOREIGN LANGUAGES

Homeschoolers study foreign languages for many reasons, and preparation for college admissions is number one. Competitive colleges usually require the equivalent of at least two years foreign language study. Very selective colleges recommend three or four years. Many homeschoolers study Latin, Spanish, or French so they can include it on their high school transcript.

While college provides a major stimulus, there are other reasons to learn foreign tongues. Two of our survey respondents write about moving to countries with principal languages other than English. Some teenagers plan service, mission, or pleasure trips to Mexico, France, Germany, or African countries. Speaking the foreign language eases and enhances the journey.

Others polish their foreign language skills to travel through time. Homeschoolers tackle ancient Greek and Hebrew to read the Bible in the original. They learn Russian to read Tolstoy or French to savor the nuances of Gallic poetry.

Finally, some people study foreign languages for fun. They enjoy learning and piecing together the unique vocabulary and syntax of a new language the same way others enjoy mastering a Beethoven sonata or creating a quilt. We call these people foreign language hobbyists, and they emphasize that creating a reason to learn a second language must be your first step.

> How about learning enough Italian to communicate with Grandma in her native tongue? Or acquiring sufficient Russian or Japanese to correspond with a pen pal?

Motivation

Foreign language hobbyists tell us that two elements provide motivation. First, listen and practice daily. Foreign language learners need frequent exposure to the new tongue. The daily activity can be anything—reviewing flash cards, listening to music in the target language, watching foreign language television, perusing *French Reader's Digest* with a translating dictionary close at hand, doing Latin grammar exercises, or speaking Spanish. The more students know, the more their confidence increases, and the more they want to know.

Second, hobbyists tell us to tie foreign language learning to a goal, ideally a fun goal. Consider a trip to Europe within the next two to four years, tied to learning French or German or Spanish. Or consider somewhere closer to the United States, such as Mexico and French-speaking Canada. Of course, travel is not the only potential goal. How about learning enough Italian to communicate with Grandma in her native tongue? Or acquiring sufficient Russian or Japanese to correspond with a pen pal?

Which Language?

A whopping 90 percent of those responding to our survey chose Spanish, with good reason. Spanish clearly ranks as the de facto second language in the United States. In the Southwest, as well as in Florida and even New York City, Spanish permeates everyday life. In these predominantly Spanish communities, it's not uncommon to see signs and government documents printed in English and Spanish, to hear Spanish radio and television programs, and to find Spanish books and tapes in libraries. There are also large populations who speak little or no English, only Spanish. Prevalence of this language means that students nationwide have easy access to formal Spanish educational materials. Students in the Southwest, Texas, and Florida also have frequent opportunities to use the language in everyday life.

The second most frequently studied language, according to our survey respondents, is Latin. The language of Cicero, famous Roman orator, owes its popularity among home educators to several factors. First, Latin study makes English grammar more understandable and increases English vocabulary. That explains why Latin students score 15 percent higher than others on the verbal portion of the Scholastic Assessment Test, the principal college admissions test. Second, unlike other languages, Latin is a dead language, with no living speakers today. Pronunciation is not as critical as with Spanish or French. With little pressure to "say it right," students study Latin principally to acquire a reading knowledge, giving them direct access to 1,500 years of Western thought. And finally, excellent home-school instructional resources exist for Latin, probably better than for any other language.

The third most popular language with our survey respondents is American Sign Language (ASL), the language of the deaf. As the fourth most-used language in the United States, the public has grown increasingly interested in ASL over the past several years. It is everywhere. Increasingly, employers look for applicants who can communicate with the deaf, and television stations use signing in their advertising and programming. Hundreds of colleges now accept ASL as fulfillment of their foreign language requirements. Homeschoolers, taking note of the snowballing interest in ASL, usually take classes through support groups and local junior colleges.

In deciding which language to study, homeschoolers have to carefully consider their resources. Foreign language study can be expensive and can also require substantial time and energy. For that reason, consider having all children in the family study the same foreign language. Also, strongly favor any language with which the parents have experience. You may think your high school French has evaporated, but even rudimentary knowledge can help your teenagers.

Teens with definite goals should choose a language consistent with those goals. Employers tell us that Japanese is a good choice for future computer engineers. Those planning a stint in the military will be well served by Arabic, German, or Russian. Future physicians,

> Hundreds of colleges now accept American Sign Language as fulfillment of their foreign language requirements.

Languages the survey respondents study—in order of popularity—include:

+ Spanish (more than 90 percent of respondents)
+ Latin (more than 20 percent)
+ American Sign Language
+ German
+ French
+ Greek
+ Gaelic
+ Italian
+ Japanese

nurses, and veterinarians should study Latin, the source of 95 percent of medical vocabulary. Classically trained singers usually learn German, French, and Italian. Those planning missionary work in Africa might consider Swahili and other widely spoken African languages.

Total Immersion

Several of our survey respondents report problems learning foreign languages. Belinda confesses, "We keep trying to learn Spanish, but it is not working. We need a tutor or something. We will keep plugging away until we figure out how to get it done." Marla agrees, saying, "We are not particularly successful with foreign language. The best resources are home-shopping shows that describe items in Spanish, then in English."

Marla has come close to a solution with the home-shopping shows—she simply needs to expand upon it. We have all heard of children or teenagers transplanted to a foreign country who learn a second language in a year or two. They watch television. They use their new language all day, every day. They listen, respond, and

HOW WE DID IT

We studied Spanish as a family formally in Guatemala and Honduras. Nathan returned to Honduras for three weeks for more immersion study. Leana will be taking Spanish at the local university this fall. Andrea and I will work together with a variety of materials, combining it with studying English grammar.

—AMY IN PORTLAND, MAINE

somehow work through difficult situations. This is the ideal way to learn a foreign language.

For those who cannot afford a move to France or Spain, hobbyists recommend learning techniques that resemble living in a foreign country. These techniques are called total immersion.

Total immersion goes beyond using a formal curriculum and tapes. Total immersion for home educators involves doing as much as possible every day in the target language. Label everything in your home in the target language. Learn common greetings, and use them routinely. Listen to foreign language music and watch foreign films. Amy explains how they combine program language learning with total immersion techniques: "I think the Learnables [a cassette-tape foreign-language program] is the best, but it is very important to draw from a variety of materials. Books on tape are great if you can find them at the right level. Of course, the very best is an immersion course in the appropriate country."

Create a personal connection to keep interest high. Some families invite a bilingual friend to dinner every week. Others host foreign exchange students. Kim found a relative to help. "[Our daughter] is learning from her German grandmother and a language program with tapes. I have also bought German grammar books and readers that I have found in thrift stores."

Total immersion takes a lot of planning and effort. Many families look for outside help, instead. Laura in Colorado uses computer programs and Web sites.

Kristin's teenagers enroll in classes for homeschoolers held at a nearby junior college. Terrie in Texas employs a computer program and a tutor for Spanish. See end-of-chapter Resources for frequently recommended programs.

QUICK & EASY

Find a foreign pen pal for your teenager from a country in which they speak the language you are studying.

THE ARTS

No doubt about it: Homeschoolers are artsy people. Almost every survey respondent reports that their teens spend time daily on music, dance, drama, drawing, painting, or sculpture.

Music

Tess in Pennsylvania explains why her teens study music: "Studies show that playing a musical instrument helps with math understanding and may contribute to maintaining your mental faculties in old age." Whether music study improves your grasp of algebra or not, many parents find it hard to ignore the window of opportunity for learning to play an instrument. Younger students learn more quickly than older ones, and teenagers learn better than adults. Practical considerations aside, many teens find an emotional outlet in music difficult to duplicate elsewhere.

MONEY SAVER

Call the foreign language departments of local colleges and universities and ask about campus clubs for Spanish, French, German, and so on. Often these organizations welcome community participants.

Janice, who has been homeschooling since 1991, describes her teenagers' music experiences. "Between two teens, we have provided private lessons in piano, violin, and drums. Guitar has been self-taught. Other activities include youth symphony, community orchestra, music camp, church praise band, symphony concerts, and occasional rock concerts. My son's band, playing Christian rock, had their first public performance on the Fourth of July. He spends all of his free time on music."

Many parents, like Janice, provide private music lessons, but they do not stop there. Almost all respondents report exposing their teenagers to a range of musical experiences. Martha, who lives in a small town in New Jersey, says, "Our children take private instrument lessons, play in the orchestra and small ensembles, and sing in choirs." Belinda in Toledo, Ohio, writes, "Our son has taken guitar lessons for about six months. He has also been in two musical plays through the Community Theater. We do music appreciation in the car when we are traveling, and lots of singing at home."

Sharon, an unschooling mom in Canada, describes her fourteen-year-old son's experience. "He's had three years of weekly keyboard and percussion sessions with a music mentor. He has grown up with a variety of music, mostly classical, and has attended many concerts. He jams with homeschool friends and composes original piano music."

> Whether music study improves your grasp of algebra or not, many parents find it hard to ignore the window of opportunity for learning to play an instrument.

Learning to play more than one instrument is also common. Claudia reports, "[Our son] is studying toward grade 6 theory and practical recorder, and he has played in competitions and concerts. He has also taken two years of piano lessons and two years of saxophone lessons. He taught himself guitar this last year."

Music education sometimes extends to community productions and technical work. Lauren writes, "Our eighteen-year-old takes voice lessons and participates in musical theater. Our fifteen-year-old learns music sound systems with a professional musician friend."

Visual Arts

As a group, home educators express less interest in drawing, painting, and sculpture than in music. Unless they have an artistically talented teenager, they take a casual approach. Jane reports, "Our son does not draw much now that he has a guitar in his hand, but he used to draw a lot. He has all kinds of books and art supplies. We

MOST POPULAR INSTRUMENTS

Instruments that proved most popular with our survey respondents include:

+ Piano
+ Guitar
+ Violin
+ Voice
+ Recorder

have just set up lawn chairs at the lake and spent the day drawing. We got videos on techniques. We also studied photography and went on nature shoots."

Denise says, "We do art appreciation with museum visits, art books, Sister Wendy Beckett's books, and photo exhibits put on by an aunt, uncle, and grandmother. We took a pottery class, and also draw and sculpt at home. Many of our survey respondents mention homeschool co-op art experiences. Claudia provides art classes when her teenagers request them.

Karleen describes her children's art education: "Mandy carries a sketchbook with her and draws as inspiration strikes her. She has also studied drawing using Mark Kistler's *Imagination Station* on PBS and Mona Brookes' *Drawing with Children*. Both girls learned ceramic painting with a good friend of ours."

Visual Performing Arts

Community activities abound for drama and dance. Homeschoolers attend performances, act in drama productions at church, and take co-op classes with other homeschoolers. Karleen writes, "Both girls participated last year in the Guild Builders, a community children's theater group, and will again this year. Our homeschooling 4-H club has chosen drama as our special focus this year. We will do many of the activities out of Lisa Bany-Winters' book, *On Stage: Theater Games and Activities for Kids,* and Kay Hamblin's *Mime: A Playbook of Silent Fantasy.* In addition, the teens want to write and produce a play. Finally, we have plans for a Shakespearean reader's theater with the county homeschooling teens."

Dance, also popular, goes beyond ballet and tap. Opportunities range from aerobic Jazzercise to swing. Kate says her son took ballroom dancing last summer. Folk dancing is popular, and many communities provide free opportunities to learn square dancing, clogging, reels, Scottish sword dancing, and so on.

Donna in Canada says that the visual performing arts, specifically acting and associated activities, form the framework for her son's homeschooling. "He does not study visual performing art—he lives it. He is an actor and is very involved in the technical aspects of the entertainment industry." If Donna's son finds his eventual occupation through his teenage passion, he will not be the first.

MONEY SAVER

Learn the self-taught instruments. While it is possible to learn any instrument on your own, certain instruments lend themselves to self-teaching. These include guitar, recorder, bagpipes, harmonica, and many folk instruments. The recorder, a very inexpensive starter instrument, has serious literature written for it.

LIVING WELL

HEALTH, NUTRITION, AND physical education, often taught as separate classes in school, integrate seamlessly into most homeschools.

Health and Nutrition

"Keep it simple," say most of our survey respondents. Laura writes, "We make menus every two weeks, and our teens plan well-balanced meals. They also help cook."

Sarah reports, "We don't [formally] cover health and nutrition. He learns on his own by watching Discovery and The Learning Channel and reading magazine and newspaper articles."

Carrie describes her family's approach to health and nutrition: "We did a unit on body and health. Mostly, we discuss issues when they come up, particularly during an illness. We read food labels, discuss articles we run across, and research things that we find interesting. As a family, we practice homeopathy and use natural and herbal remedies when possible. Also, we always use doctor and chiropractic visits as opportunities to get information."

Jane says they use some published materials. "We had a school health book we covered last year, along with videos and other books from the library. This year I have a college book and some tapes and software. We will also go to the kitchen and grocery store and read labels."

Physical Education

With work, family activities, and individual and team sports, homeschool teenagers build the habits of lifetime fitness. Ron describes typical homeschool physical education. "My daughters swim, ski, ride their bikes, and extensively show Arabian horses. They also do a lot of ranch chores. We feel that it is important to learn some sports that they can pursue the rest of their lives."

Similarly, Donna's son's activities would keep anyone fit. They include "building soundproof walls, hanging lighting for shows (up and down ladders), rollerblading, cycling, basketball, gardening (building, digging, trimming trees, weeding), transferring cinder blocks, delivering flyers, walking friends' dogs, and hiking."

Carrie's teenager also lives an active life. "Our daughter taught herself yoga from a book and practices daily. We also join our home-school group in sports, take private tennis lessons, participate in the Presidential Physical Fitness Program, bicycle, skate, golf, and so on. We are an athletic family."

For formal sports training, many home-schoolers prefer martial arts. More than 30 per-cent of our survey respondents mention karate or tae kwon do or similar activities in connection with physical education. Tess writes, "As a family, we take kung fu and tai chi. Ted studies kung fu six days per week for forty-five minutes each les-son through Chinese Martial Arts of Carnegie, Pennsylvania."

QUICK & EASY

For couch potatoes, rent dance and exercise videos at the library. Then do them!

Many youth groups provide outlets for physi-cal activity. Our son regularly completed the mile run and other fitness challenges through the Civil Air Patrol Cadet Program. Jane describes her teenager's physical education, largely connected to the Boy Scouts. "He goes on Scout outings, rides bike with his dad, and we go canoeing. He and his dad took a trip in the Smoky Mountains and talked to people who hike the Appalachian Trail. He did the biking, backpacking, and canoeing merit badges in Scouts."

Community groups also provide opportunities to hone skills and keep in shape. Ron's daughters take gymnastics classes at the local high school and at their community recreation department. YMCAs and private gyms offer many activities, such as tennis, racquetball, and swimming. Churches often field volleyball teams and sponsor bowling leagues. Trina in Pennsylvania says her teens play on public school soccer teams. They also play church baseball and join local softball leagues. Bill in Canada mentions adult baseball and curling leagues as other possibilities.

Serious competition exists for those who desire it. Our son par-ticipated on a U.S. diving team that traveled to meets all over the

> Intense physical activity provides fun for everyone and one additional benefit—exhausting workouts diffuse teenage and family tensions.

nation. Based on this experience with a parks and recreation department team, the diving coach at West Point attempted to recruit him. Similarly, Patty in Anchorage writes about her teenager's precision skating for the Alaska state team. Homeschoolers who wish to qualify for NCAA sports should review the National Collegiate Athletic Association's Initial Eligibility Procedures for Homeschool Athletes. (See Resources for contact information.)

Probably the most important part of teenage physical education is creating fitness habits for a lifetime. Involve everybody—Mom, Dad, teens, and younger children. Intense physical activity provides fun for everyone and one additional benefit—exhausting workouts diffuse teenage and family tensions.

RELIGIOUS EDUCATION

ABOUT FACE! WE now journey from the physical to the metaphysical. Home educators who study religion fall into two groups. The first group concerns itself primarily with inculcating the family's beliefs, be they Christian, Jewish, Muslim or of some other faith. They would agree with Bill, who says, "Religion is important and integrated into all parts of teaching."

The second group studies religion as just another social studies course. They learn about religion to understand history, psychology, economics, and literature. Lauren explains, "We are not members of an established church, but I do read about religious beliefs of different faiths worldwide. We have learned about holidays of others and how religion has affected history."

Our survey respondents learn about religion using books, instructional materials, and discussion. Regardless of approach, homeschooling parents find themselves dealing with difficult questions when discussing religion with teenagers. Fortunately, free expert help lies right outside your front door—at your local churches, synagogues, and temples.

DRIVER EDUCATION

IF YOU TOOK driver education two or three decades ago in public school, you should know that much has changed. First, most school districts, tightening the purse strings, no longer offer free driver education. Even if you have access to high school classes, do not be surprised if they either charge for driver training or do not offer it at all.

Where should you go? Home educators have two alternatives for classroom and behind-the-wheel training. Several companies and independent-study high schools now offer excellent parent-taught driving courses (see the end-of-chapter Resources for specifics). Unfortunately, not all motor vehicle departments and insurance companies recognize these courses. As an alternative, check your Yellow Pages for local private companies that offer driver education. It will not be cheap, but as Mary Pride, homeschool mother and author, points out, "This is the only school subject that, if you fail to master it, could result in your or someone else's death." If you have to pay the money to get it right, do it.

That leaves the second big change over the past two to three decades for teens behind the wheel. State laws for licensing drivers under the age of eighteen have tightened up considerably. Some states now require not only completion of a driver education class, but also proof of school enrollment. This is supposed to prevent teens from dropping out of regular school. Unfortunately, it can create a paperwork hassle for home educators. If you encounter this roadblock at your motor vehicle department office, contact your statewide support group for advice on how to prove "enrollment" as a full-time homeschooler.

The extras fit into each homeschool differently. Some teenagers spend hours daily making music or perfecting martial arts moves. Others draw or practice skating or gymnastics for most of each day. Incorporate those extras that fit your situation, and leave the rest for adulthood.

SIMPLE STARTING POINTS

✦   *Visit your local library and evaluate the foreign language resources.* What books, audiocassette programs, and videotapes do they have?

✦   *Watch a familiar film, such as* The Wizard of Oz *or* Star Wars, *in the language you plan to study.* Or listen to music in your target language.

✦   *If your teenagers play an instrument, make certain they also sing and listen!* Sing, either at home with CDs or with a community choir. Listen to good music on the radio or from the library. Attend local concerts. Both singing and listening are free, and both enhance musical development.

✦   *Try one of the Art Unit Studies, specifically written for teenagers, found in every issue of* Homeschooling Today.

✦   *List your teenagers' current physical activities, whether related to work or play.* Remember, you can call it all "school."

RESOURCES

Foreign Languages

American Sign Language Institute, Suite 3B, 242 West 27th Street
    (between 7th and 8th), New York, NY 10001
Artes Latinae, 800-392-6453, http://www.bolchazy.com
Calliope Books, Route 3, Box 3395, Saylorsburg, PA, 610-381-2587

Destinos (Spanish) and French in Action, Public Broadcasting
    System, 800-257-2578, http://www.pbs.org
Latina Christiana, Catholic Heritage Curricula, 800-490-7713,
    http://www.sonnet.com/chc/lati1.htm
Learnables, 800-237-1830,
    http://www.home-school.com/Mall /ILC/Learnables.html
Power-Glide Language Courses, 801-373-3973,
    http://www.powerglide.com
The Rosetta Stone, 800-788-0822,
    http://www.therosettastone.com
Silverstein, Ruth et al. *Spanish the Easy Way.* Barron's, 1996.
Stewart, David. *American Sign Language the Easy Way.* Barron's,
    1998.
Wheelock, Frederick M. and Richard A. LaFleur. *Wheelock's Latin*
    (Harper College Outline). HarperCollins, 1995.
World of Reading (in many languages), 404-233-4042,
    http://www.wor.com

Music

Ben-Tovim, Atarah and Douglas Boyd. *The Right Instrument for
    Your Child.* Trafalgar Square, 1996.
Davidson Music Courses, 913-262-6533,
    http://www.davidsonmusic .com
Gindick, John. *Country Blues Harmonica for the Musically Hopeless.*
    Klutz Press, 1984.
Homespun Piano Courses, 800-338-2737,
    http://www.homespuntapes.com
Learning to Read Music, 800-243-1234, http://www.audioforum.com
Pogue, David and Scott Speck. *Classical Music for Dummies.*
    IDG Books, 1997.
Sethna, Dhun. *Classical Music for Everybody.* Fitzwilliam Press,
    1997.
Zeitlin, Ralph. *Basic Recorder Lessons.* Music Sales Corporation, 1997.

Visual Arts

Beckett, Wendy. *Sister Wendy's Story of Painting.* DK Publishing, 1994.

Butterfield, Mona and Susan Peach. *Photography* (An Usborne Guide). EDC Publications, 1987.

Janson, H. W. *History of Art.* Harry N. Abrams, 1999.

McCloud, Scott. *Understanding Comics: The Invisible Art.* Harper-Perennial, 1994.

Metzger, Phil. *Perspective Without Pain/3 Volumes in One.* North Light Books, 1992.

Reece, Nigel. *The Usborne Complete Book of Drawing.* EDC Publications, 1994.

Strickland, Carol. *The Annotated Mona List: A Crash Course in Art History from Prehistoric to Post-Modern.* EconoClad Books, 1999.

Visual Performing Arts

Bany-Winters, Lisa. *On Stage: Theater Games and Activities for Kids.* Chicago Review Press, 1997.

Davidson, Diane. *Shakespeare on Stage.* Learning Links, 800-724-2616, http://www.learninglinks.com

Hamblin, Kay. *Mime: A Playbook of Silent Fantasy* (out of print, check library and used bookstores)

Physical Fitness

Fitness at Home, 315-585-2248, http://drk3@cornell.edu

Home School Family Fitness, 651-636-7738, http://www.umn.edu /home/whitn003

NCAA Guide for the College-Bound Student Athlete, Initial Eligibility Procedures for Homeschooled Student Athletes, 317-917-6222, http://www.ncaa.org/cbsa/home_school.html

The President's Challenge Youth Physical Fitness Programs, 800-258-8146, http://www.indiana.edu/~preschal/

Religion

Many home educators will used religious materials specific to their faith, for example Catholic catechism materials. In addition, home educators may purchase religious instructional materials from the many Christian homeschool suppliers, like A Beka and Alpha Omega. We make no attempt to list those materials here. To branch out, for comparative religion studies, check out the following titles.

Anders, Max. *30 Days to Understanding The Bible in 15 Minutes a Day.* Thomas Nelson, 1998.

Ellsberg, Robert. *All Saints: Daily Reflections on Saints, Prophets, and Witnesses for Our Time.* Crossroad Publishing, 1997.

Rosten, Leo. *Religions of America: Ferment and Faith in an Age of Crisis.* Simon & Schuster, 1975.

SuperStar Teachers Great World Religions, Audio and Video Versions, 800-832-2412, http://www.teachco.com

Driver Education

Berardelli, Phil. *Safe Young Drivers: A Guide for Parents and Teens.* Nautilus Communications, 1996.

Help! I Want to Drive and *Help! My Teenager Wants to Drive,* two books sold as a set by National Driver Training Institute, 800-439-1231, http://www.nationaldrivertraining.com

Keystone National High School Driver Education, 800-255-4937, http://www.keystonehighschool.com

Magliozzi, Tom. *Car Talk.* Dell Books, 1991.

University of Nebraska-Lincoln Driver's Education, 402-472-4321, http://www.unl.edu/conted.disted

Web Sites

Go Driver, Free Driver's License Written Test Preparation, http: //www.godriver.com

New Driver, http://newdriver.spedia.net/

Online Study Guide for Student Drivers, http://golocalnet.net/ drive/

9

TAILORING HOME-SCHOOLING TO MEET YOUR FAMILY'S UNIQUE NEEDS

In This Chapter

+ Depressed finances and trying times

+ Single parents and full-time work

+ Stay-at-home dads

+ Special academics

+ Physically challenged teens

+ When family size makes a difference

+ Simple starting points

+ Resources

W*HEN NEWSPAPER REPORTERS* ask about home education, they often assume that all homeschooling families consist of a working father with an adequate income, a stay-at-home mother, and two or three healthy, able children. Questions that interest homeschool travelers about special circumstances seldom arise. Yet more than 80 percent of our survey respondents deal every day with one or more uncommon situations. These include limited funds, single parenthood, stay-at-home fathers, gifted and special needs teenagers, and single-child and large families. Those who responded to our survey describe their challenges and suggest solutions for the journey.

DEPRESSED FINANCES
AND TRYING TIMES

SEVERAL TRAVELERS, WHO count every penny and live from paycheck to paycheck, creatively homeschool with free community resources. Katy says, "We educate our children on a very tight budget so we use the library and Internet, free books, yard sales, and the thrift store."

Ron keeps his goals in sight. "We homeschool on very little money. We just do what we can afford within our budget and make our children's education our first priority."

Beth in Indiana tells us that they are a missionary family going to college. She comments, "No income means no money for outside resources. We buy used books and write our own curriculum. The library and the VegSource Internet bulletin board have been the most helpful in our situation. Home education has prepared us for the mission field. We now know how to learn at home and how to rely on our family unit for everything."

> Several travelers who count every penny and live from paycheck to paycheck creatively homeschool with free community resources.

Carrie in Florida lists outstanding strategies for homeschooling with limited funds. She writes: "Homeschooling on tight money has always been an issue for us. We recycle, solicit donations from local businesses (paper products, and so on), and buy used books, games, and materials. We do a lot within a small budget. We have a couple of local museums that offer annual memberships, permitting frequent inexpensive trips. Some of these have let us purchase our membership by volunteering."

Tess plans ahead, buying materials she can use for more than one child. She also receives substantial help from local school districts. "This year we had extra money, so I purchased items for our son that will still work for our two-year-old when she reaches high school age. We have been fortunate to live near schools supportive of home education. Our northern California district supplied us with books, supplies, a supervising teacher, and field trips. In Pennsylvania, we use school textbooks for free."

Susanna writes not only about spending as little as possible, but also about dealing with family sickness and death. "We homeschool on a minimal budget, but the curriculum has been there when our children needed it. Our local homeschooling community has provided generously in the past. However, the homeschooling Internet community is now a more valuable resource. Our family has also experienced trying times. My daughter has had approximately fifty hours of surgery. In addition, we have taken care of a disabled parent and dealt with a death in the family. Home education has made all this easier to deal with."

Molly also deals with chronic illness. She describes how they mesh home education with family responsibilities. "We spend a big chunk of our time caring for my parents and helping with my handicapped sister. We handle this with careful planning. Homeschooling means the boys have much more time to help around the house with their grandparents and to hang out with their aunt."

One money saver, indeed one moneymaker all homeschool families should consider are part-time jobs for their teens. Unlike typical high-schoolers whose employment too often compromises education, most homeschooled thirteen- to eighteen-year-olds can easily schedule ten to twenty hours of paid work each week. Over two years, our daughter earned enough working at a dry cleaner to fund an exchange trip to Australia. Other teens work and contribute to family finances, build college savings, and purchase supplies for hobbies and special projects.

QUICK & EASY

Always remind grandparents and other extended family that you appreciate educational gifts for birthdays and the holidays. Suggest reference books, magazine subscriptions, educational games, and scholarships to educational summer camps.

SINGLE PARENTS AND FULL-TIME WORK

Parents whose work schedules conflict with their commitment to home education agonize over how to best spend their time. Some find full-time work incompatible with homeschooling. Viola, who has six children, lives in a log cabin in a rural mountainous area. She writes: "I worked part time, either as a bookkeeper or selling books on eBay [an Internet auction site]. I was on the computer too long, and it was too much."

Belinda, a single parent who has home-schooled since 1994, talks about the pluses and minuses of juggling work and teaching. "I have to work to support us and direct my son's home education at the same time. As a single mother, I have no one to consult or to share the teaching load. I get no feedback—sometimes I like that. With limited time, I cannot do all of the un-school things I would like to. My thirteen-year-old son has to take responsibility for completing his work with little supervision. We do school when I get home from work. Although I have no social life, I love spending time with my boy. It has been difficult because I have had to arrange day care instead of warehousing him in public school while I work."

Karleen also knows about coordinating work and homeschooling. "I just came home from a full-time job, working forty hours per week the last five years while homeschooling. For the first four years, my husband was home with the girls. He mainly supervised, and I did all lesson planning. This last year my in-laws and parents supervised. I still had to check their work and so on. It was very difficult for all of us. Eventually, my workload was too much.

MONEY SAVER

Call your local school district and any local private schools and ask what they do with their discards—textbooks, desks, laboratory equipment, gloves, encyclopedias, and audio- and videotapes. Many give these away or sell them for a nominal price.

HOMESCHOOL ALMOST-FOR-FREE CURRICULUM FOR TEENS

✦   Volunteer as a computer docent at the library or at local public and private schools or at your church if you are a computer expert (computer science).

✦   Construct history, geography, and government unit studies around real books from the library (social studies).

✦   Volunteer with a political campaign (social studies).

✦   Volunteer at a local science museum, veterinary clinic, or college science department (science).

✦   Keep a daily journal, write for real-life purposes, and select your own reading at the library (English).

✦   Call local colleges and universities and ask about speaker programs and free concerts and art exhibits (social studies, music, art).

✦   Tune into foreign language programming on radio and television (Spanish).

✦   Trade any needed private tutoring for housework, yard work, child care, or pet care (math, foreign language, music lessons).

✦   Join community groups. Genealogical societies will teach you research techniques, amateur radio clubs electronics, and computer interest groups computer science (social studies, science, computer science, and much more).

✦   Ask about book discussion groups at the library and at local bookstores (English).

✦   Get a job (math, independent-living skills).

✦   Apply for scholarships for summer camps and for summer college classes for teens (science, math, history, art, English).

✦   Join 4-H or Scouts (science, social studies, language arts, art, and much more).

✦   Join a church with programs for teenagers (religious studies, physical education, social studies).

Unlike typical high-schoolers whose employment too often compromises education, most homeschool teens can easily schedule ten to twenty hours of paid work each week.

Benefits of my working? My husband got closer to the girls during the time he was home with them, and the girls learned to teach themselves. My most helpful resource has been a database to plan my year. Lesson plans have kept us on schedule. We usually finish school within a couple of weeks of the original plan."

Single parents learn to network effectively. Donna writes: "As a single parent, I am fortunate to have a fairly close family, extended family, and support network. My most helpful resources have been family, extended family and an electronic-list support group."

Several of our survey respondents run home businesses, in-home day care being the most frequently mentioned income source. Sarah, who homeschools a son, age fifteen, and a daughter, eleven, describes her experience. "I do part-time day care and before and after school care. My children help with this—walking to and picking up from the bus stop, and helping with the baby I care for. It is hard to schedule homeschooling on the two days a week I have the baby. My children work independently on those days. I am not always free to go places, and my time is limited. We cope by opting out of some classes and field trips or by taking the baby with us. My job allows me to earn money while still homeschooling. Unfortunately, sometimes homeschooling does not get top priority anymore."

Carrie does publishing, graphic arts, and other contract work from a computer at home. She writes: "Most of the time, it has been easy to juggle work with homeschooling. However, on occasion, my work demands many hours in a short period of time. Homeschooling either goes on without me or ceases for a few days. Sometimes my three children, ages six to fourteen, work on the things they can do independently. It can cause stress and tension. On the plus side, our older children are learning to help the younger."

Karla has been homeschooling since 1996 in suburban Indiana. She agrees with other at-home workers that organization is key. She says, "I work part time at home as a piano teacher, so our schedule often feels very tight. I handle it by keeping us on a very regular schedule to fit everything in."

Anita in Illinois incorporates her home education into her business. "I operate a cake-decorating business out of my home. The children learn how to run a business and to be flexible when holidays and other rush times arrive. Homeschooling has allowed our teenagers to see how much work private enterprise involves. They see the difference between gross income and net pay. Of course, cake decorating gives us more money to spend on education."

HOW WE DID IT

Denise is a military wife. That makes her an off-and-on single parent, one who also deals with frequent moves. She writes: "I am a single parent sometimes as my husband goes out to sea often. I handle it the best way I can. If it means staying up late to finish something, I do. My children will never be at this stage again, so I try to live in such a way that I have no regrets. I might add that I have no paying job, and I do not often volunteer my time away from my family. I handle my husband's absences and our frequent moves by emphasizing the positives. Writing to Dad when he is gone is English. Tracking the ports he visits brings geography to life, and meeting new people is always a learning experience. Homeschooling is very helpful in our situation. If we had been tied down to a school district, we would not have been as free to move. Without our moves, we would have missed wonderful experiences. Our children are closer and their education does not stop and start with each move and each new school with its different expectations. Their education just follows along with us."

STAY-AT-HOME DADS

WHEN HOME EDUCATION was less common, one never heard of a stay-at-home dad homeschooling his children. Now not only do some fathers assume primary responsibility for home education, there's even an online magazine called *Homeschool Dad*. It is filled with projects and articles of particular concern to homeschool fathers, including those who act as the primary teacher and facilitator.

> Now not only do some fathers assume primary responsibility for home education, there's even an online magazine called Homeschool Dad.

Bill has two grown children and three boys, two of them teenagers, at home. He has been homeschooling since 1991 and lives in a small town in British Columbia, Canada. He writes: "I am a stay-at-home dad. My wife works, and I look after the house and homeschool. I also work part time as a school bus driver from 7:00 to 9:00 and 2:30 to 4:30. I sometimes feel out of place at homeschool meetings because I am often the only dad there. We have a support group and do activities together, like field trips. It's me and the rest of the moms. We get along great, and I am considered 'one of the girls.' I do have to have a good sense of humor. And I have had to explain to our children why Dad stays home while Mom works."

SPECIAL ACADEMICS

DO YOU HAVE an academically talented teenager who begs for mental challenges? Or one who cannot sit still? Or a teen who has been labeled ADD, dyslexic, or otherwise learning impaired? Or a physically disabled child? If so, you are not alone. Families nationwide have found solutions.

Gifted and Talented

Nobody likes the elitist word "gifted," home educators least of all it seems. Maybe that comes from being around children and realizing that every single one of them has special gifts. So, let's try the term "academically talented." This section deals primarily with academically talented teens—those who find grade-level materials boring and those who take advanced, college-level course work—as well as those who score high on IQ tests.

Jane describes how home education benefits their fourteen-year-old son. "The school gifted program was one day per week—clearly not enough. With homeschooling, the sky is the limit. Best of all, we have eliminated stupid busy work." Karleen, mother two academically advanced girls, agrees on the superiority of home education over public schooling. "We tune into their abilities and learning styles. With homeschooling, we can customize learning to interests and abilities. They go into as much depth as they desire in areas of interest. They use approaches and resources that work best for them. For example, both prefer real books and hands-on experiences to textbooks."

Molly in Gunnison, Colorado, writes about their family: "I have two identified gifted children, one in the 150+ IQ category. It has been hard occasionally because well-meaning friends think I push them too hard. They push themselves. We like to let the girls go as fast and far as they can and then if we want to spend months on a sidetrack, I know we have time. We will be using college courses for more subjects as they mature."

Janice sees her role as clearing a path for her academically talented son. She says, "It has been challenging to meet our son's needs. I sometimes have to be a 'pushy' mom to make sure our son is challenged. Early admission to a local community college has been very helpful, and homeschooling has been beneficial. Without it, Steven would have been a straight-A student, but would not have reached his potential. He has thrived with one-on-one tutoring and self-directed learning."

Academically Labeled Teens

Learning difficulties such as dyslexia and attention deficit disorder (ADD) motivate many families to begin home education. Some see problems miraculously disappear, once the student leaves school. Others find that a combination of patience, one-on-one instruction, and appropriate materials and pacing can make a world of difference.

Claudia uses labels to describe her situation, but avoids them with her children. "I have two children who would have been diagnosed as dyslexic, one with ADD. I let them learn at their own pace and try different methods until something works. We allow that just as some people never learn to play a musical instrument and are still okay people, so not being able to read does not disqualify you from being a neat person. Funnily enough, learning to read music was the turning point for both of them in learning to read words. We treat each family member as an individual with strengths and weaknesses, and search for individual solutions without labeling. Our best resources have been people, places, libraries, and open minds and loving hearts."

Kristin, homeschooling for four years, believes in individual instruction. "Our daughter, sixteen, has learning difficulties. She has improved enormously in the one-to-one environment. We alternate between feeling overwhelmed and knowing that we can do better than the public school. We just keep working. One on one does the trick."

At the same time, some parents have doubts. Rena has been homeschooling her thirteen-year-old son for three years. She writes: "I have a teen who was not getting what he needed from school. At home he works at his own level and is not so discouraged with himself. I always wonder if we do enough because progress is slow."

Others, like Trudy, succeed with a bits and pieces approach. She says, "I have an ADD/dyslexic child who has never been in school. I think my son does better at home with individualized instruction that he would in school. We were told 'dyslexic children hate to read.' He's a prolific reader. He has a short attention span, is impulsive, and gets frustrated easily. At home, he can learn in bits and pieces."

Annette also works one on one. "Although not diagnosed, I believe James is mildly dyslexic. At home, he is able to relax and concentrate. I have seen his dyslexic tendencies greatly improve over the course of a year. For instance, when copying math problems to his notebook, he would often copy the problem incorrectly. When I graded his papers, I would circle these and we would always correct them before moving on to the next lesson. In public school, he would have simply gotten a bad grade, and that would be the end of it. By constantly correcting these types of errors, he is beginning to see that slowing down, concentrating and paying attention will help him in the long run."

Karleen points out that communication and sensitivity go a long way. She writes: "One of our daughters, although gifted, is a very energetic, emotional, and noisy person. I have little doubt that some teacher along the way would have counseled us to test her for ADD. We handle it by tuning into her needs. She has always been able to concentrate on things that interested her. With other subjects, she would become antsy very quickly. When that happened, I would let her change activities or simply do something physical. She is always tapping her fingers or feet to some inner music. This would drive my other daughter and me crazy because we are easily distracted by noise. Each of us worked on being sensitive to each other's needs. Over the years, our noisy daughter learned to leave the room to make her sounds. And my other daughter and I now tolerate the sounds for a longer period of time."

SIMPLE TECHNIQUES TO DEAL WITH LEARNING DIFFICULTIES

✦ Keep him company; work one on one.

✦ Work at student's ability level, not necessarily at grade level.

✦ Work at appropriate pace; slow down and speed up as needed.

✦ Adapt to his learning style.

✦ Emphasize areas in which your teen shines.

PHYSICALLY CHALLENGED TEENS

DO DEAFNESS, BLINDNESS, mental retardation, chronic illness, or other disabling conditions preclude home education? Certainly not. While ten years ago, it was difficult to find homeschoolers in similar situations, the growth of homeschooling and the advent of the Internet have changed everything.

Best advice for those dealing with physical handicaps? First, give yourself a support system. Look two places—within the homeschooling community and within groups of parents who deal with similar disabilities. Second, schedule breaks and respite care at least weekly. Tired parents cannot provide optimal care and education.

WHEN FAMILY SIZE MAKES A DIFFERENCE

SINGLE-CHILD FAMILIES and large families face different homeschooling challenges. Camille in Hawaii writes: "We have an only child, now thirteen. There are no older children to help teach or do housework. And she has no one to keep her company when I go to the office or do other errands."

Loneliness can be a problem for families homeschooling only children. These parents usually need to make greater efforts to satisfy their teenager's need for companionship. Kate, who lives in the greater Los Angeles area, volunteers some solutions. "We have an only child, now fifteen and always homeschooled. I have sought out and included other youth in enrichment trips to museums, concerts, and sporting events. Boy Scouts has been an integral part of our homeschooling. Support groups and church associations have also been very helpful."

HOW WE DID IT

We find that our learning-disabled son does better out of school than in. He learns best with one-on-one attention. He progresses because we will not let him get away with laziness. Of course, we have modified his program to fit his needs, to stretch him intellectually without being overwhelming. It took most of the first year of homeschooling for Ted to see academic success. He is now a reader. And this summer's work on fractions has shown him that he can do math.

It will probably take another year or two to iron out writing difficulties. Ted has always been a difficult child. Always. A lot of time he is no fun to be around. When he was little, I decided that I did not want to homeschool him because he was such a challenge. Unfortunately, school does not help. In our experience, schooling leaves Ted worse off. If he is going to make it in life, I am the only one who will put forth the effort to instill necessary skills. So I go on. Sometimes he is just delightful. The most helpful resources I have found have been on the Internet. One excellent site on learning disabilities simply says to use what works and ignore what does not. It has given me the courage and expert backing to follow my gut instincts.

—TESS IN CANONSBURG, PENNSYLVANIA

Large families, of course, deal with an entirely different set of challenges. Marta details some of the trade-offs. "Seven children (all daughters) means homeschooling with limited funds. I have learned to use the public library, to make my own materials, and to accept used and donated items. Scheduling is difficult. When the girls request an activity outside the home, I have to ask, 'How much does it cost?' and 'How will you get there?' Often the time and transportation to one activity conflicts with another. The girls have had to learn to work on their own since I cannot work with each of them all the time. They help each other with both academics and household chores."

> Loneliness can be a problem for families homeschooling only children. These parents usually need to make greater efforts to satisfy their teenager's need for companionship.

Marta, homeschooling her brood since 1997, continues, "Despite the problems, homeschooling is best for large families. I no longer think about organizing around the school schedule. My husband's only day off is Monday, so that is his day with the girls. When they were in school, half the day was wasted. Now he sees more of our daughters. And family trips can be any time."

Tom and Sherry Bushnell in their article from the *NATHHAN News*, "Hints for Mothers of Many Children," say that the two most important things that mothers in large families can do are stay rested and take time to plan. I agree. Sounds like good advice for all homeschooling special situations.

SIMPLE STARTING POINTS

✦ *Write down how you would homeschool your teenagers if you only had $25 per child per year.* Even if you have unlimited funds, you may surprise yourself with creative educational strategies.

+ *Make a budget for homeschooling.* Include expenditures per child per year and decide what items will be purchased with the money allocated. Ask you teenagers for budget suggestions and listen carefully to their ideas.

+ *If you are giving up a salaried job to homeschool, research work-at-home opportunities.* Those who create successful situations often begin with an inventory of their own assets and skills.

+ *If you have a special-needs teenager (such as academically talented, dyslexic, physically challenged), network with others to learn about helpful approaches and resources.* Begin with the reading listed below under Resources.

+ *If you have an only child or a large family or if you are a single parent or a homeschooling stay-at-home father, realistically assess the potential problems.* Find support and decide how to handle those problems at the onset.

RESOURCES

Living Within a Budget

Books

Dacyczyn, Amy. *The Complete Tightwad Gazette: Promoting Thrift As a Viable Alternative Lifestyle.* Random House, 1999.

Hendrickson, Borg. *How to Write a Low-Cost/No-Cost Curriculum for Your Homeschool.* Mountain Meadow Press, 1995.

Kenyon, Mary Potter and Lisa Laurance. *Homeschooling from Scratch: Simple Living—Super Learning.* Gazelle Publications, 1996.

McCoy, Jonni. *Miserly Moms.* Holly Hall Publishing, 1996.

Morgan, Melissa and Judith Waite Allee. *Homeschooling on a Shoestring.* Harold Shaw Publishers, 1999.

Williams, Jane. *How to Stock a Home Library Inexpensively.* Bluestocking Press, 1995.

Catalogs

Used Books and Curriculum

The Back Pack, 252-244-0738, http://www.thebackpack.com
The Book Cellar, 800-338-4257, e-mail bookcellar@juno.com
The Book Peddler, 800-928-1760,
    e-mail The Book Peddler@juno.com
The Homeschool Publishing House, 508-892-4307,
    http://www.bravewc.com/hph
Home School Used Book and Curriculum Exchange,
    http://www.homeschoolusedbooks.com
Laurelwood Publications, 540-554-2670,
    e-mail Laurelwood@juno.com
Library Shelf, http://www.libraryshelf.com
The Swap, http://www.theswap.com
Twaddle Free Books, 804-749-4859

Academically Talented

Books

Galbraith, Judy, James Delisle, and Pamela Espeland. *The Gifted Kids Survival Guide: A Teen Handbook.* Free Spirit Publishing, 1996.
Olenchak, Richard. *They Say My Kid's Gifted: Now What?* Prufrock Press, 1998.
Webb, James T. *Guiding the Gifted Child: A Practical Source for Parents and Teachers.* Gifted Psychology Press, 1989.
Yahnke, Sally. *The Survival Guide for Parenting Gifted Kids.* Free Spirit Publishing, 1991.

Periodicals

Gifted Child Today, 800-998-2208, http://www.prufrock.com
    Gifted Education Review, 303-670-8350.

Support

National Association for Gifted Children, 202-785-4268,
http://www.nagc.com

Special Needs and Learning Difficulties

Books

Armstrong, Thomas. *The Myth of the A.D.D. Child: 50 Ways to Improve Your Child's Behavior and Attention Span Without Drugs, Labels, or Coercion.* Plume, 1997.

Crook, William G. *Help for the Hyperactive Child.* Professional Books, 1991.

Davis, Ronald D. *The Gift of Dyslexia.* Perigree, 1997.

Herzog, Joyce. *Choosing and Using Curriculum for Your Special Child.* Greenleaf Press, 1996.

Moore, Raymond and Dorothy. *School Can Wait.* Brigham Young University Press, 1989.

Reichenburg-Ullman, Judyth. *Ritalin Free Kids.* Prima Publishing, 1996.

Rosner, Jerome. *Helping Children Overcome Learning Difficulties.* Walker and Company, 1993.

Seiderman, Arthur S. and Steven E. Marcus. *20/20 Is Not Enough.* Mass Market Paperback, 1991.

Turecki, Stanley, M.D. *Difficult Child.* Bantam Doubleday Dell, 1989.

Support

ADD Action Group, providing alternative solutions for ADD, learning difficulties, dyslexia, and autism, 212-769-2457

Children and Adults with Attention Deficit Disorder (CHADD), 800-233-4050, http://www.chadd.org

Homeschooling Kids with Disabilities,
    http://members.tripod.com/~Maaja
NATHHAN (NATional CHallenged Homeschoolers Association
    Network), 206-857-4257, http://www.nathhan.com
PAVE (Parents Active for Vision Education), 800-PAVE988,
    http://www.pave-eye/~vision.com

Uncommon Situations: Small, Large, Military, and Single-Parent Families Plus Homeschool Dads

HomeSchool Dad Magazine, an online publication,
    www. homeschooldad.com
Military Home Educators Network,
    http://www.geocities.com/Heartland/Village/6678/
NATHHAN (see above)

Web Site

Federal Resources for Educational Excellence (FREE),
    http://www.ed.gov/free/

Part Three

KEEPING THE LEARNING JOURNEY FUN AND SUCCESSFUL

10

RESOURCES FOR YOUR

LEARNING JOURNEY

In This Chapter

✦ You already have great resources

✦ Creating a home learning environment

✦ Helpful supplies

✦ More helpful resources

✦ Simple starting points

✦ Resources

W HEN WE FIRST consider homeschooling, many of us reach for our checkbooks. We think about buying curriculum, paper, pencils, lab supplies, and turning at least part of our home into something that resembles school. Read this chapter before you sign that first check, though. You may find that your home already contains most of the items experienced home educators say they cannot live without.

YOU ALREADY HAVE GREAT RESOURCES

LOOK AROUND YOUR home. Check out every room including the kitchen, garage, and yard. If you see books, magazines, an encyclopedia, dictionaries, an atlas, a radio, and perhaps musical instruments or sports equipment, you already have great resources. So long as you can find pens, sharpened pencils, and paper, you have the makings of a fine homeschool, without spending another cent.

We asked our survey respondents, "If you had to homeschool on an island and could only take ten things with you, what would they be? In other words, what items do you have in your home that you consider invaluable for home education?" Answers range from serious articles like dictionaries to frivolous can't-live-without-it items like chocolate. The answers reflect, above all, the incredible diversity of home educators.

Denise responds, "I had to laugh when I read this question. We *are* on an island, and we moved here without our household goods so we had to really think hard about what to bring. Here is our list: computer, TV-VCR, keyboard for piano-playing son, guitar for our daughter, textbooks we could not find at the library, maps and posters, blow-up globe, dictionary and thesaurus, Norton anthologies, and telescope and microscope."

Karen, like Denise, lives in a very rural area. She thought carefully about the most important items for their homeschool. She writes, "We live thirty miles from the nearest large grocery store and fifteen miles from the nearest country library, which is only about 900 square feet." Karen's top-ten island-resource list includes: "Computer and Internet access; history and science software; lots of books; American School course; telescope and star chart; cable TV; VCR and tapes for the Discovery Channel, History Channel, the Learning Channel; CD player and music from different composers; woodworking tools; and automotive tools."

TOP-TEN ISLAND RESOURCES

Number after each item indicates how many respondents out of 104 included this item on their top ten lists:

✦ Pens, pencils, and paper (85)

✦ Computer with Internet access (68)

✦ Bible or other holy book (52)

✦ Home library/lots of books (45)

✦ Dictionary (40)

✦ Piano/musical instruments (38)

✦ Encyclopedia (35)

✦ TV/VCR/CD player (32)

✦ Art supplies (32)

✦ Atlas/wall maps/globes (28)

Amy, homeschooling since 1984, lists her ten essential items as "A piano, a library of great fiction, a travel agent, a computer, songbooks, camping equipment, a CD player, a set of encyclopedias, a sewing machine, and colored pencils." Only half-jokingly, she adds, "We would make paper out of local wood pulp."

Many who responded to this question emphasize hands-on materials, whether for music, art, or science. Johanna, homeschooling since 1992 in Minnesota, says she would take a set of colored pencils, drawing paper, notebooks, origami paper, laptop computer, at least one musical instrument, model rockets and engines, and batteries. Sharon in North Vancouver, British Columbia, lists her top resources—a computer with Internet access, dictionary, duct tape, vegetable seeds, complete works of Shakespeare, baseball equipment, cookbook, notebooks, pens, radio.

Other respondents put more emphasis on books. Molly who homeschools her children on a large cattle ranch in Colorado, says, "I couldn't imagine homeschooling without our 2,300-plus volume library." Kim reports that they would take the scriptures, the computer, Shakespeare's complete works, violins, music, paper, art supplies, *Little Women, David Copperfield,* and Puzzle Books. Lauren in Ithaca, New York, also prominently features books on her list, which she says includes an encyclopedia, a computer, the *American Heritage Dictionary,* a shortwave radio, art supplies, colored pencils, collections of literature, and an atlas.

Interestingly, only twelve respondents out of 104 mention curriculum and textbooks on their top-ten lists. Only two respondents talk about including a desk, two others a chalkboard or whiteboard. One specified a filing cabinet. Most respondents favor computers, books, and hands-on resources over traditional school hardware.

Janet, an unschooler in Oregon with five children, so closely integrates home education and life that she finds it difficult to specify ten items. She writes, "I don't think of things as invaluable for homeschooling as much as invaluable for life. For example, our family unicycles, so our unicycles are very important. If you call our riding physical education, then I suppose they are invaluable for homeschooling. Our daughter is a very knowledgeable birder, so her binoculars and spotting scope are very important. But I would never call her birding homeschooling—it is just a life activity."

CREATING A HOME LEARNING ENVIRONMENT

Even those on tight budgets can create rich home learning environments. Of course, books and magazines and catalogs—lots of reading material—usually pervade rich learning environments. Just as important, however, stimulating homes include attitudes and practices and organizational techniques conducive to learning. Here are questions that outline significant areas.

+ Are books accessible throughout your home?

+ Can you find important references when you need them?

+ Do you have areas or rules that allow for both quiet and noisy activity? Do you have a place for the musician who practices for four hours as well as provision for the voracious reader who demands extended quiet time?

+ Do your teenagers have your undivided attention several times each day?

+ Do you encourage friends, neighbors, and relatives of all ages to visit and discuss their lives and concerns?

+ If you have a computer, is your teenager's access commensurate with his needs? (Ask the same question for television.)

> When building your learning environment, think not only about what to include but also about how to include it.

It makes no sense to own encyclopedias that remain stacked in an inaccessible closet. Having a piano and television in the same room doesn't work if you never turn the television off. Frequent discussion with a wide range of people enhances listening, speaking, and critical thinking skills. When building your learning environment, think not only about what to include but also about how to include it.

Reference Materials for Teens

Even though most of us have library and Internet access, it is important to keep reference materials at home for your teenagers. Browsing at the library and surfing the Internet cannot replace in-depth experience won over time with even just a few convenient references.

Essentials

Most of our survey respondents mention basic references as the backbones of their home libraries. These include dictionaries, encyclopedias, thesauruses, quote books, atlases, and almanacs.

Dictionaries top the list. With hundreds on the market, selecting one or two can be trickier than you think. Useful dictionaries include not only pronunciations and definitions, but also sections on etymology or word origins, definitions of common foreign words and phrases, drawings and pictures, and quotations showing how authors like Shakespeare used different words. Good dictionaries are attractive and fun to browse. Lauren has shopped and compared. She writes, "I am a fan of the *American Heritage Dictionary* for ease of use, etymological information, sections on linguists, illustrations, and so on." Many report that this dictionary doubles as a mini-encyclopedia.

> Browsing at the library and surfing the Internet cannot replace in-depth experience won over time with even just a few convenient references.

Acquiring several dictionaries makes sense. Some families own a small desk-copy edition for quick reference and a larger volume for in-depth definitions. Dictionaries, like all other books, reflect the views of their editors. As teens mature, they will find it interesting and educational to compare definitions of the same word in different dictionaries.

After the dictionary, most families think about getting an encyclopedia. These come in two forms, book or CD-ROM and—in the case of books—two sizes: small one-to-three volume editions and large multi-volume sets, such as the *World Book Encyclopedia* or *Encyclopedia Britannica*. Encyclopedias excel at giving readers an overview of a subject. Usually you will have to consult specialized references to explore topics in more depth. For that reason, you may want to invest in a small, one-to-three volume encyclopedia and move to a larger set only if you find that inadequate. Above all, shop for an encyclopedia with your teenagers to ensure you buy one they find both attractive and easy to use.

The third general reference most families homeschooling teenagers buy is a thesaurus or synonym finder. A thesaurus looks much like a dictionary. Instead of definitions, however, it lists synonyms or word substitutes. Thesauruses help writers find the right term, avoid irritating repetition, and create clear and informative prose. Many professional authors would give up their dictionary before their thesaurus. Synonym finders, like dictionaries and encyclopedias, come in different formats, so preview several before purchasing one.

MONEY SAVER

Libraries replace their encyclopedias every year or two. Call to ask when and how used sets will be sold. You may find a bargain.

Will your teenagers be writing speeches, newsletter articles, reports, or papers? Or do they simply enjoy new twists on old sayings and ideas? If so, you will want to invest in at least one book of quotations. The most well-known quote book is *Bartlett's Familiar Quotations*. In addition, a host of others now flood the market, many of them specialized for certain uses or occasions. *The Book of Positive Quotations* contains uplifting messages, and *3,500 Good Quotes for Speakers* provides observations and witticisms that add spice to speeches. Check used bookstores for a good selection.

After the dictionary, encyclopedia, thesaurus, and quote book, think atlas. How many times do you look up locations worldwide? In our household, we refer to atlases to understand current and historic events, preview travel locations, and relate geographic details like rivers and mountain ranges to states and countries. While the big all-inclusive atlases in bookstores may look appealing, consider instead buying a student world atlas for quick reference plus one or more specialized atlases, depending on your family's interests. Look for a student atlas that includes political subdivisions, like state and country boundaries, as well as topographic features, like deserts, lakes, and mountains.

Our final basic reference, an almanac, picks up where the encyclopedia and atlas leave off. Almanacs, compiled annually, specialize in up-to-date facts and figures. They include current political maps, statistics on national and international issues, science updates, election returns, synopses of important recent events. Tables in one current almanac detail endangered species in 1999, life expectancy in the United States from 1950 to 1997, poverty statistics by state, a time line of second millennium events, obituaries of famous people who died in 1999, and much more.

> Many of our survey respondents value field guides, books filled with pictures and descriptions of stars, reptiles, birds, insects, rocks, and other parts of the natural world.

Specialized References

With dictionaries, atlases, and other general references in place, you will want to add specialized references. Home educators find at least three uses for specialized references—browsing, entertainment, and research. Of course, consider first those sources most applicable to your children and their interests. Marta recommends *The Math Kit,* which she says is "a wonderful resource book with everything you want to know from simple calculations to trigonometry." Emma's daughter constantly browses *The Little-Brown Book of Anecdotes,* which they found at a used bookstore. Carolyn prefers to stock up on pre-1960 reference books. Many of our survey respondents value field guides, books filled with pictures and descriptions of stars, reptiles, birds, insects, rocks, and other parts of the natural world.

Sources of Bargain Books

Homeschool travelers typically build reference libraries throughout their journey, over several years. To do this inexpensively, make a list of items of interest, and keep it with you at all times. Then look for reference materials as well as curricula and other instructional materials at all of the following locations.

+ *Amazon.com.* This well-stocked online bookstore offers discounts across the board, reasonable shipping, and great service.

+ *Barnes and Noble.* They offer an educator's discount card for a percentage off any title you use in your homeschool. Other bookstores, especially educational supply stores, may have a similar deal. Always ask.

HOW WE DID IT

Specialized references our survey respondents recommend include an unapologetic mixture of the generic and specific!

+ Bibles (different translations)

+ Bible concordances and commentaries

+ *Complete Works of Shakespeare*

+ Field guides, such as the *Peterson Guide to Wildflowers*

+ *Gray's Anatomy*

+ Greek mythology anthologies

+ *History of Us* by Joy Hakim

+ History textbooks

+ Reader's Digest reference books

+ Specialized dictionaries (law dictionary, music dictionary)

+ Specialized encyclopedias (*Oxford Music Encyclopedia,* for example)

+ *The Story of Civilization* by Will and Ariel Durant

+ Time lines

+ *Write Source, Elements of Style, St. Martin's Handbook* and other grammar references

✦ *Friends, neighbors, and relatives.* Remind them at least twice yearly to give you first right of refusal on any books they plan to discard or donate to charity. Or ask if you can help clean their basement or attic. You never know what you will find, and most people like assisting with educational endeavors.

✦ *Garage, rummage, church, and yard sales.* Of course, you will sift through many boxes of books before you find one on your list, but books sell for dimes and quarters at garage sales.

✦ *Library sales.* Most libraries receive regular book donations. In addition, they turn over their own stock, books that no one checks out any longer. Our local library handles a small part of their surplus with a rack of used books for purchase every day. They also schedule book sale Saturdays every two months, when they unload thousands of titles. A friend of mine got a two-year-old encyclopedia (*World Book*) for $25 at a library sale.

✦ *School discards.* Unfortunately, many schools tote old books to the Dumpster when new editions arrive. Others have resale facilities, open to the public, where they either give away discards or sell them for very low prices. We have acquired foreign language tapes, laboratory equipment, classical music, and educational games as well as books at these facilities. Call your school district and ask what they do with discards. Even if they dump them, they may allow you to sift through them first.

✦ *Thrift shops.* Check the bookshelves of local Goodwill and other outlets for classics, reference books, and old texts.

✦ *Used book stores.* Make regular visits to local used bookstores, which rival new bookstores in two areas. Prices for used books—and sometimes used music—range from 25 to 75 percent of new books.

MONEY SAVER

Hunt used bookstores to locate essential references. Stock up on several dictionaries and quotation books.

Just as important, used bookstores carry hard-to-find out-of-print titles.

✦ *Used curriculum sales.* Many local and state homeschool groups sponsor curriculum exchanges at least once per year. In addition, check with used curriculum vendors, many of which operate nationwide and worldwide. See the list at the end of chapter 9.

Homeschool Resource Guides

To build your home library past the reference and curriculum stage, review one or more resource guides. In the 1980s, we only had two resource books—Mary Pride's *The Big Book of Home Learning* and Donn and Jean Reed's *The Homeschool Sourcebook*. Now we have many more from a wide range of compilers. In addition, all of the national homeschool publications also include resource review columns. For example, *Homeschooling Today* has book, software, and multimedia review columns in every issue.

Resource guides contain in-depth descriptions and evaluations of curricula, references, real books, and hands-on materials, together with prices and purchasing information. Check your library for one or more of the titles suggested under Resources at the end of the chapter.

HELPFUL SUPPLIES

Begin with the basics—paper, pens, and pencils. Then expand. For math, think rulers, protractors, compasses, and graph paper. For writing and art, stock construction paper, staplers, colored markers, binders, folders, and so on. Most of us have no problem obtaining these resources. Unfortunately, many of us have problems finding them once we get them home.

In our homeschool, if we were unable to locate a pencil, we could not accomplish much. We designated a single closet for writing instruments, all kinds of paper, rulers and protractors, desk supplies, art materials, and so on. To save and to avoid buying items we already had, we all used the same supplies, and we returned materials to the organized closet after use.

Desks and Other Workspaces

Several years ago, a television reporter visited our house to do a story on homeschooling. They asked whether they could videotape our teenagers "doing school." We had a tough time accommodating their request. I explained that our son and daughter read on their beds or a couch and completed math assignments at the kitchen table. For other projects, they might use a worktable in the basement or garage. Both the reporter and his cameraman were dumbfounded to learn that neither of our children routinely used their bedroom desks.

Some fathers feel the same way—that learning occurs best in the "school" position—sitting at a table, for example. When asked if her children use special workspaces, Darla writes, "No, though Dad has complained that they should. When he wins—or should I say when he is home—they use the dining-room table."

Darla's husband would probably approve of Laura's household. Her teenagers use an office, which has two desks.

In contrast, more than 80 percent of our survey respondents say their teenagers shun desks. Carrie, homeschooling a fourteen-year-old daughter, writes, "She has a library table, bulletin board, and shelves in her work area. Actually, though, she works all over the house. Often she starts a project one place, then moves to another area to do something else." Marla reports, "We have tables in a schoolroom, but our teens work throughout the house. They do not have a specific place, but the tables do allow them to leave materials spread out." Ellen says her daughter has no special workspace, using only a basket and shelf for her school stuff. Gina confesses, "Our teens have desks, used as storage, not as study space."

MORE HELPFUL RESOURCES

WHILE YOU CAN homeschool without the following resources, enough home educators use them to warrant inclusion here.

Computer

As we move into the new millennium, we find an exponentially increasing amount of information via computer, either through software or the Internet. Chapter 11 details educational options available to families who integrate computers into their homeschooling.

Just three to five years ago, buying a computer represented a major investment. We would tell homeschooling families without computers to budget carefully and save for one. The Internet offered good educational Web sites and research opportunities. Educational software motivated teenagers to learn on their own.

Two things have changed. First, computer software and Internet sites are not just good; they are so outstanding that it is difficult to imagine homeschooling without them. Second, computers now cost less than some bicycles, television sets, or musical instruments. Most families can afford one.

Calculator

Homeschooled teens usually study algebra by age fourteen or fifteen. Although experts argue over the educational value of supplying a calculator to an early- or middle-years child, most agree that bogging students down with complicated multiplications and divisions while they learn advanced math creates unnecessary frustration.

Computers now cost less than some bicycles, television sets, or musical instruments. Most families can afford one.

Do you need a fancy graphing calculator? Not for most students. A basic model with the four arithmetic operations (addition, subtraction, multiplication, and division), plus log and exponential functions, will do the trick. If your teenager studies trigonometry, you should upgrade to a calculator with the trig functions: sine, cosine, and tangent.

Television and VCR

So many of our survey respondents use educational videotapes that it is almost as difficult to imagine homeschooling without a television and videocassette recorder as without a computer. Chapter 11 describes educational uses of the TV-VCR combination.

Audiocassette Tape Player

Home educators bring audio books, music, great lectures, speaking practice, and foreign language drill into their homes for less than $20 when they purchase a basic audiocassette tape player. Kinesthetic and auditory learners much prefer hearing classic literature to reading it. Budding musicians not only listen to the Greats, they tape themselves to determine how to improve their playing. Teens writing speeches will want to practice by taping themselves. Most libraries carry foreign language tapes, which you can play at home or in the car.

Musical Instruments

As we described in chapter 8, many home educators devote time and monetary resources to music. Whether you pay for lessons or not, you will probably find that if you keep enough musical instruments around, sooner or later your teenagers will experiment with one or more of them.

Pianos are nice, but you need not crowd an expensive keyboard into your living room to encourage music making. Instead consider recorders, harmonicas, tin whistles, ukeleles, and African drums. Just make them available and watch what happens.

Art Supplies

Many of our survey respondents say they could not homeschool without art supplies. They keep stashes of construction paper, posterboard, tape, glue, paint, and markers together and make them readily available. At least three survey respondents comment on how often their teenagers use colored pencils.

Supplies for your trip? You have many and can gradually acquire the remainder. Plan ahead and buy as your budget permits.

MONEY SAVER

Watch your local newspaper classified ads for used computers. Compulsive upgraders buy new hardware every year or two. Better it should go to you for a couple of hundred dollars than to the dump!

SIMPLE STARTING POINTS

✦ *Compile a deserted island list for home education.* Ask your teenager to do the same. What do you absolutely have to have? What do you need? What does your teenager need?

✦ *Make a list of reference books and other needed titles.* Watch for these at library, garage sales, and homeschool used book sales.

✦ *Before you buy—even used materials—review several different dictionaries, encyclopedias, and atlases at the library to learn about different features.*

✦ *Browse one or more of the homeschool resource guides listed below.* Decide what additional curriculum or instructional materials you will need to purchase.

✦ *Discuss workspace with your teenagers.* List options. If they want a special space, help them create it.

✦ *Call your local and statewide support groups and ask about the next curriculum exchange or used materials sale.*

RESOURCES

Homeschool Resource Guides

Bell, Debra. *The Ultimate Guide to Homeschooling.* Word Books, 2000.

Duffy, Cathy. *Christian Home Educators' Curriculum Manual: Junior/Senior High 1997–98.* Grove Publishing, 1997.

Leppert, Michael and Mary. *Homeschooling Almanac, 2000–2001.* Prima Publishing, 1999.

Pride, Mary. *The Big Book of Home Learning: Teen and Adult.* Crossway Books, 1999.

Reed, Donn and Jean. *Home School Sourcebook,* 3rd Edition. Brook Farm Books, 1999.

Rupp, Rebecca. *The Complete Home Learning Source Book: The Essential Resource Guide for Homeschoolers, Parents, Educators Covering Every Subject.* Three Rivers Press, 1998.

Wade, Theodore E. *The Homeschool Manual: Plans, Pointers, Reasons and Resources,* 7th Edition. Gazelle Publications, 1998.

General Catalogs with Homeschool Resources

The Elijah Company, The Elijah Company 888-2-ELIJAH, http://www.elijahco.com

John Holt Book and Music Store, 617-864-3100, http://www.holt-gws.com

Web Sites

The Education Source, http://www.edusource.com
Homeschool Resource Guide,
    http://members.home.net/cthomeschool/guide.htm

Favorite Home References

Allen, John. *Student Atlas of World Geography.* McGraw Hill, 1999.

American Heritage Dictionary of the English Language. Houghton Mifflin, 1992.

Bartlett, John. *Bartlett's Familiar Quotations: A Collection of Passages, Phrases, and Proverbs Traced to Their Sources in Ancient and Modern Literature.* Little Brown, 1992.

Byrne, Robert. *1911 Best Things Anybody Ever Said.* Fawcett Books, 1988.

Chapman, Robert, Editor. *Roget's International Thesaurus.* Harper-Collins, 1992.

Clark, Sandra. *A Dictionary of Who, What, and Where in Shakespeare: A Comprehensive Guide to Shakespeare's Plays, Characters, and Contemporaries.* NTC Publishing, 1997.

Cook, John, Editor. *The Book of Positive Quotations.* Fairview Press, 1997.

Crystal, David. *The Cambridge Encyclopedia.* Cambridge University Press, 1997.

Givis, Steven. *Dictionary of Legal Terms: A Simplified Guide to the Language of Law.* Barron's, 1998.

Gorton, Julia and Nicholas Price. *The Student World Atlas.* Lodestar Books Dutton, 1994.

Gray, Henry. *Gray's Anatomy: Anatomy, Descriptive, and Surgical.* Running Press, 1991.

Hamilton, Edith. *Mythology: Timeless Tales of Gods and Heroes.* Warner Books, 1999.

Henry, Matthew. *Commentary on the Whole Bible.* Hendrickson Publishers, 1991.

Kipfer, Barbara Ann, Editor. *21st Century Dictionary of Quotations.* Dell Publishing, 1993. Also the *21st Century Synonym and Antonym Finder.*

Lebtecht, Norman. *The Book of Musical Anecdotes: Hundreds of Classic and Little-Known Stories about the World's Greatest Composers and Performers.* Free Press, 1985.

Leclerc, Paul (Preface) and Paul Fargis, Editor. *The New York Public Library Desk Reference* (3rd Edition). IDG Books, 1998.

Merriam-Webster's Biographical Dictionary. Merriam-Webster, 1995.

Reagan, Michael and Bob Phillips. *The All-American Quote Book.* Harvest House, 1995.

Rodale, J. I., Nancy Laroche, and Faye C. Allen. *Synonym Finder.* Warner Books, 1986.

Sadie, Stanley. *The Norton/Grove Concise Encyclopedia of Music.* Norton, 1994.

Schonberg, Harold. *The Lives of the Great Composers.* Norton, 1997.

Shakespeare, William and David Bevington, Editor. *The Complete Works of Shakespeare.* Addison-Wesley, 1997.

Shakespeare, William and Hugh Rawson and Margaret Miner. *A Dictionary of Quotations from Shakespeare: A Topical Guide to over 3,000 Great Passages from the Plays, Sonnets, and Narrative Poems.* Meridian Books, 1996.

Strong, James. *The New Strong's Exhaustive Concordance of the Bible.* Thomas Nelson, 1997.

Urdang, Laurence. *The Timetables of American History.* Touchstone, 1996.

Wetterau, Bruce. *The New York Public Library Book of Chronologies.* IDG Books, 1994.

Zimmerman, John. *Dictionary of Classical Mythology.* Bantam Books, 1983.

See also: Many Peterson Field Guides on rocks, birds, wildflowers, stars, trees, insects, mammals, and other natural science topics.

11

THE LEARNING JOURNEY MERGES ONTO THE INFORMATION SUPERHIGHWAY

In This Chapter

+ The computer: your information superhighway vehicle

+ Plug in and zone out?

+ Armchair voyages: Africa and other great trips

+ Simple starting points

+ Resources

$\mathcal{M}$OST OF OUR survey respondents report using more technology now in their homeschools than when they began their journeys. Travelers incorporate educational videos into their history and science units, and their children take classes online. More often than you might think, eager teenagers drag their reluctant parents into the twenty-first century with their enthusiasm for interactive computer programs, informative Web sites, and instant e-mail communication.

Over the last ten years, we have seen an explosion of educational software and videos. Many companies have developed titles specifi-

TEENS TALK

I love using computers. I play games, write, and sometimes make graphics for my Web site. I use the Internet to talk to friends, work on my Web site, and visit other sites for a variety of purposes.

—ELLEN, AGE SEVENTEEN, IN NORTH PLAINFIELD, NEW JERSEY

cally for home educators. From one company, you can buy an entire kindergarten through grade 12 curriculum on a single CD-ROM. In addition, cable channels like The Learning Channel, Discovery, and The History Channel join traditional broadcast stations like PBS to provide outstanding history, geography, science, and art programming. Most turn around and sell these programs as educational videos, which many libraries now stock.

We live in an age of technology so pervasive that we sprinkle everyday conversation with countless computer terms. Dot-com has become a synonym for electronic commerce. Hard drive refers to mental capacity as well as computer disk space. Even the dictionary definition of the word "home" now includes "the starting position of a cursor on a computer monitor." Of course, you can ignore it all. Homeschoolers still succeed with traditional methods. Nevertheless, videos, software, and the Internet can make your homeschooling job easier. Learning becomes not only fun but also addicting. Whether you use technology for curriculum or for enrichment, you will probably benefit when you include videos and computers in your homeschool.

THE COMPUTER: YOUR INFORMATION SUPERHIGHWAY VEHICLE

Some families find so many uses for computers that they own two or three. Trina, homeschooling four children ages twelve to nineteen, says they use their computer for writing assignments, SAT practice, e-mail, research, games, and online classes. Ron's thirteen-year-old daughter drills math, learns keyboarding skills, writes to

HOW WE DID IT

Principal ways our survey respondents use computers to enhance their home-schooling include:

TIMESAVING APPLICATIONS

+ Word processors
+ Drawing programs
+ Desktop publishing

RESEARCH

+ Encyclopedias and other software
+ Internet research

INSTRUCTION

+ Teaching CDs for math, science, history, and more
+ Online classes

SOCIALIZATION

+ E-mail
+ Chat

RECREATION

+ Edutainment software
+ Interactive Internet games

LEARNING COMPUTER TECHNOLOGY

+ Building hardware
+ Programming

Success with self-directed learning may be one of the best reasons to incorporate computer technology into your home.

pen pals, prints calendars, makes organizational lists, and explores the Web—all via computer. Carolyn's son uses computers away from home, both word-processing and art programs, at his volunteer and paying jobs.

Michaela's fifteen-year-old daughter employs timesaving applications, such as word processing, desktop publishing, and drawing software. Michaela also buys educational software and programs to drill typing and math. It doesn't stop there. She says her daughter enjoys her online classes and uses chat and e-mail programs to keep in touch with friends far and near.

We asked our survey respondents what percentage of learning occurs with the computer, either online or with software. Approximately two-thirds say that up to 20 percent of learning occurs with computers. Just under one-quarter categorize half of their teenagers' learning as computer-mediated. On the average, families using computers report equal use of the Internet and educational software. A few parents say the Internet too much resembles bad parts of town, and they restrict computer use to software only.

Almost all families find that computers facilitate the homeschooling journey and encourage self-directed learning. Our survey respondents report many examples. Reluctant writers become prolific authors when you offer the word processor as an alternative to pencil and paper. Teenagers tackle difficult subjects like trigonometry and foreign languages with self-instructional software. Homeschoolers also take online high school and college classes.

Technically oriented adolescents teach themselves programming and Web-page design, proving that computers have become the ultimate teach-yourself device. Many computer-literate individuals become competent primarily through trial-and-error and self-instruction. Home educators, of course, appreciate that teaching oneself anything builds confidence. Success with self-directed learning may be one of the best reasons to incorporate computer technology into your home.

Soaring into Educational Cyberspace

Research probably tops the list of reasons for using the World Wide Web and other Internet resources. For any subject of interest, your teenagers can now find nearly unlimited information online. Web surfers talk with Civil War buffs, tour the White House, investigate colleges, research environmental problems, and discover family history—all without having to get dressed.

> Web surfers talk with Civil War buffs, tour the White House, investigate colleges, research environmental problems, and discover family history—all without having to get dressed.

With millions of Web pages online, Internet research skills come into play. Just as the inability to use the index of an atlas compromises the usefulness of that reference, the inability to use a search engine puts much of the Internet out of reach. You can learn to surf, to point-and-click, in fifteen minutes (five minutes if you are under ten years of age!). But Internet research skills extend far beyond surfing. Effective researchers employ search engine technology and simultaneously exercise the discipline not to chase after every tangent. They combine these skills with surfing to quickly locate needed information. No one learns all the tricks of searching overnight. If you and your teenagers lack these skills, spend several hours with the tutorials of two to three Web search engines to learn effective techniques.

If you would prefer a gentler introduction to the Internet than surf engines provide, check out home education portals or gateways. These Web sites, maintained by homeschooling publishers and other interested parties, let you bypass search engines. Portal publishers search the Web for you and provide links to interesting and educational content. Typically, they review sites and filter so that they link

TEENS' FAVORITE WEB SITES

Our survey respondents report a few of their teenagers' favorite Web sites.

- ✦ American Girls, http://www.americangirl.com

- ✦ Ask Jeeves, http://www.askjeeves.com

- ✦ Atrium Center for Classical Studies, http://web.idirect.com/~atrium

- ✦ Big Idea, Interactive Adventures and Games, http://www.bigidea.com

- ✦ Disney, http://disney.go.com

- ✦ History Channel, http://www.historychannel.com

- ✦ Martha Stewart, http://www.marthastewart.com

- ✦ Sonique, an audio player, http://www.sonique.com

- ✦ Star Wars, http://www.starwars.com

- ✦ The Teen Homeschooler, http://www.eatbug.com/homeschool

only to content that meets their criteria for excellence. Both beginners and experienced Internet denizens will want to visit one or two favorite homeschool gateways each month to see what's new. Check the end-of-the-chapter Resources for a list of homeschooling portals.

Staying Closer to Home with Software

Some families restrict their teenagers to applications and educational software. Applications software includes word processors, desktop publishing and drawing programs, Photoshop, databases, and spreadsheets. Applications software is the tool that allows you to accomplish a particular project, such as writing a paper. Educational software, in contrast, teaches specific subjects. A subset of educational software, edutainment titles educate and entertain at the same time.

We discussed learning how to use applications software in chapter 6. Now let's think about the education and edutainment titles that beckon from the shelves of computer and office-supply stores and the glossy, colorful ads in homeschooling magazines. What is worthwhile? What works?

TEENS' FAVORITE SOFTWARE

- ✦ Adobe Illustrator
- ✦ Algeblaster 3
- ✦ American Girls Premiere 2nd Edition
- ✦ Carmen Sandiego Series (Where in the World?)
- ✦ Chess Master 5000 Classic
- ✦ Creative Writer 2
- ✦ Deer Hunter II
- ✦ DK Eyewitness History of the World
- ✦ Dr. Brain Series
- ✦ Hasbro Civilization II Series
- ✦ King's Quest Series
- ✦ Learning Company Trail Series (Oregon Trail, Yukon Trail, Amazon Trail)
- ✦ Logical Journey of the Zoombinis
- ✦ Oddworld: Abe's Exodus
- ✦ Photoshop
- ✦ Starcraft
- ✦ Stars Wars Episode I Insiders Guide
- ✦ Ultimate Civil War
- ✦ You Don't Know Jack Series Trivia Games

To answer those questions, bring on the reviewers. Most of the homeschool resource books listed at the end of chapter 10 include software reviews. For more current evaluations, read the national homeschool magazines listed in the chapter 1 Resources, which include educational software reviews. After reading the reviews, carefully peruse the software advertisements in homeschooling magazines as well. Many publishers have developed products specifically for the home education market. Finally, check online. Begin at an excellent Web site titled Learningware Reviews, maintained by homeschooling mother Juline Lambert.

Many families also find excellent software the same way they find good curricula—by word of mouth. Talk to your friends and see what they recommend. In addition, ask questions about various software packages on Internet homeschool discussion boards.

After arming yourself with review information and personal recommendations, you may want to preview software in the vendor hall at home education conferences. Publishers and software developers welcome your questions and comments. And they invite you to take their products for a test drive. My rule of thumb? If I cannot understand and learn to use a piece of software in fifteen minutes at a conference, it is too complicated.

POPULAR EDUCATIONAL SOFTWARE

✦ Artes Latinae

✦ Music Ace

✦ Stars and Stories

✦ Typing Tutor 99 Platinum Edition

✦ World Book Deluxe

The first piece of software many families purchase is an encyclopedia. Fortunately, most encyclopedia publishers now market software equivalents. CD-ROM versions occupy a fraction of the space of the equivalent hard copy. Most of our survey respondents say that they prefer the *World Book Deluxe Encyclopedia*. The *Homeschooling Today* reviewer writes, "Finally—a CD-ROM encyclopedia worth recommending."

Computer Use and Teenagers

Whether learning with software or the Internet, our survey respondents have mixed feelings about regulating their teenagers' computer use. Approximately half feel the need to restrict time and access. They cite two problems—addictive behavior that excludes the real world and dangerous Internet sites.

> Many families also find excellent software the same way they find good curricula—by word of mouth.

Trina describes how the computer snares her teenagers: "They become so involved in what they are doing they lose track of time." Leanne writes, "We limit the time they spend on the computer because we don't think it should be the focus of their day. I prefer that they read for pleasure and get lots of outdoor exercise." Jeannette also limits time, explaining that computers are hard on the eyes. She adds, "Our children also limit themselves because they prefer their real-world activities."

Other families find no need to set limits. Candace and Brian, homeschooling two teenagers in Texas, say, "Limitations are natural limitations. They cannot go bowling and use the computer at the same time."

Carrie agrees, noting that computer use is just one of many activities her teenagers engage in. "None of our three children have been excessive or compulsive with the computer. They go in spurts playing one thing or another and then switch to another game or activity. Like all things, they immerse themselves for a while. When they are saturated, they move on to something else."

Ron avoids providing games and encourages viewing computers as tools, no different from books and pencils and paper. He comments, "We have not had to limit computer time because neither girl spends a lot of time there. We have no computer games to draw them away from books and such, and we don't plan to own any. Also, they schedule their own time. I think they see the computer as a tool to do, find, or type something. When they complete their task, other activities beckon."

Kate explains her mixed view of her son's hours on the computer. "Since computers are our son's main area of interest and he takes computer classes, I am not sure that limiting his time makes sense. On the other hand, sometimes he gets into a game-playing mode and I consider, in my worse moments, taking a sledgehammer to the device."

Certainly, games seem to cause the most problems. I had to remove several from my own machine before I could write this book. If you are concerned about addicting computer use, try deleting mindless games from the desktop. Or use games as motivators.

> If you are concerned about addicting computer use, try deleting mindless games from the desktop.

Marla says that she puts fun stuff off limits if traditional schoolwork and chores are not completed.

Carrie sees all the positives: "We are not uncomfortable with our teens using a computer. They will need all the computer skills they can develop because most jobs will require computer utilization. There is a wealth of opportunity for the computer-literate."

Many parents say that dangerous Internet content causes more concern than time. Kay writes, "We don't limit time; we limit content. We have our son's computer set up to log all Internet usage, so he knows we are aware of what he does."

Cruising the Net can be as hazardous as cruising the streets of a large city because the Internet contains everything good or bad that you can find in any town. Many parents say that the trick is to find good content and restrict access to negative influences. Some families achieve this goal by not allowing the Internet into their homes. Others use a combination of strategies to provide access to wholesome education and entertainment.

> Supervision and parental involvement probably work better than all the filters.

Filters provide some reassurance. Janice writes, "Our Internet provider uses a filter to eliminate unwelcome sites." You can buy filters for your machine or get them at the Internet service provider level. Mayberry USA is one provider that advertises safe Internet access. Of course, while filters provide some protection, you want your young adults to be safe in any situation. In conjunction with filter use, Janice says that they have taught their teenagers to be discerning and aware of dangers.

Supervision and parental involvement probably work better than all the filters. Lydia writes, "Our teens are always supervised." Molly agrees, saying that Web access is an adult-supervised activity in their home. Denise uses a library technique, keeping their computer in a well-traveled area of their house. She adds, "I also trust them to use common sense."

PLUG IN AND ZONE OUT?

TELEVISION PROVOKES MORE controversy than computer use. Many families who log on first thing each morning will not have a television in their homes. Cheryl explains, "We have never owned a TV, mostly because we would not be self-disciplined enough to turn it off and build relationships within the family. We rent a TV for one week per year during the Thanksgiving holidays. Whatever videos we watch then last us the year."

Marta has a similar view. "We rarely use TV or videos. I feel we learn more quickly using other methods. We will sometimes watch a dramatization of a literary work."

Others avoid broadcast and cable networks and restrict viewing to videotapes. They control content in much the same way as do families who use software but not the Internet. Tess writes, "When our children were in public school, everyone plugged into the tube, zoned out, and fought over the remote controller. So we had the cable service disconnected. We cannot get any reception where we live, so now we rely on videotapes. That gives us control over the content, which is important in a household with a two-year-old. Every week we get new tapes from the library that we incorporate into our program. Sometimes we borrow others from friends or a video rental place."

Molly agrees with limiting access to television. She writes, "We see about one video per week, but avoid network television. We will watch the 'Civil War' series this year. We used travel videos for geography last year."

In other homes, television use ranges from casual to serious. Certainly, for those who take the trouble, the Public Broadcasting System (PBS) and several cable channels (The Learning Channel, Discovery, A&E, and History) provide outstanding educational content. *The American Experience* on PBS, classical music on A&E, and science programs on Discovery bring to life many textbook subjects.

Jeannette remarks, "We use TV and videos—movies of classics, news, weather, and popular movies. In addition to entertaining all of us, programs spark interest in history, good literature,

The American Experience on PBS, classical music on A&E, and science programs on Discovery bring to life many textbook subjects.

MONEY SAVER

Search the Internet using keywords like "free educational videos" or "educational video rentals." Many companies and some government agencies send free videos on request.

and current events in other parts of the world. We discuss how to confront our culture when it conflicts with our faith."

Hal and Ellen in Kalamazoo, Michigan, say, "When PBS has appropriate programming or we find videos pertaining to their studies, we incorporate them into our homeschooling. Our children are very interested in the visual arts and they will pay attention to a video sometimes before they will read a book. The visual presentation also enhances recall. Our teens remember what they see." Jane agrees, saying, "We use videos as often as I can find quality ones because they break up the reading and make it come alive."

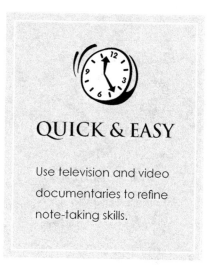

QUICK & EASY

Use television and video documentaries to refine note-taking skills.

ARMCHAIR VOYAGES: AFRICA AND OTHER GREAT TRIPS

PROPERLY MANAGED, BROADCAST and cable television programs can enrich almost any area of study. Even better, video presentations turn boring material into fascinating subject matter. Reading about the geography of Africa cannot compare with watching several travelogues and documentaries. And surely Shakespeare would rather have us see his plays than read them.

Let's look at a sampling of homeschooler's favorite educational stations.

Public Television

PBS rates high with our survey respondents. Programming enriches almost every high school subject area. Perusing my television schedule this week, I see biographies of Andrew Carnegie and Eleanor Roosevelt; performances of the New York and Vienna Philharmonic Orchestras; episodes of *Nature* on buffaloes, otters, and whales; and

> Reading about the geography of Africa cannot compare with watching several travelogues and documentaries. And surely Shakespeare would rather have us see his plays than read them.

classic movies like *Adam's Rib* and *Arsenic and Old Lace.* The PBS companion Web site provides enrichment in the form of teacher resource materials and background documents.

Discovery Channel

The program *Wild Discovery,* among others, brings the natural world into our living rooms with scientific programming on subjects ranging from dragonflies to reptiles to mammals. Other favorite programs include *Sci-Trek* and *Science Mysteries.* Home educators whose teenagers prefer a low-key approach to biology and earth science will find a wealth of material here. Spin-off channels like The Learning Channel, Animal Planet, Discovery Health, and the Travel Channel can provide or enrich not only science instruction, but also history and geography learning.

A&E

This channel and its spin-offs, The History Channel and the new Biography Channel, complement the Discovery "family." Where Discovery focuses on the natural world, A&E and its associated channels concentrate on history, literature, and music. Recent programming includes *The Crossing* (a Revolutionary War episode in the life of George Washington), an accompanying biography of the first president, and a dramatization of the nineteenth-century English classic, *Pride and Prejudice.* Associated A&E and History Channel Web sites include study guides and other educational enrichment materials.

To get the most out of television programming and videos, watch them with your teenagers and discuss what you see. For history overviews, such as the recent multipart series on the history of New York City, watch programs several times. Discussion helps teens understand cause and effect, and repetition mentally fixes names, places, and dates. If you doubt this, see how much of the dialogue of *Star Wars* or *The Wizard of Oz* your children can recall. Always follow up on interesting programming. Investigate interesting topics in more depth, at the library and online at associated Web sites.

Video Instructional Materials

Every national homeschooling magazine I receive has new video instructional materials advertised in each issue. Dozens of publishers have joined the grandfather of instructional videos for homeschoolers, A Beka Books. Instead of learning algebra with a textbook, home educators can now choose one of several video algebra series. The same holds true for other difficult subjects, such as Spanish or government or chemistry. While not the least expensive educational alternative, video instruction does provide a way to cover material with your teen that you do not want to relearn yourself.

Online resources, software, television programming, and education videos provide both basic instruction and enrichment. In our increasingly technological society, it only makes sense to add some of these tools to your travel kit.

> Discussion helps teens understand cause and effect, and repetition mentally fixes names, places, and dates. If you doubt this, see how much of the dialogue of *Star Wars* or *The Wizard of Oz* your children can recall.

SIMPLE STARTING POINTS

✦ *Evaluate the usefulness of television and computers for your situation.* Which subjects would you rather not teach? Which areas do your teenagers resist learning by traditional methods?

✦ *If you plan to limit computer access, discuss why and how with your teenager.*

While not the least expensive educational alternative, video instruction does provide a way to cover material with your teen that you do not want to relearn yourself.

✦ *Soar into cyberspace with your teens.* Learn to surf. Begin with areas they find interesting and point-and-click, following links to find good Web sites. Bookmark those worth return visits.

✦ *With your teenagers, do the tutorials* accompanying at least two search engines listed here in Resources. Practice basic search techniques, focusing first on hobbies or fun, easy school subjects.

✦ *Read reviews of educational software.* You can find these either in national homeschooling magazines or at online review sites, like Learningware Reviews.

✦ *If you decide to use television and videos in your homeschool, begin building a video library.* Peruse your TV schedule and make a list of programs to tape.

RESOURCES

Books

Dinsmore, Mark and Wendy. *Homeschool Guide to the Internet: Your Roadmap to the Information Superhighway.* Holly Hall Publishing, 1997.

Glavac, Marjan. *The Busy Educator's Guide to the World Wide Web.* Nima Systems, 1998.

Jones, Steve. *The Internet for Educators and Homeschoolers.* ETC Publications, 2000.

Winn, Marie. *The Plug-In Drug: Television, Children, and the Family.* Penguin, 1985.

Web Sites

Keep in mind that Internet addresses (URLs, or Uniform Resource
Locators) change. If a URL below leads you to a dead link, try
the site title in one of the search engines.

Reviews

Learningware Reviews, http://www.learningwarereviews.com
Newsweek's Parents Guide to Children's Software,
     http://www.newsweekparentsguide.com
Screen It! Entertainment Reviews for Parents, http://www.screenit.com
Superkids Education Software Review, http://www.superkids.com

Home Education Portals or Link Farms

B. J. Pinchbeck's Homework Helper, http://www.bjpinchbeck.com
Coyle's Where in the Web?
     http://www.geocities.com/Athens/Aegean/3446/
Eclectic Homeschool Online, http://www.eho.org
Happy Homeschooling, http://www.ij.net/tshoaf/hhs/
Homeschool Support on the Internet,
     http://www.geocities.com/Athens/8259/
Jon's Homeschool Resource Page,
     http://www.midnightbeach.com/hs/
Kids' Web, http://www.kidsvista.com/
Webschooling, http://www.webschooling.com/

Search Engines

Google, http://www.google.com
HotBot, http://www.hotbot.com
Search Engine Watch, http://www.searchenginewatch.com
Yahoo, http://www.yahoo.com

Kid-Safe Search Engines

Alta Vista Family Finder, http://www.altavista.com
Excite's Magellan, http://www.magellan.excite.com
GOGuardian, http://www.go.com

Software

MGM Software (Free Educational Software),
    http://www.mmsoft.com

Filtering Software

Cyber Sentinel 888-835-7278, http://www.securitysoft.com
We Blocker, http://www.we-blocker.com

Online Courses

Beginners' Guide to the Net,
    http://l2lpd.arin.k12.pa.us /linktuts/bgtoc.htm
Internet 101, http://www2.famvid.com/i101/internet101.html
WannaLearn (links to online tutorials and courses),
    http://www.wannalearn.com

Educational Videotapes

The American Testimony (history), 281-565-7711
Chalk Dust Company, 800-588-7564, http://www.chalkdust.com
Free Clutter Educational Videos,
    http://www.freeclutter.snap.com/videos.html
Home Education Video Network,
    http://www.hevnvideo.com/HEVN.nsf
    /HEVNInitial?OpenNavigator
Interactive Mathematics, 800-694-6858,
    http://www.personal-learning.com
National Geographic Videos, http://www.nationalgeographic.com
Saxon Algebra on Videotape, 800-284-7019,
    http://www.saxonpub.com

School of Tomorrow Science Videos, 800-976-7226,
   http://www.schooloftomorrow.com

Catalogs

Edusoft, 619-562-6812, http://www.eudsoftonline.com
Lawrence Productions, 800-421-4157, http://www.lpi.com
National School Products, 800-627-9393
S&S Software, 520-384-3844

12

HOMESCHOOLERS' TOP THREE DESTINATIONS

> ## *In This Chapter*
>
> + Support groups
>
> + Your local libraries
>
> + Your community: a microcosm of your world
>
> + Simple starting points
>
> + Resources

$\mathcal{H}$OMESCHOOLERS TRAVEL, LITERALLY, every day. They attend support group functions, use libraries, and participate in a wide range of community activities.

Most of our survey respondents say they belong to at least one homeschool association, usually a local one. Many also join regional, state or provincial, and national groups. Some find support on on-line bulletin boards and mailing lists.

As a destination, libraries rate just as high as support groups. "We almost live there," Emma in Georgia writes. Who can blame them? Families homeschooling teenagers list more than twenty free educational services available at libraries.

Finally, community activities—such as 4-H, Scouts, volunteering, and co-op and college classes—provide expertise, service opportunities, entertainment, and social outlets for the journey. Freed from conventional school constraints, most homeschooled teenagers take advantage of a wide range of community resources.

SUPPORT GROUPS

HOMESCHOOLERS FIND SUPPORT at different levels. Local and regional groups provide social outlets and educational activities, like co-op classes. State and provincial associations usually publish legal information and other helpful literature, monitor state legislatures, and sponsor conferences. National groups watch federal legislation and court decisions that affect home educators. The largest national group, the Homeschool Legal Defense Association (HSLDA), provides legal advice to their members. HSLDA and other national groups also facilitate communication among state groups and often provide information to the media.

Approximately 80 percent of our survey respondents belong to local support groups. Sixty percent have joined state or provincial groups. Just under 30 percent claim affiliation with one or more national groups. Close to half of our survey respondents participate in supportive Internet bulletin boards and mailing lists.

Gina in Stevens Point, Wisconsin, explains her involvement: "We joined the local group to interact with real teenagers. I like the state group for educational resources. I love Internet groups for real support, encouragement, and advice, at my convenience."

Johanna in Minnesota writes, "I belong to the state group to keep abreast of local and statewide events as well as legislative developments that could impact homeschooling families here. I visit Internet homeschool boards for a sense of connection to the larger homeschooling community and to investigate high school homeschooling options."

Support groups are not just an American phenomenon. Claudia in New Zealand looks to her national support group for political representation and information. She finds personal support and activities for her teens at the local level. She says Internet mailing lists provide similar personal support plus stimulating discussion.

Some families never join support groups. They do not have time, see no need, or have had bad experiences. Others cannot find a group with a compatible educational philosophy. Marta, mother of seven, writes, "I cannot commit myself because I am too busy with my children." Tina says, "I have not found support groups supportive. In fact, they can be discouraging." Jane in Tennessee explains, "Most support groups are too conservative for our taste."

Many support groups cater to early- and middle-years children. Kate in California writes, "We no longer participate in the local support group because my son has outgrown the activities and field trips offered."

Karleen, once heavily involved with a local support group, found it more work than she anticipated. She says, "I started a group because I needed to talk with other home educators. I also wanted to help others. Unfortunately, after a while, I was the primary organizer. I burned out, and that group folded after four years. If I need support, I talk with a couple of other parents here who have teens. Or I use Internet bulletin boards."

Local and Regional Groups

Local homeschool support groups vary tremendously. Some cater primarily to families with young children, others to families with teenagers. An estimated half of such groups require adherence to a particular educational philosophy or religious viewpoint. Others welcome all home educators. Many local support groups publish newsletters describing field trips, classes, resource centers, speakers, and used curriculum exchanges—in other words, enough activities to keep you busy every day of the week. Our respondents report that membership in these groups costs from $4 to $20 per year. In contrast, many free support groups meet informally in homes and parks to discuss problems and share resources.

> Many local support groups publish newsletters describing field trips, classes, resource centers, speakers, and used curriculum exchanges—in other words, enough activities to keep you busy every day of the week.

Denise in Hawaii describes her religiously affiliated group: "I belong to my local support group, and I serve in two ways, as newcomer welcomer and membership coordinator. I started the group because I wanted to get to know other Catholic home educators in our area." Anita also prefers sectarian local support. She writes, "We started a support group. We needed an academically based group that was Christian. We gathered twenty other like-minded families, and we became one of two couples in leadership."

Carrie in Florida belongs to an inclusive association. "Our local homeschool group encourages any type of homeschooling style families choose. I prefer the open group over the religious group in our area, because I think it affords more variety, and does not require that we subscribe to values that are not our own."

Obviously, not all support groups are created equal. If you join one, remember that the worker bees are all busy volunteer parents who homeschool their own children. If you join, expect support, of course. But also expect to help others, to be supportive.

You may find exactly what you want in your vicinity—or not. If you find local support lacking, remember that many groups begin with two or three mothers brainstorming over coffee and tea at a kitchen table. Consider starting your own group. Lauren in New York did it. "I started the local support group almost eleven years ago. I was new to the area. People I met said, 'Oh, there are lots of homeschoolers around here,' but I could not find them! I put an announcement in the newspaper. That was the beginning. I simply wanted to find other adults, and my children needed other home-schoolers to interact with."

Karla recently organized a new group to meet her specific needs. She writes, "I have started a homeschool group that begins activities this month. The existing group did not meet my standards for be-havior, discipline, attitudes, and so on. So I have started a group that is by invitation and interview only, set up much as a church might interview potential members, so that all families understand and agree with our expectations."

Claudia set up an inclusive group. "I formed a new support group because the one I was in at the time was a branch of a national organization which became exclusive, not by religion, but by political viewpoint. The political litmus test interfered with local activities. Several of us formed a breakaway group, which we set up with definite inclusive rules, based around local support and activities."

State and Provincial Groups

Because homeschooling legalities center around state laws and regulations, many state groups focus on providing interpretations of educational statutes as well as monitoring legislation. They may also refer new home educators to local support groups, publish informative newsletters, organize statewide conferences, and otherwise help local support groups network with each other. Donna in Ontario, Canada, reports, "We belong to the provincial group because of the experience, knowledge and support they provide, not to mention the great yearly conference and quarterly newsletter."

Some home educators, without access to a compatible local group, may find the nearest sup-port for their efforts through a state association. Emma in Georgia says that the best support for

Not all support groups are created equal. If you join one, remember that the worker bees are all busy volunteer parents who homeschool their own children.

> If you find local support lacking, remember that many groups begin with two or three mothers brainstorming over coffee and tea at a kitchen table.

homeschooling her teenagers comes from her statewide newsletter and annual conference.

California, where I live, resembles many other states in that homeschoolers can choose from more than one statewide support and networking group. All three groups here publish excellent newsletters and provide referrals to local support groups. One offers classes for new home educators throughout the year. The other two sponsor huge statewide conferences.

Kate emphasizes the importance of working with a statewide organization. She explains, "My husband and I maintain a paid membership only in the state group [rather than a local or national group]. I believe every home educator should join and volunteer with their state organization to maintain our right to homeschool." Annette in Arkansas agrees. "I support our state association because they consistently lobby for better state homeschool law and keep us informed of changes and needs within our state."

National Groups

Several national homeschooling groups exist, each with a different focus. The Homeschool Legal Defense Association defends and promotes the rights of families to direct their children's education. HSLDA has a staff of attorneys, and paying members of HSLDA receive legal advice and support should they have a problem with their homeschooling. The HSLDA Web site primarily refers readers to Christian statewide organizations and resources. The National Center for Home Education, a division of HSLDA, networks homeschooling organizations in all fifty states for rapid response to federal issues. They also act as a clearinghouse for homeschool research and provide information to the media and other interested parties.

The National Home Education Research Institute concentrates on numbers, producing statistics and technical reports on home-schooling. They see themselves as a research clearinghouse, ready to educate policy makers and the public about homeschooling.

Confused yet? Just one more. The Internet-based National Home Education Network (NHEN) was formed to expand the general public's image of homeschoolers. They see home educators as a very diverse group, and they encourage the distribution of information from a variety of viewpoints, rather than promoting one philosophy over another. They say, "We respect that what is best for one homeschool family isn't necessarily best for another." They maintain information files and conduct resource referral from their Web site.

In addition, national associations exist for various religious and ethnic homeschool subgroups, such as the Jewish Home Educators Network and the Native American Homeschool Association. The number of national homeschool organizations outside the United States continues to grow. See the end-of-chapter Resources for specifics.

E-mail and Internet Groups

Karen in Washington belongs only to an e-mail support group. She says, "They fit my style of homeschooling. I learn a lot about the different curricula and techniques that are available."

> Internet groups and online mailing lists fill a support-group gap for many home educators. Those who can find no compatible groups locally usually can find experience and good advice online—any time of the day or night.

Marla in Wyoming also finds the best support online. She explains, "The local support group, tiny as it is, will not accept members of my church. We have few homeschoolers locally. I use the Internet to meet like-minded people for support and ideas."

Internet groups and online mailing lists fill a support-group gap for many home educators. Those who can find no compatible groups locally usually can find experience and good advice online—any time of the day or night. Virtual friendships form quickly as homeschooling parents worldwide share ideas.

My online experience dates from 1991, first with the now defunct Prodigy Homeschool Bulletin Boards, more recently as a co-host at Kaleidoscapes, one of many World Wide Web home-schooling discussion boards. In addition, I keep abreast of statewide developments through an e-mail loop for county contacts of our state support group, and I monitor national developments through yet another electronic mailing list. Boards and lists exist for different religious groups, for learning difficulties, for writers for various homeschooling publications, even for families using certain curricula. No matter what your interests or questions, you can find a discussion board or mailing list devoted to it.

YOUR LOCAL LIBRARIES

If you think of libraries as merely places to borrow books, you have missed 90 percent of what they offer. Of course, library shelves contain thousands of useful titles for reading and research. In addition, almost all libraries now participate in Inter-Library Loan, a program that enables you to obtain almost any title on loan—not just from other nearby libraries, but from outside systems as well. I often wonder why people do not preview textbooks this way. Get that Saxon Math book Inter-Library Loan, and try it out first. Just ask at the front desk. Your librarian will give you a form to complete, usually asking simply for author and title.

Our survey respondents list an amazing variety of learning activities and resources at their libraries. Obviously big libraries will offer more services than small ones. Nevertheless, it pays to ask about all these resources, no matter what size your library. If they don't provide it now, perhaps they will in the future. Ways those responding to our survey use their libraries include:

+ Reading magazines
+ Borrowing books
+ Borrowing books on tape
+ Buying used books
+ Borrowing music and foreign language CDs
+ Borrowing educational computer games
+ Playing educational computer games at the library
+ Viewing art and history displays
+ Participating in teen summer reading programs
+ Using meeting rooms
+ Attending lectures
+ Borrowing sheet music
+ Participating in book discussion groups
+ Finding community resource information
+ Using the reference section
+ Consulting the reference librarians
+ Taking free classes
+ Borrowing videos
+ Using homeschool resource files
+ Using the Inter-Library Loan system
+ Using computers—word processing
+ Accessing the Internet
+ Doing volunteer work

For all their advantages, some parents urge caution when visiting libraries. Viola in Nevada explains, "We don't use the local library much. I do not like the trend toward a lack of censorship in the library, especially as it applies to trash on the Internet."

In addition to regular libraries, teenagers have the intellectual maturity to use specialized libraries and collections. If you live near a college or university, visit their main library the next time your teen needs to research a question or new interest. Most large colleges and universities also have specialized libraries for science or history or music, for example.

> In addition to regular libraries, teenagers have the intellectual maturity to use specialized libraries and collections.

There is more. Most towns, cities, and counties have local history collections—either in a historical society library or museum. Visit and peruse the resources. Family History Centers, libraries operated by the Latter-Day Saints Church welcome visitors for family history research. Church libraries carry many titles you will never find at the local public library. To review curriculum, call your local school district and ask if they have an educational library open to the public.

Libraries are precious treasures—education for free. Bring smiles, flowers, and even cookies when you visit. Make certain your librarians know that you appreciate their efforts.

YOUR COMMUNITY: A MICROCOSM OF YOUR WORLD

AS THEY VENTURE into their communities, homeschooled teenagers first get their feet wet in the real world. In our case, many days our son and daughter spent more time away from home than if they attended school. They participated in 4-H and Civil Air Patrol meetings. They sang in the church choir and attended youth group activities. They joined other teenage homeschoolers for co-op classes. They volunteered regularly at hospitals, churches, museums, libraries, and soup kitchens, and irregularly at fairs and hot-air balloon festivals. They took weekly group music theory lessons. In the spring, they played on baseball and softball teams. They enrolled in college classes, and they worked paying jobs.

In similar fashion, many of our survey respondents report that their homeschoolers make the world their classroom with community activities, volunteering, alternative homeschool programs, and college classes.

Community Activities

Susanna in Illinois, lists her thirteen-year-old son's activities. They include YMCA swim team, military base swim team, Prairie State Games (state-level Olympic-type competition), Boy Scouts, 4-H, USS swim meets, junior college–sponsored science classes, and junior goodwill games. Cheryl, homeschooling two teenagers, says they participate in church youth group and various homeschool support subgroups, such as a Teen Club and Chess Club. Molly's thirteen-year-old daughter uses several community resources. She does gymnastics

TOP FIVE YOUTH PROGRAMS

Our survey respondents listed these five youth programs most frequently:

+ Church youth groups, particularly AWANA
+ 4-H
+ Scouts
+ Team sports
+ Camp Fire

SURVEY RESPONDENTS' VOLUNTEER SITES

- ✦ Library
- ✦ Church
- ✦ Nursing homes/hospitals
- ✦ Community drama groups
- ✦ Tutoring programs
- ✦ Nature preserves
- ✦ Recycling programs
- ✦ Radio stations
- ✦ Children's sports
- ✦ Zoos
- ✦ TV stations
- ✦ Political campaigns
- ✦ Camps
- ✦ Preschools
- ✦ Food banks

through the recreation department, dances with a local troupe, plays in a nearby college orchestra, and participates in 4-H.

Most communities offer many activities for teenagers. Check first with your local 4-H and Scouting organizations. Then branch out to your parks and recreation department, library, and local colleges. If applicable, find activities at your church and local homeschool support group. Do a little research and networking. Community outlets can make what high schools offer look very limiting.

Volunteering

Eighty percent of our survey respondents report that their teenagers volunteer from two to twenty or more hours per week. Karen lists her sixteen-year-old son's and fourteen-year-old daughter's volunteer activities. They include recycling every month, collecting cans of food twice a year for the needy, and helping Dad at work in the local emergency room. Anita's teenage daughter volunteers at a tutoring program and at a nature preserve. She also works for her church at the renaissance fair every year.

The two most popular venues, libraries and churches, provide many opportunities for service. At libraries, teenagers repair and stack books, act as computer docents, conduct storytelling, create special-events displays and posters, and work with Friends of the Library on used book sales. Teens also perform many useful volunteer services at churches, including office work and computing, gardening, cleaning, room-painting, child care, teaching vacation Bible school, and running the sound system.

Volunteering can count as "school." Our daughter worked four hours weekly at a veterinary clinic, doing everything from taking vital signs on cats and dogs to observing autopsies. She learned to make up inoculations and identify microscopic parasites. We called it life science.

Teenage volunteers sample working conditions in various fields. At hospitals, they see doctors, nurses, and technicians close up. In television and radio stations, they go behind the scenes and observe exactly how managers juggle programs, personnel, and advertisers. Early exposure to different environments helps them further explore certain occupations or rule them out at an early age.

QUICK & EASY

Enter the search term "family volunteering" into a search engine like www.google.com to read online articles about how your family can volunteer together.

Homeschool Programs

Although not an option in some areas, some families homeschooling teenagers use alternative education programs, especially for subjects in which they lack expertise. These programs take many forms. Homeschool support groups offer co-op classes, and private individuals offer courses. In addition, some public and charter high schools allow homeschoolers to take one or two classes.

Approximately half of our survey respondents use alternative education programs. Although most teens average four to eight hours weekly in these programs, two of our respondents report that their children spend up to twenty hours each week in alternative education. Except where public schools make classes available, funding almost always comes directly from parents, either in the form of direct payments to teachers or volunteered time.

Several of our survey respondents explain how and why they use alternative education programs.

Pauline in Kentucky writes, "My daughter will be starting a biology class for high-schoolers taught by a homeschooling mom. It is her own private business."

Sarah reports, "Our homeschool co-op and academy help with subjects I do not feel comfortable teaching. It makes our son accountable to someone else. We consider it good practice for college classes. He takes science, higher math, speech, and computer programming. Our co-op classes are free. We trade teaching time. For classes at our local homeschooling academy, we pay each teacher individually."

Kate tells us about her son's experience. "We currently attend a math class sponsored by a local private independent-study program. We pay $40 a month. My husband also taught a biology class and plans to teach chemistry to a group of homeschoolers. Each family contributes money for the supplies. The math class takes four hours each week. The lab portion of biology took six hours a month."

> Volunteering can count as "school." Our daughter worked four hours weekly at a veterinary clinic, doing everything from taking vital signs on cats and dogs to observing autopsies. She learned to make up inoculations and identify microscopic parasites. We called it Life Science.

Anita's daughters take classes at public school. She has mixed feelings about it. "It's good that my daughters have a decent German teacher. On the other hand, they get the negative influences of school. They can easily regress into doing just what it takes to make an A instead of doing their very best."

Not every family with programs available finds them useful. Johanna explains, "We don't use alt-ed programs. There are several large co-ops in our area, but they often have long waiting lists and seem quite rigid in approach. No programs are offered by our school district, which has a long history of being particularly unfriendly to homeschooling families."

> Before you enroll your teen in any public school homeschool programs, always ask exactly what schools require of you.

She continues, "Even if good alt-ed programs were available, we probably would not use them. First, I think it would take too much time. Right now we rarely have enough hours in the day to accomplish all we want to do. Second, I would be uncomfortable taking part in any public-school–sanctioned program. They almost always come with strings attached."

Johanna makes a good point about programs through public schools. Many offer free textbooks and access to special activities like sports or band or choir. In return, however, some require weekly or monthly reports and standardized testing. Before you enroll your teen in any public school homeschool programs, always ask exactly what schools require of you.

College at Age Thirteen?

At a recent graduation ceremony for Florida State homeschoolers, the emcee read a short description of each of more than forty teenagers receiving diplomas. More than 90 percent of them had taken college classes concurrent with their high school homeschooling. Several had accumulated more than a year's worth of college credits.

Homeschooled teenagers take college courses for several reasons. Amy in Maine explains, "Our teenagers enroll in college classes to be independent from us and to boost their confidence in their ability to do well at conventional-style schooling." Janice adds, "My teens take one or two college classes each semester for the challenge, to start accumulating college credits, to ease into a classroom environment before full-time college enrollment."

Some families find that college classes offer subjects and resources not available even at large high schools. Molly in Colorado says, "Our teen takes college classes. It's the only way to get music theory." Kate, in California, reports, "Our son takes eight semester hours per quarter at our local community college. Having recently received a huge grant from Microsoft, they have wonderful computer science classes. We cannot begin to reproduce all the equipment he has access to at college."

Lauren, across the country in New York state, relates a different experience. "Our daughter took three college classes one semester. She audited them—no credit, no payment. She took them for the content and the experience of college classes. Her art history professor volunteered to write a college recommendation for her."

Jill in California writes about supervising the college experience of young teenagers. "My daughter enrolled in an American Sign Language class for two semesters at a local junior college. She was fourteen at the time. Because of her age, my husband sat at the back of the class reading."

Unfortunately, some states make it difficult for homeschooled teenagers to take college courses. Monica in Wyoming reports, "Our local community college does not allow homeschoolers to take classes without a GED. And in our state, no one under eighteen can take the GED." If you find yourself in a similar position, consider correspondence and online colleges. Many institutions nationwide will allow your teenager to enroll in courses. See end-of-chapter Resources for contact information.

College classes, community activities, libraries, support groups—the world is wide open for your teenagers.

SIMPLE STARTING POINTS

✦   *Contact every local support group in your area, go to their meetings, and ask about activities for teenagers.* When you join a local support group, ask how you can help. If you cannot find a compatible group, don't give up. Consider forming your own group. Post library notices, ask existing groups to refer people to you, and advertise in the newspaper to locate like-minded families.

✦   *Visit one or more online homeschool support group Web sites.*

✦   *Request literature and sample newsletters from all state homeschooling organizations.* Join one or more to learn about proposed education legislation and to get information about conferences, curriculum exchanges, and seminars.

✦   *Make a trip to your library, interview the librarians, and learn about all of their services.* In addition, visit one or two college or other specialized libraries in your area.

✦   *Call community youth organizations to learn about participation.* Church youth groups, 4-H, and Scouts rank high, so begin there.

✦   *Using the list of volunteer activities in this chapter, brainstorm options with your teenager.* Even organizations without established volunteer programs welcome eager teenage helpers who are available during the daytime.

✦   *If you have older teenagers ready to try a college class, collect catalogs from local community and private colleges to see what classes your teens might enroll in.*

RESOURCES

National Organizations

Check for more organizations and updates at:
The Eclectic Homeschool Organization Web site,
    http://www.eho.org/national.htmcheck
Catholic Homeschool Network of America, P.O. Box 6343,
    River Forest, IL 60305-6343,
    http://www.geocities.com/Heartland/8579/chsna.html
Homeschool Legal Defense Association, P.O. Box 3000,
    Purcellville, VA 20134, http://www.hslda.org
Islamic Homeschool Education Network, 241 Meadowbrook
    Drive, Bolingbrook, IL 60440, e-mail mshgofil@aol.com
Jewish Home Educators Network, c/o Lisa Hodge Kander, 2122
    Houser, Holly, MI 48442, http://snj.com/jhen
Latter-Day Saint Home Educators Association, LDS-HEA, 2770
    South 1000, West Perry, Utah 84302, http://www.ldshea.org
National Center for Home Education, P.O. Box 3000, Purcellville,
    VA 20134, http://www.hslda.org/nationalcenter
National Challenged Homeschoolers Associated Network, 5383
    Alpine Rd. SE, Olalla, WA 98359
National Home Education Network, P.O. Box 41067, Long Beach,
    CA 90853, http://www.nhen.org
National Home Education Research Institute, P.O. Box 13939,
    Salem, OR 93709, http://www.nheri.org
Native American Homeschool Association, P.O. Box 979, Fries, VA
    24330, http://expage.com/apge/nahomeschool

International Groups

Association of Canadian Home-Based Education, Suite 145, 35-
    2855 Pembina Hwy, Winnipeg, Manitoba R3T 2H5, Canada,
    http://www.flora.org/homeschool-ca/achbe

Education Otherwise, P.O. Box 7420, London, N9 9SG, United
Kingdom, http://www.education-otherwise.org

Homeschoolers Australia, P.O. Box 420, Kellyville NSW 2155,
Australia, http://homeschool.3dproductions.com.au/support
/homeaust.html

Volunteering

Ryan, Bernard. *Participating in Government: Opportunities to Volunteer* (Community Service for Teens). Ferguson Publishing, 1998. Also, *Helping the Ill, the Poor, and the Elderly; Increasing Neighborhood Service* and related titles by the same author.

Online Discussion Boards and Support

See chapter 4 Resources—Online message boards

Independent-Study College Courses

See chapter 15 Resources

13

THE HOME FRONT

$\mathcal{H}$OME EDUCATION CREATES conflicting demands. As you discuss writing or math with your teen, younger siblings clamor for attention. Educational projects fill every corner, homes get messy, and household chores increase. And there's more. Teenagers, with their many activities, require transportation more often than younger children. In addition, teens need guidance to manage their days. Planning and scheduling take time from history and science. Demands on the primary teacher or facilitator do not end there. Husbands need time with their wives—away from children. Finally, many homeschool parents say they need time alone.

Certainly the primary teacher has responsibilities beyond academics that threaten to overwhelm the most capable among us. Almost all homeschooling parents admit struggling with these issues. Our survey respondents, in the midst of their journeys, talk candidly about the challenges and suggest interesting solutions.

ACCOMMODATING YOUNGER TRAVELERS

TODDLERS AND EARLY- AND MIDDLE-YEARS children want to join anything interesting happening in the house. Curiosity about the teen and adult world drives their learning, and you will not want to discourage it. At the same time, you need individual time with your thirteen- to eighteen-year-olds to tackle difficult academics, discuss mature topics, and work on complicated projects. Here we offer effective coping techniques. On a related tangent, our survey respondents also discuss how the homeschooling experience differs for oldest, middle, and youngest children.

Tactics of Inclusion and Diversion

Some families handle younger siblings by including them in activities. Others prefer diversions, such as Legos and videos. In some instances, inclusion is the diversion.

Marta, mother of seven girls ages two to seventeen, describes her bag of tricks. "I sometimes give our younger children their own work to do in parallel to what the older ones are doing. For example, they have coloring books and workbooks that they use while the older ones are doing written work. I have educational computer games aimed specifically at our younger children. They play while I teach. I also have a French cartoon teaching video for the little ones. They watch this every day, so that they become comfortable with simple phrases and conversations in French. This gives me a half-hour to work with one of the older girls without interruptions."

HOW WE DID IT

Here are some ways homeschooling parents occupy younger siblings while they work with older ones:

✦ Give younger children their own workbooks, pencils, crayons
✦ Do "school" with younger siblings first
✦ Let the younger ones listen
✦ Legos, blocks, and cuisenaire rods
✦ Books with tapes
✦ Story tapes
✦ Friends to visit
✦ Chores
✦ Nap
✦ Playing with water in the sink
✦ Videos
✦ Computer games
✦ Puzzles
✦ Play-Doh

Claudia has homeschooled her four boys, now ages nine to eighteen, since 1986. She maintains her younger children's interest in workbooks and other materials by restricting access. "We keep certain books, paper, and other supplies for younger children separate from other toys, available only when we want to do something with the older children. The younger siblings see these items as their special homeschooling things."

Several of our survey respondents mentioned adjusting curriculum to accommodate younger learners. Many use unit studies, sometimes in conjunction with other techniques. Molly, mother of five children ages eight months to fourteen years, writes, "I have always devised units around what my oldest is studying. I fit the

> First, homeschooling parents need not think of themselves as The Entertainment Committee.

younger ones into that framework. We will all do biology this year. The two oldest will dissect while my five-year-old daughter observes and eventually leaves to play. Our three-year-old son will be off riding tractors with Dad, and I hope the baby will nap. I have trained my younger ones not to interrupt—not very often anyway! We have a big house, and that helps spread folks out. I am a firm believer in extra chores for children who cannot happily occupy themselves."

Molly makes two good points. First, homeschooling parents need not think of themselves as The Entertainment Committee.

This applies to younger children as well as teenagers. There is nothing wrong with learning to deal with boredom by creating your own entertainment. Many children, occupied with full-time school and activities, never get that chance until they reach adulthood. Homeschoolers learn this valuable lesson early. Second, except for babies and toddlers, children of all ages can be taught to respect the time of everyone in the home. Even a three-year-old can learn when not to interrupt.

Amy, with four children ages ten to nineteen, schedules activities interesting and educational to all ages—in her words, "activities that can be absorbed on many levels." Examples are reading aloud, watching educational videos, and going on field trips. Building on this idea, consider introducing some subjects that younger children can learn as fast or faster than their older siblings can. These include music, foreign languages, and games like chess.

Same Family, Different Experience

Ryan, age twenty-five and a former homeschooler, is the oldest of four sons of a close friend. Watching his parents' relaxed relationship with his younger teenage brothers, he wryly calls himself "the experimental model." According to our survey respondents, he hits the nail on the head.

Birth order affects the homeschooling experience. Mira explains, "Our first child definitely had more attention from us in the beginning and had to suffer as we developed our educational philosophy. Our second did not get as much attention but had the benefit of a very relaxed educational style customized to him from the beginning." Susanna recounts a similar experience. "My firstborn son has had to endure my exploring and finding the correct curriculums for him. My daughter has had medical problems that have delayed her, yet I have easily found appropriate curriculum for her."

> Consider introducing some subjects that younger children can learn as fast or faster than their older siblings can. These include music, foreign languages, and games like chess.

No doubt about it. Parents become better home educators with experience. During their journey, they learn how to evaluate resources and choose appropriate community activities. Then, as they focus on their younger children, they operate with confidence, not from fear. Typically, older children bear the brunt of experimentation. They also shoulder the unstated yet always-present responsibility for proving the success of home education to doubting friends and relatives.

Nevertheless, oldest children have some advantages. With higher parental expectations, a greater percentage of older children excel academically. In addition, older children seem to mature more quickly, probably because they assume responsibilities that youngest children never have, such as child care or even teaching.

Younger children benefit from their parents' experience with older siblings. In addition, many mothers say that younger children often learn by osmosis, just by listening to a lesson or discussion many deem too difficult for them to understand. Marta says, "The younger ones benefit the most since they observe and soak up all the things the older ones do." At the same time, younger siblings usually feel less pressure to achieve and perform.

Some say that reduced expectations can lead to mediocre performance. Others counter that expectations are not reduced, just different. Emma writes, "We learned with our older children that everything works out in the end. Our new expectations center not so much around specific skills as around developing a work ethic and pursuing interests in depth."

KEEPING HOUSE AND SANITY AS YOU HOMESCHOOL

AS A HOMESCHOOLING parent, you wear many hats. First come the parent and teacher hats. Then you don administrator, housecleaner, scheduler, organizer, nurse, chauffeur, cook, and chief bottle-washer hats, often all in the same day. Before you know it, you look and feel like a character in a Dr. Seuss book—smiley, animated, and confused, all at the same time. Bring yourself back to reality with the comments of experienced travelers.

Housework—A Family Affair

Our survey respondents divided equally on whether homeschooling makes housekeeping easier or more difficult. Karleen finds it easier. "If they were in school, then I would also be working full time. This way, I get my chores done whenever I have a chance throughout the day. Plus I expect our teenagers to do additional chores because they are home more."

Cheryl compares her previously schooled daughter to her homeschooled son. She writes, "When our daughter attended school, she spent so many hours on homework that she had no time to help at home at all. Keeping house is easier with our son at home because he does help out a lot."

Not all parents find keeping up with chores easier. Over two-thirds of our survey respondents say that their homes get dirtier and disorganized faster because they homeschool.

Coping strategies vary. Many decide that having a house that resembles pictures in *House Beautiful* need not be a top priority. Delia says, "We focus on learning. Our time with our children is brief. I cannot see wasting it polishing knickknacks."

> Many decide that having a house that resembles pictures in *House Beautiful* need not be a top priority.

Deanna has also redefined her priorities, writing, "Housekeeping is difficult because I have less time. However, a clean house has become much lower on my priority list since homeschooling. It doesn't bother me the way it used to!"

Some parents see their homes as places where teenagers learn independent-living skills. Jill explains, "It is difficult to have a neat house. We live here all day, busy with projects and learning. Learning is messy. Creativity is messy. We keep order because if we did not, we would not be able to find anything. Our home is a training ground for my children to learn how to keep house—how to cook, how to clean, and how to make a house a home. My goal in this season of my life is to raise healthy adults and not to have a house that looks like a model home."

We also saw our home as a training ground—especially as our children moved into their teen years. I reasoned that if I did a household task—whether painting a room, cleaning a sink, or adjusting the air in the tires—my teenagers should be able to do those jobs also. We promoted independence by insisting on at least an hour of chores each day. Our son and daughter planned menus, cooked meals, shopped for groceries on a budget, learned basic auto maintenance, helped with home improvements, repaired torn clothing, and helped with sick pets.

Some of our survey respondents, especially those who live in rural areas, report that their teenagers do up to four hours of chores

HOW WE DID IT

Here's a list of chores survey respondents say their teenagers regularly perform:

- Doing laundry
- Mowing the lawn
- Shoveling snow
- Taking out garbage
- Grocery shopping
- Weeding
- Car care
- Canning
- Pet care
- Home improvement projects
- House cleaning
- Doing dishes
- Sewing
- Planning and preparing meals
- Yard work
- Recycling
- Child care

each day. David and Micki Colfax, homeschooling parents whose sons won admission to Harvard, assigned their children so many ranch chores that all four came to view sitting down with a book as a real treat. Hard physical work creates an unexpected reward—motivation to do academic work!

Whether you view chores as necessary evils, learning opportunities, or motivators, you will need to keep a modicum of order. Most home-cleaning experts recommend regular de-junking. Unused items add to disorganization. If you want to simplify housework, simplify your life by selling or giving away anything you have not used in five years. Go through every space in your home. That means cleaning out every closet, desk, and cupboard. It also means going through the basement, attic, and garage and deciding what stays and what goes. This may sound like a backwards approach to housework, but many moms say it helps to have less to deal with.

Consider in-depth organization of one room or space each month of the year.

TIME AND RESOURCE MANAGEMENT

The logistics of homeschooling make everyone stop and think. Here the rubber meets the road, literally. Many families ask "How will you get there?" when their teenagers suggest new activities. And planning transportation fits into the larger scheme—planning household chores and family and outside activities. Although they do not have to work around school, home educators do need time and resource management skills.

> Hard physical work creates an unexpected reward—motivation to do academic work!

Getting Around

Always on the go. That describes my two home-schooled teens. Every morning after breakfast and chores, we met to decide the big question—who gets the car? We choreographed as intricately as if we were staging a classical ballet to assure that everyone made it to work and activities.

Many of our survey respondents list their cars as their primary mode of transportation. Like Aletha, they cheerfully wear their taxi-driver hats. Some get help. Amy reports, "My husband takes a couple of late afternoons off to help with chauffeuring."

Others breathe a sigh of relief when their teenagers learn to drive. Leanne writes, "Our son has his driver's license. He gets himself to his activities. He also transports his younger sister. Otherwise I do the driving or share with a neighbor."

Molly adds, "There's nothing more wonderful than your oldest child getting a driver's license! We live twelve miles from town, so transportation can be a logistical nightmare. I have been known to

HOW WE DID IT

We do chores the first thing every morning to favorite music. We like Broadway show tunes. Our teenagers find it easier than confronting a math text at 8:00 A.M.!

— EMMA IN GEORGIA

spend quite a bit of time at the library waiting for someone to finish an activity. We also transport our schoolwork to the library when several children need to be in town at different times."

Marta uses a combination of transportation strategies. "We combine several things into one outing, for example shopping while children attend music lessons. We carpool with other families. I have our girls take the bus to choir practice."

Some families make it work without Mom chauffeuring. Tess explains, "I don't drive. My husband takes everyone to kung fu and tai chi. The library is about three blocks away from our house." Deanna, who lives in Japan, writes, "We do not have a car. They take the subway." Dinah, in suburban Salem, Oregon, says her fourteen-year-old son either walks or bikes. He plans activities more than five miles away for evenings or weekends, when they have an automobile.

Planning and Scheduling Your Days

A homeschooling friend often reminds me: "Failure to plan is planning to fail." Scheduling activities and making the best use of time present challenges to many adults, most particularly those adults who did not learn these skills as teenagers. Of course, there is a big difference between most thirteen-year-olds and most seventeen-year-olds. Many older adolescents work almost completely independently. Younger teens still need guidance. Either way, most parents want their teens to develop planning and scheduling skills.

Finding a balance between parent-directed and teen planning can be difficult. Jill writes, "This year, unlike last year, I schedule my sixteen-year-old daughter's schoolwork. She was very busy last year. Although she had to check my schedule first and ask about activities, I found that she was getting lazy with schoolwork and chores. This year, we will work on planning one's time and breaking things down to bite-size tasks. This is a life skill, valuable to her future."

MONEY SAVER

Network with other home-schooling parents to form carpools.

Having a planning schedule helps. Deanna says, "We try to sit down on Monday and plan the week's work." Mira reports that they use day planners, the type found in office supply stores. Marla explains to her teenagers how to decide what comes first. "I have taught them to prioritize. There are things they need to do daily—seminary study and math. Other subjects, like reading and history, lend themselves to large chunks of time one to three times each week."

Marta, mother of seven children, writes, "They prefer a list of things to do that they can check off as they work at their own pace. I need to schedule a few classes when I work with several of them— Latin, science, music theory—so that they fit into my schedule."

Cheryl also decides the subjects taught, but leaves details up to her two teenage sons. She explains: "I don't get them up, but by 10:00 A.M. they must have eaten, finished their chores, and have started schoolwork. I don't care if it takes them all day or two hours. I make an assignment sheet from the computer on Monday. By Friday, it needs to be done. I am here for help, and we do our unit studies together. Otherwise, they are on their own. We do school four days a week. Thursday is our co-op day—no formal academics. We have lots of social things on Friday afternoon. If they have not completed their work, they stay home."

Karen, in Washington State, adjusts plans according to the weather. She writes, "We schedule differently for every season. In the summer, they work in the afternoon with the air conditioner on. In the morning, they work on farm chores or we go to town to shop. In the winter, we work on the school subjects in the morning while waiting for the day to warm up and for the ice to melt from the roads."

> When queried about daily schedules, our survey respondents fall into two groups—those who can describe their daily routine and those who say that no day is typical.

Daily Schedules

When queried about daily schedules, our survey respondents fall into two groups—those who can describe their daily routine and those who say that no day is typical.

Cheryl falls into the first group. Writing about her fifteen-year-old son's day, she says, "We begin school around 8:30 and start working through the subjects in the lesson plan book. We do math, then vocabulary, grammar, reading, and writing before lunch. After lunch, he practices piano. Then we do Bible, science, and social studies. We usually finish by 2:30 P.M. and sometimes as early as noon. He then checks his e-mail. He also plays computer games, cruises the Net, sees friends, reads car magazines, or listens to music."

Marta also runs a tight ship. Here is one of her teenage daughter's days:

7:30–8:00	Breakfast. Morning prayer with family.
8:00–11:00	Music theory with Mom and sisters. Algebra—check with Mom on assignment or with questions, did problem set on her own. Preparation for Shakespeare class. Snack.
11:00	Internet class on Shakespeare.
12:00	History, Greek, or literature. Help with lunch.

1:00 P.M.	Lunch. Help with cleanup.
2:00	Biology class with Mom.
3:00	Latin class with Mom.
3:30	Free to study, read, do chores, practice cello.
6:00–9:45 P.M.	Orchestra rehearsal.

Belinda, a single parent, builds homeschooling her thirteen-year-old son around her work schedule. She reports, "From 6:30 A.M. to 2:30 P.M., I am at work. Kevin does his schoolwork from his assignment sheet. He also sleeps late and plays outside until I get home. Sometimes he goes to the library with one of his adult siblings. My twenty-eight-year-old daughter lives with us, and she helps occupy him while I am at work. From 2:30 to 5:00 P.M. Kevin usually does what he wants. Around 5:00 P.M. we have dinner and then do school. It usually takes a couple of hours to check his work, read, and go over new stuff. We are very unstructured—as much as we can be and still get the job done."

Susanna says they have no typical days. Here she lists a previous day's activities for her son, age thirteen.

6:00 A.M.	Got up, ate breakfast, did chores.
9:00 A.M.–12:00 noon	Robotics class at local junior college.
12:00–12:45 P.M.	Lunch.
12:45–3:00 P.M.	Schoolwork.
3:00–6:30 P.M.	Swim practice and supper.
6:30–8:00 P.M.	Free time.
8:00–9:00 P.M.	Boy Scouts.
9:30 P.M	Bed.

Dinah operates a day care in her home. She reports, "We never have a typical day. Yesterday, our fourteen-year-old son did two lessons in Saxon math. We read for thirty minutes from the Bible. He listed his goals for this coming school year, including special projects he wanted to undertake. He wrote letters to Grandma and

As your teenagers mature, discuss priorities and let them practice making their own schedules.

Grandpa, thanking them for letting him spend the summer with them. He also wrote a professional letter to Grandpa's boss, thanking him for a learning opportunity. He accomplished all this while helping me—picking up toys, changing diapers, fixing dinner (it was his day), working on a combustion engine, practicing guitar, and bathing his youngest brother."

No matter what your situation, you can find a routine that fits your family. As your teenagers mature, discuss priorities and let them practice making their own schedules. Plan with them, and practice the fine arts of negotiation and compromise to make time for everything.

Time with Your Spouse

Some of our survey respondents report that they feel no need to schedule time with spouses, away from children. However, a substantial majority, about three-fourths of those who answered our questionnaire, say time alone with spouses is essential. Some have special times every day. Others rely on "dates" every week or at least once per month. Amy writes, "We have tea and walk together every morning." Susanna says that she tries to get out with her husband without their children a couple of times per month, even if it is only to the store.

Lydia reports, "I try to set bedtime for about 9:30. Then we get a couple of hours to ourselves. We usually sit outside or watch a movie."

Leanne describes how she and her husband make time for each other. "Each week we have one morning breakfast out and one evening dinner or cup of coffee at a restaurant. We walk two miles, three to four times per week. In addition, three times a year we go away for a weekend in a motel. For our anniversary, we go out for a really fancy dinner, a movie, and an overnight trip. Doing these things is how my husband looks out for my well-being, and I appreciate it!"

Time for Yourself

You know the old saying. If you do not take care of yourself, you will not be able to take care of anyone else. Of course, homeschooling can make it very difficult to meet your needs. Some parents sneak time alone. Molly comments, "I get maybe an hour per week. I hide at the library." Many busy moms use their alone time for exercise. Laura says, "I work out, and that takes about an hour a day." Some block out part of the day. Emma confesses, "I warn everyone not to bother me between 1:00 and 2:30 in the afternoon. That is when I read, walk, and play piano."

Siblings, housework, schedules, family and personal needs—the home front presents unexpected challenges to all homeschooling families. No one approach works best for all. Experienced travelers often arrive at solutions by trial and error, eventually finding the most productive strategies that allow them to remain in balance or at least juggle successfully. Above all, our homes provide training, where our teenagers learn the realities of hard work, planning, negotiation, and compromise.

SIMPLE STARTING POINTS

✦ *Decide how you will occupy younger siblings.* Peruse homeschooling catalogs, and gather learning resources and toys. Give some of these a special "stamp." Put them away and save them for times you and your teens really need to focus.

✦ *Think about at least one learning activity your entire family can do together.* Depending on your children's ages, consider videos, foreign language instruction, music appreciation, art, reading aloud, field trips, and even sports.

✦ *Discuss chores with your teenagers.* Certainly, they should be working at least as hard as you do! Divvy up household jobs. Make them part of the daily schedule.

✦ *Think about your comfort level with respect to daily schedules.* How much responsibility should your teenagers assume for planning their time?

✦ *Talk with your spouse about how much time you spend together now.* Is it enough? Brainstorm and discuss ways to keep your marriage alive while you homeschool.

✦ *Remember to take care of yourself.* Make time for activities that feed your spirit and renew your enthusiasm.

RESOURCES

Books

Aslet, Don. *Clutter's Last Stand.* Writer's Digest Books, 1984. *Also The Cleaning Encyclopedia, Make Your Home Do the Housework,* and others.

Cabellero, Jane A. *A Handbook of Learning Activities for Young Children.* Humanics Publishing Group, 1987.

Campbell, Jeff. *Talking Dirt: America's Speed Cleaning Expert Answers the 157 Most Asked Cleaning Questions.* DTP, 1997.

Dobson, Linda. *Homeschooling: The Early Years.* Prima Publishing, 1999.

Eisenberg, Ronnie. *Organize Your Family.* Hyperion, 1993.

Gee, Robin. *Entertaining and Educating Your Preschool Child.* EDC Publishing, 1987.

Gettman, David. *Basic Montessori: Learning Activities for Under-Fives.* St. Martin's Press, 1998.

Henry, Shari. *Homeschooling: The Middle Years.* Prima Publishing, 1999.

Herzog, Joyce. *Including Very Young Children in Your Homeschool.* Joyce Herzog, 1998. Also *Multilevel Teaching.*

Kizer, Kathryn. *200+ Ideas for Teaching Preschoolers.* New Hope Publishers, 1997.

Leman, Kevin. *The New Birth Order Book.* Fleming H. Revell, 1998.

Schofield, Deniece. *Confessions of an Organized Homemaker.* Betterway, 1994.

Wilson, Bradford. *First Child, Second Child: Your Birth Order Profile.* Kensington, 1983.

Winston, Stephanie. *Stephanie Winston's Best Organizing Tips: Quick Simple Ways to Get Organized and Get on with Your Life.* Fireside, 1996.

Catalogs

Jeff Campbell's The Clean Team, 800-717-2532, http://www.thecleanteam.com

Tooling Around, 408-286-9770

The Urban Homemaker, 303-750-7230

Organizational Tools

Steward, Jennifer and Harris, Gregg. *Choreganizers: The Visual Way to Organize.* Nobel Books, 1995.

Web Sites

Crayola Family Play Activity Homepage, http://www.familyplay.com/activities

Gryphon House Online, http://www.ghbooks.com/activity

Idea Box, http://www.theideabox.com

Little Explorers, http://www.enchantedlearning.com/dictionary.html

14

COMPLEMENTING PUBLIC AND PRIVATE SCHOOLING

In This Chapter

- ✦ Part-time homeschooling
- ✦ Menu-approach home education
- ✦ Afterschooling
- ✦ Simple starting points
- ✦ Resources

$\mathcal{M}$ORE OFTEN THAN you might think, I run into parents who say, "I wish I could homeschool." Take one of my e-mail correspondents. She cannot convince her husband of homeschooling's merits. He is dead set against it. Wisely, she will not proceed until they agree. In another case, a friend recently sent her teenagers back to public school. She prefers home education, but had to return to full-time work after her husband's unexpected death. Sometimes a mother's chronic illness or disability precludes homeschooling. In other families, both parents work full time just to pay the rent. They cannot give up the free child care and supervision school offers. Still other parents think home education looks like a good idea, yet they hesitate to make the final leap. Many situations lead parents to believe they cannot homeschool full time, even though they desperately want to.

As it turns out, families in all of the above situations can participate fully in their children's education. Part-time homeschooling, menu-approach home education, and "afterschooling" all offer ways to remediate, supplement, and enrich your teenager's learning. To complement full-time schooling, you need only two things—the desire to be part of your teenagers' education and the willingness to spend time working with them. Here we outline your options and then suggest approaches and resources to satisfy your goals.

PART-TIME HOMESCHOOLING

MOST PEOPLE HAVE no idea that part-time home education exists. Somebody at the school district office tells them homeschooling is all or nothing, and they pursue the idea no further. "Not so fast," say the part-timers.

First, let's define part-time home education. Part-time homeschoolers typically attend school for part of each day, usually in either the morning or the afternoon. This group differs from homeschoolers who take one or two classes to supplement homeschooling. Part-time homeschoolers usually work much more closely with schools to assure that all subjects are covered in ways schools find acceptable. In a typical case, Jason takes science, foreign language, and math each morning at his high school. Evenings, at home with his parents, he covers English and history and Bible. Another example? Maria studies history and language arts with her mother in the morning. She attends high school in the afternoon, taking math and science and physical education, when her mother begins working her second-shift job.

Some school districts work willingly with parents who want to try part-time arrangements. To determine whether yours is one, check three places. First, query members of local support groups to find families who have similar arrangements. They can tell you whom they talked to and how they went about it. Second, call your local state homeschooling association. They will usually be able to refer you to applicable laws and regulations. You need to read these and understand your rights before you proceed to step three.

Third, call both the principal of your local high school and your school district administrative offices. Ask them about making arrangements for part-time homeschooling. Before you call, always have in mind exactly what you want—which classes and which time periods. Also, ask whether the school will recognize your homeschool credits and grant a diploma. In many states, schools have no obligation to recognize courses you teach at home. In those cases, your student would not earn a diploma from the school. As will be explained in chapter 15, this is not a major problem. You will simply do what many full-time home educators do—write your own transcript.

Although not for everyone, part-time homeschooling allows some teenagers to experience the best of both worlds. And it creates a way for some parents caught between a rock and hard place to homeschool.

MENU-APPROACH HOME EDUCATION

FOR A VARIETY of reasons, some families send their teenagers to school one year, homeschool the next, back to school the following year, homeschool the next, and so on.

> Although not for everyone, part-time homeschooling allows some teenagers to experience the best of both worlds. And it creates a way for some parents caught between a rock and hard place to homeschool.

In some cases, families experiment, looking for the best educational venue. Marta explains, "My oldest daughter spent ninth grade in Catholic school, tenth grade at home, and eleventh grade in public school. She plans to graduate from public school. She loved her Catholic school experience. Except for her online Shakespeare class and her computer Web site, she was unhappy and unmotivated and unproductive at home. My husband and I decided to send her to the public school for eleventh grade. She has been happy there."

> Never assume that returning to school in grade 11 or 12 will allow your teen to receive a diploma from an accredited school.

Marta continues, "I have not been satisfied with her academic performance in any of the settings. She did make it to the honor society this year, though. Perhaps if she had been younger, we would have stuck with homeschooling. We felt, however, that she could not afford to do nothing for another year at home. For her, homeschooling was not the answer. She has to prepare for college. She has trouble motivating herself (result of years of institutional school?) and resents Mom trying to motivate her. She does find peers, grades, and other school trappings a little motivating. Maybe things would be different if we had started sooner. I will never know, and I do feel a little guilty about the whole thing."

Other parents rotate their children in and out of school for philosophical reasons. They want them to work in classroom groups and experience the discipline of traditional academic environments. At the same time, they know home education provides benefits that schools cannot duplicate. So they homeschool every other year.

Menu-approach homeschooling also works well for families that need extra income. The children attend school every other year while mom works full time. Mom takes alternate years off to homeschool.

Families with teenagers have to be particularly careful with menu-approach home education. Never assume that returning to school in grade 11 or 12 will allow your teen to receive a diploma from an accredited school. Beginning in what would be your teenagers' ninth-grade year, have a clear understanding with your school about recognizing homeschool credits. If they commit to accepting homeschool coursework, get it in writing.

AFTERSCHOOLING

WE WERE AFTERSCHOOLERS before I knew it had a name. I bought workbooks and did "school" with my children in the summertime to assure their math and reading did not regress. We took family field trips to zoos and museums. We stocked our home with educational games, toys, and supplies. We read aloud. We helped with homework and science projects. We funded music lessons and team sports participation.

Donna, now a full-time home educator, afterschooled also. She explains, "I guess that without knowing it, I did afterschool. Our family has always been into learning and education. In retrospect, we homeschooled while our son was still in school. Of course, afterschooling made switching to homeschooling a breeze, relative to what it could have been. One thing about afterschooling was hard, though. Everyone around us thought we were so weird."

Denise writes, "I think we always supplemented with afterschooling when our oldest three were in public school. I thought everyone who cared about their children did the same. We went over homework and played learning games. We always took the same field trip the school did to reinforce what they missed because of distractions that twenty-five classmates present. We went to the library weekly and read all the time to our children. Benefits? I gained plenty of confidence that I could homeschool and do a better job. I know now that learning takes place everywhere, not just in a classroom. Drawbacks? My children were gone for the best hours of the day. Afterschooling did lead us to homeschool full time when I realized that they didn't need school to learn. Amazingly, full-time homeschooling was easier than handling the problems school creates and better for them, too."

Just as Denise points out, most concerned parents are after-schoolers. They offer formal instruction outside of school, either with homework support or purchased curricular materials. They constantly look for ways to remediate problems and enrich education. They maintain rich learning environments at home. Often they become temporary full-time home educators during summer break.

> Afterschooling lets parents practice home-schooling, sometimes leading to full-time home education.

Afterschooling offers wonderful opportunities for families who cannot consider home-schooling, even on a part-time basis. In addition, afterschooling lets parents practice homeschooling, sometimes leading to full-time home education. Read on for ideas on choosing the best approaches and resources.

You Don't Have Much Time . . . Where Do You Want to Go?

If your teens attend school full time, you know the drill. They sit in class six to seven hours and tackle homework for one to three hours each evening. Factor in daily transportation, meals, and personal care. Your thirteen- to eighteen-year-old already spends nine to twelve hours each day getting an education. In addition, adolescents, like everyone else, need time to relax and pursue their own interests. All in all, afterschoolers have severe time constraints. They have to pick their approaches and materials carefully.

First, think about a goal for your afterschooling. Obviously, time precludes teaching a comprehensive curriculum. Proceed with caution. Your teenagers should not come home from school just to face more school at home. Are there obvious gaps in your teens' educations? Do they have difficulty keeping up? If so, you provide remediation. Are you worried that public school ignores Christian education? Think about supplementing with a Bible study course. Do your academically gifted teenagers find high school work boring? You can enrich their curriculum with unit studies and special projects.

Decide whether you will be providing remediation, supplementation, or enrichment. Depending on your teenagers, you may choose all three—remediation for math, supplementation for music theory, and enrichment for history, for example. Let's check out the various subject areas and see how you might approach afterschooling.

Math

Many children seem to do fine in math until they hit algebra. All of a sudden, their grades drop from A's and B's to C's and D's. Parents and teachers blame unproven instruction methods, poorly written textbooks, incompetent instructors, and anxiety-inducing testing. It is no accident that the terms "math" and "remediation" frequently occur in the same sentence.

Of course, fixing blame does not solve the problem. Identifying deficits and addressing them in a nonthreatening atmosphere does. I have tutored dozens of teenagers and adults in math—usually at the level of first-year algebra. Almost without exception, failing algebra students have problems with basic arithmetic. They cannot add, subtract, multiply, and divide quickly and accurately. In addition, most cannot calculate fractions, decimals, and percents and apply them to real-world situations. Algebra, the next step, is nothing more than abstract arithmetic. If your teens have a shaky grasp of arithmetic, expect algebra to put an end to their math learning.

For teenagers who need math remediation, home educators suggest the following approaches to solidify arithmetic skills and build confidence in algebra.

> Your teenagers should not come home from school just to face more school at home.

> It is no accident that the terms "math" and "remediation" frequently occur in the same sentence.

✦ *Work one on one with your students.* Resource teachers, private tutors, and even companies that specialize in raising school grades agree with homeschooling parents. They all say that working with students individually solves more than half of all academic problems.

✦ *Work at an appropriate level.* It makes little sense to struggle with algebra homework when your student cannot reliably multiply six times seven or calculate a percent. To build skills, back up to the point where your teenager finds the going easy.

✦ *Play games.* Both board and computer games offer drill disguised as fun. Teens especially enjoy fast computer games.

✦ *Use manipulatives, hands-on materials.* M&Ms, pennies, Monopoly money, rulers, and construction paper cutouts can work well for modeling math problems.

✦ *Relate math to everyday life.* Cook or work on home-improvement projects to learn fractions, and budget or play the stock market with fake money to practice arithmetic.

✦ *Ignore vacations.* Many forget the math they learn during the school year each summer. Do some math every week.

While many parents worry about remediation, another group—parents of math whizzes—seek enrichment materials. Mental math, math history, and recreational math pick up where school leaves off. Mental mathematicians learn to calculate in their heads, without pencil and paper or calculator. You can find excellent self-instructional mental math programs in any large bookstore. Or consider building a thematic unit around a math history topic. Explore abacuses, Egyptian numbering systems, or the many ways mathematicians determine the value of pi (the ratio of the circumference of a circle to its diameter). Recreational math—solving challenging, sometimes off-the-beaten-track problems—presents additional alternatives. Our end-of-chapter Resources suggest helpful titles.

Reading

Reading deficits become painful by high-school age. Teenagers who stumble over words suffer every day they attend school. They find English class difficult. Even science and history learning are compromised because those subjects rely heavily on reading.

You may have a teenager who reads slowly or never reads for pleasure. Adolescents without identified learning disabilities most often slip through the cracks at school. They know enough to get by and too much to warrant special education. At the same time, their minimal skills constantly limit them.

Almost all home educators will tell you that you improve reading skills by reading. "Fine," you say, "but he won't read anything!" Homeschoolers have found many approaches that create readers out of non-readers. Two, in particular, head most lists.

> Adolescents without identified learning disabilities most often slip through the cracks at school. They know enough to get by and too much to warrant special education.

First, read aloud. That's right. Read aloud to your teenagers. Do it fifteen to twenty minutes daily for a year or more. Pick book and magazine selections the whole family can enjoy and discuss. Listening to books on tape provides a variation on the read-aloud theme. Either way, building an appreciation for the written word may lead to reading for pleasure.

Second, encourage reading by providing materials that interest your teen. Begin with their outside activities. Do they play sports, skateboard, draw, adore *Star Trek* movies, or tinker with car engines? No matter what the activity, you can find magazines and books related to it. Shop for high-interest items to leave around the house. Try *The Guinness Book of World Records* or *The Top Ten of Everything.*

Reading enrichment usually takes care of itself. Good readers frequent libraries and bookstores. Many beg their parents for certain titles for holidays and birthdays. To help avid readers branch out, feed their habit. Help them find community book discussion groups. Ask your high school English teacher for summer reading lists, and obtain suggested reading lists from colleges of interest.

Writing

Writing frustrates many adolescents. Overzealous grammarians and usage police—high school English teachers—too often create environments where students resist putting any thoughts on paper. Chapter 5 contains suggestions for dealing with teenage writer's block. These work equally well for afterschoolers as they do for home educators.

> Overzealous grammarians and usage police—high school English teachers—too often create environments where students resist putting any thoughts on paper.

Recommendations for writing remediation and enrichment overlap. Just as readers improve by reading, writers improve by writing. Forget grammar lessons, and help your adolescents find real-world reasons to write. Daily journals make a good beginning and create first draft material your teen can use many other places. A friend of mine encouraged her sixteen-year-old to begin a family newsletter. Every month now her daughter writes articles and edits the work of others. Your teenager may prefer a twenty-first century writing task—building a Web page. No matter what the objective, suggest additional writing to your schooled teenagers frequently. They may surprise you with what they produce when they write for themselves and when they know no one will grade their work.

Science

Most teenagers who have trouble with science also have difficulty with math, reading, or both. Work on reading and math skills to see science grades improve.

Regardless of your assessment of your son's or daughter's science skills, consider science enrichment activities all around you. Visit science museums. Play computer and board games with science themes. Work on special projects at home, such as building model rockets or experimenting with electronics kits. Find a volunteer job at a zoo, veterinary clinic, hospital, or university laboratory. Invest in field guides and take nature hikes. Check into science videos, computer software, and Internet sites for more help.

Gifted scientists will need your support for science fairs and other science competitions. Too often parents find that schools announce these events and provide registration forms, leaving the rest up to them. Even if you have no science background, do not despair. Begin at the library and on the Internet, using "science project" as a search term. Whether your budding scientist wants to investigate insects, reptiles, lasers, or stars, many resources describe exactly how to proceed. For additional assistance, help your teenager locate a mentor for his project. This is not easy and often calls for adult networking skills. Begin by asking everyone you know—including your teen's science teacher and the science departments at nearby colleges and universities.

QUICK & EASY

Use amazon.com to find titles on obscure topics for teenagers. Also, if your teen likes one author, this Web site can recommend titles with similar themes and styles.

History and Geography

Success with history and geography in school depend on three factors: reading ability, memorization skills, and motivation to learn. As an afterschooler, you can enhance all three. We discussed improving reading above. Let's focus here on memorization and motivation.

Typical history and geography classes are filled with names, places, and dates. Most students need help memorizing facts. To build a good knowledge base, look for educational card, board, and computer games. Our children particularly enjoyed the board game Where in the World, but there are many others. Also, buy map puzzles, which provide solid geography orientation in a fun format.

In addition, help your teenagers deal with that next history test with memorization aids. Show them how to make flashcards and time lines. Teach them how to construct acronyms, like H-O-M-E-S to memorize the names of the Great Lakes—Huron, Ontario, Michigan, Erie, and Superior. Discuss word associations, relating an unknown fact to a known one. For example, to memorize Lincoln as the capital of Nebraska, picture a Lincoln Continental cruising the prairie.

As your teenagers develop memorization techniques, nurture their love of history and geography. Discuss the history that led up to current events. Visit history museums and watch history videos, many available for free at your library. Find good historical fiction for avid readers. Travel and note geographic features. Discuss how rivers and mountains and other topographic features influence history. Read chapter 7 for more history and geography enrichment ideas.

Foreign Language

Despite years of formal foreign language instruction, too many high school graduates remain fluent only in English. Afterschooling makes a real difference here. At home, increase foreign language exposure with music and videos. Peruse homeschool catalogs and buy additional instructional tapes. Subscribe to magazines like *Reader's Digest* in the foreign language. Invite foreign language speakers into your home. Travel to a country where they speak the language your teenager is studying. All of these enrichment activities will give your teen an advantage.

Afterschoolers also find ways to study languages not offered in most high schools. They study Hebrew at the local synagogue or American Sign Language in adult community education classes. I used to say that possibilities are limited only by your location. However, with many free foreign language courses on the Internet, that is no longer true. Not only can your teens take Internet courses in hundreds of languages, they can also find native speakers with whom to correspond.

Religious Studies

In the United States, too many public schools have interpreted separation of church and state to mean freedom from religion—all religion. This means they teach history with only passing references to religious influences and never adequately explain how religious faith affects individuals and societies. At the same time, more than 90 percent of Americans say that faith plays a role in their lives, and famous historians say Western civilization rests on two pillars—the Greco-Roman world and the Judeo-Christian tradition. Those from other emerging cultures in the United States have the same complaint—their views get no playtime in schools. Regardless of your perspective, it is easy to see why many families see a gaping hole in public school instruction with respect to religion.

Not only can your teens take Internet courses in hundreds of languages, they can also find native speakers with whom to correspond.

For these reasons and others, many parents feel it is essential to enrich their teenagers' public school education with religious studies at home. Some prefer one of the many popular courses that have been developed for home educators. If this interests you, check out Mary Pride's *Big Book of Home Learning,* Volume 3, for excellent reviews. Others use materials supplied by their churches and synagogues. Still others take a hands-on approach, studying comparative religions by visiting diverse religious institutions in their community. Let your goals dictate your activities in this area.

Helping Your Teens Pursue Interests

By the time our children reach adolescence, they have definite likes and dislikes. Some spend hours drawing or writing. Others program computers far into the night. Still others surf or snowboard for days on end.

Afterschooling parents recognize that learning outside of school may encompass almost any topic imaginable. They support their teenagers' interests and enthusiasms, even the nonacademic ones. In the process, they foster self-directed learning.

> Afterschooling parents recognize that learning outside of school may encompass almost any topic imaginable.

How do you accomplish this? How do you create a lifelong learner? First encourage self-directed activity—anything your teenagers do when no one is telling them what to do. Self-directed activity eventually leads to expertise. At this point, teenagers know more about their subjects, academic or nonacademic, than anyone around them. As they begin to teach themselves and network for additional resources in their community, they become self-directed learners. It is a great gift—and the best reason to afterschool your apprentice adults.

SIMPLE STARTING POINTS

✦   *Define what you want to accomplish through part-time home education, menu-approach schooling, or afterschooling.* Set reasonable goals, especially for afterschooling. Keep in mind the limited hours available, and choose activities wisely.

✦   *Attend one or two large homeschooling conferences or curriculum fairs where you can see a wide variety of resources.* Interview everyone there—the vendors, the speakers, the participants—to learn how to remediate, supplement, and enrich your teenager's education.

✦   *If you cannot attend a conference, read homeschool resource guides to locate fun and helpful materials.* Consider educational games, videos, and hands-on materials for all subjects.

✦   *Review pertinent chapters of this book to find ideas and resources for different subject areas.*

✦ *Help your teenagers explore their interests, even if they look nonacademic.* Buy related books, and help your teens find community groups related to their interests.

✦ *Reconsider afterschooling every year.* Think about it as a prelude to full-time homeschooling. Review the reasons you cannot homeschool full time. As teens mature, reasons for not homeschooling sometimes vanish.

RESOURCES

Books with Enrichment Suggestions

Griffith, Mary. *The Unschooling Handbook: How to Use the Whole World as Your Child's Classroom.* Prima Publishing, 1998.

Leppert, Michael and Mary. *Homeschooling Almanac 2000–2001.* Prima Publishing, 1999.

Llewellyn, Grace. *The Teenage Liberation Handbook: How to Quit School and Get a Real Life and Education.* Lowry House, 1998.

Pride, Mary. *The Big Book of Home Learning, Junior High Through College,* Fourth Edition. Home Life, 1999.

Enrichment Goodies for Teens

Aristoplay Educational Games, 800-634-7738,
    http://www.aristoplay.com
Audio-Forum Say It by Signing Video, 800-243-1234,
    http://www.audioforum.com
Blackstone Audiobooks (classics on cassette), 800-729-2665,
    http://www.blackstoneaudio.com
Castle Height Press Hands-On Science, 770-218-7998,
    http://www.flash.net/~wx3o/chp/
Creative Teaching Associates, 800-767-4282,
    http://www.mastercta.com

Fun-Ed, 626-357-4443, http://www.excellenceineducation.com

Institute for Math Mania, 800-NUMERAL,
     http://members.aol.com/rmathmania

Lewis Educational Games, 800-557-8777

Radio Shack Electronic Kits, http://www.radioshack.com

15

MOVING ON

In This Chapter

- ✦ Defining graduation
- ✦ Granting a diploma
- ✦ Preparing for college
- ✦ Off to work!
- ✦ Uncle Sam wants you!
- ✦ Technical training and apprenticeships
- ✦ Simple starting points
- ✦ Resources

$\mathcal{T}$HE TEEN YEARS seem to fly by quickly for homeschooling parents. One minute we watch our early- and middle-years children climbing trees, building forts, and exploring pond life. The next day, we turn around and find them almost grown, looking at colleges, careers, and other adult opportunities. As we approach this next phase in our journey, we realize that we have done more than choose an educational option. We have created a lifestyle of learning for both our children and ourselves.

Our learning lifestyle continues as our nearly grown teens explore the paths that will lead them into adult life. As home educators, we have had time to know our children well. We know their strengths, their goals, and their dreams. We consider their assets as we help them make decisions about their lives after homeschooling.

Homeschoolers' college and career options differ little from those of teenagers who attend the local public high school. Like their schooled peers, some homeschoolers enter the workplace, some seek vocational or technical training, and others begin college. In addition to these traditional paths, today's young people have a growing variety of new options. The number of distance-learning, internship, and apprenticeship programs increase every year. The resource section of your local public library provides excellent references to explore schools and programs that might suit your teen.

Although opportunities for our children are nearly limitless, homeschoolers do have some unique situations to deal with. Our society and institutions are set up with traditional schooling in mind. While colleges and universities generally view home education favorably, we need to consider problems that homeschooled teens may encounter in the greater community.

DEFINING GRADUATION

PICTURE A FAMILY on a long automobile trip. Mom and Dad sit in the front seat with their youngest, a four-year-old son. Two older children, sharing the backseat, occupy themselves with reading and games. The youngest fidgets. Every ten minutes, he asks, "Are we there yet?" He focuses entirely on the destination.

Parents homeschooling teenagers also focus on the end of the journey. And, although they know their children will graduate at age seventeen or eighteen, they are often unsure how to define graduation. Unlike the front-seat traveler above, parents frequently ask, "How will we know when we're done?"

Public schools make it simple. Complete X number of units over four years with passing grades, and you get a diploma. (For discussion purposes, one unit equals one credit which equals a one-year high school course. Two high school credits equal one college credit.) Some home educators copy the traditional high school format. Leanne says her teenagers will graduate when they complete 22 credits in the usual high school subjects, as well as a few credits in subjects specific to their interests. Deanna, homeschooling in Japan, writes, "We joined Clonlara [an independent-study school]. Their requirements are four units of English, ½ unit of speech, two units of math, one unit of U.S. history, ½ unit of American government, ½ unit of geography, three units of science, one unit of PE, and nine electives for a total of 22 units."

As a home educator, you can rely on similar external criteria to decide when your teenagers have completed high school. If your children enroll in an independent-study school, they will, of course, meet the requirements of that program. Alternatively, you can adopt the graduation requirements of any high school, local or not.

Some families rely on testing to tell them when their teens have reached the destination. All states offer some form of the GED (tests of General Educational Development). The GED is not difficult. Most thirteen- to fourteen-year-old homeschoolers breeze through it. A few states, like California and Pennsylvania, offer more difficult high-school-equivalency diploma tests. Query your state homeschooling organizations about high school equivalency exams if working to pass a test interests you and your teenager.

> You need not rely on typical high school requirements or test scores.

You need not rely on typical high school requirements or test scores. There are alternatives. They all begin with the radical idea that homeschooling families, not an outside institution or agency, determine when their teenagers are done. Donna explains that she will grant a diploma when both she and her son feel that he has progressed sufficiently and achieved enough to earn one. She frankly says, "It is completely subjective."

Some families consider their children graduated when they meet requirements for college admissions. Other families base completion on age. When their teens reach sixteen, seventeen, eighteen, or nineteen, they call it quits. One of the most interesting approaches I have heard to date comes from a homeschooling mother who told her teens that they will graduate when they have a self-supporting skill. Her oldest daughter became a piano tuner to work her way through college. Her son built a Web-page design business.

Still other parents envision a natural, unforced progression. Kay explains, "We are not planning on a graduation from homeschool, but a gradual transition into college instead. As our son reaches a certain level in each subject, he will continue that subject in college, until he is a full-time college student. After that, he can transfer to the college of his choice."

GRANTING A DIPLOMA

DO HOMESCHOOLERS NEED a high school diploma? The answer is, "Sometimes." Do they need a diploma from an accredited school? The experience of thousands of families indicates that that answer is, "Almost never." Every homeschooler can have a document verifying graduation from high school because—as the principals and administrators of small private schools—all homeschool parents can create their own diplomas.

HOW WE DID IT

Our homeschool group made a diploma patterned after the public school. It acknowledges that [the teenagers] have finished the requirements of the parents, then our pastor and homeschool coordinator sign it along with the parents. It is more for the child to have than for schools or anyone else.

—LISA IN FLORIDA

HOW WE DID IT

I began fretting about the diploma issue when my daughter turned thirteen. We had always homeschooled and didn't feel like we wanted an independent-study program. But I feared the day would come when my daughter might want one, so it was important to me. What a surprise when I read that there was nothing in our law that said I couldn't issue my own! Even more of a surprise was a comment from my mother, a schoolteacher for over thirty years. She volunteered to help design the diploma! All three of us, grandmother, mother, and graduate, had a wonderful time creating a personalized diploma.

—NANCY IN WASHINGTON STATE

Homeschoolers earn diplomas several ways. Some test out, earning an equivalent diploma by passing the GED or a state test like the California High School Proficiency Exam. Although a few people connect the GED to high school dropouts, others realize that many high school graduates could not score well on this comprehensive test.

Grant, a homeschooling father in Oklahoma, holds a position that requires him to interview many young people every year. He sees the GED in a different light and writes, "I cannot tell you how many people with high school diplomas I have interviewed who have a difficult time reading a job application. A diploma means only that the person sat in a classroom for a certain number of hours. On the other hand, a GED tells me that the person can read and write and that he has basic skills and knowledge. Personally, I do not depend on any piece of paper when considering someone for a job, but I sure don't attach a stigma to someone who comes in with a GED."

Some homeschooled teenagers receive diplomas from umbrella schools and independent-study programs. Yet another group of families, perhaps the majority, grant their own diplomas. In our case, we fired up the word processor, designed one, and issued the diploma. Janice plans something similar, writing, "I will order a blank diploma from HSLDA, and my husband and I will sign it." Dinah reports, "We have registered our homeschool as a private school and will grant our own diploma from Winston Christian Academy."

> If you have granted a homeschool diploma, your teenager can answer "yes" to the diploma question on most job applications.

Skeptics question whether homeschool diplomas are recognized—by colleges, employers, the military, and so on. That depends. College admissions officers rely primarily on transcripts, test scores, and letters of recommendation. Most never ask about diplomas because typical applicants, high school seniors, do not yet have them. Employers care mostly about experience. If you have granted a homeschool diploma, your teenager can answer "yes" to the diploma question on most job applications. Seldom does anyone ask to see the actual document. And, interestingly, employers never seem to phrase the question this way: "Do you have a diploma from an accredited high school?"

Historically, the military cares more about diplomas than either colleges or most employers. Military regulations pertaining to homeschoolers are in state of flux, with every recent change in favor of homeschoolers. Contact local recruiters for current information. If you know your son or daughter plans to enlist in the army, navy, marines, or air force, consider using an accredited diploma-granting independent-study program or making sure your teenager earns at least sixteen college credits during high school.

PREPARING FOR COLLEGE

MANY YOUNG PEOPLE want a college education, and homeschoolers are no exception. "We have yet to come across one college that would deny admission to an otherwise-qualified young person simply because they were homeschooled," Martha in Nebraska relates from her own experiences. Although the door is open, many colleges and universities expect homeschoolers to prove they can succeed as well as traditionally school applicants. Preparation makes the road less rocky for both teens and parents. Because colleges have individual requirements, it is impossible to provide a comprehensive guide for everyone. Instead, we will highlight common concerns.

Research It

Begin learning about college just as you learned about home education. Read, talk to experienced people, and visit colleges of interest. Many admissions officers tell us that the ninth grade year is not too early. Your teenager can contact them—either by phone or via the Internet—to obtain initial information and get on their mailing lists.

Look at schools of interest, and read their entrance requirements carefully. They will talk principally about courses of study, standardized test results, and letters of recommendation. They may mention a diploma or GED, but many copy Harvard's policy, which states that a diploma is not necessary for admission. The few colleges that require diplomas accept GEDs.

Researching colleges involves assessing location, programs of interest, educational philosophy, competitiveness, cost, and other factors. Many will also want to consider alternatives such as part-time schooling, online college, and distance learning. For a detailed treatment, see the end-of-chapter Resources, and read my book, *And What About College? How Homeschooling Leads to Admissions to the Best Colleges and Universities.*

Summarizing the Experience

Homeschoolers applying to four-year colleges need to think about how to present their experiences to admissions committees. Families report success with both transcripts and portfolios. Transcripts list courses and often credits and grades. Portfolios, on the other hand, resemble scrapbooks. They include work samples, awards, photos, programs, reading lists, and so on.

If your teens enroll in independent-study high schools, these programs provide transcripts when they issue diplomas. Kate explains, "I work with my private independent-study program. I provide information, and they produce a snazzy-looking transcript." All other homeschoolers (not associated with ISPs) write their own transcripts or compile their own portfolios.

> Keep in mind, though, that all transcripts look different. No set format exists, and your home-made transcript will not stand out like a sore thumb.

Transcripts intimidate many families because they realize that colleges scrutinize them closely. Keep in mind, though, that all transcripts look different. No set format exists, and your home-made transcript will not stand out like a sore thumb. Many home educators have found that computers generate professional-looking transcripts. Or, if you prefer, several companies serving homeschoolers sell blank transcript forms. Look at your own transcripts, and ask friends if you can see theirs for ideas. Copy a format that appeals to you. Again, for more detailed assistance, including directions for computing credits, see *And What About College?*

Some teens look better with a portfolio than a transcript. And some colleges, especially those that based their reputations on innovative programs, prefer applicants with portfolios. When in doubt, call colleges of interest and ask. Your teen may end up submitting a transcript to one college, a portfolio to another.

Of course, you can avoid explaining or reporting your high school homeschooling to anyone, and your teenager can still attend college. Karen in Washington state explains, "My teens will be going to a junior college initially, so I haven't worried about transcripts." In other cases, homeschooled teens simply take classes for one to three semesters as non-degree-seeking students at colleges of their choice. This usually requires nothing more than a willingness to pay tuition.

Some colleges also have minimum age requirements for non-degree students or require applicants to take placement exams. After non-degree-seekers accumulate one to three semesters of college credit, they apply for admission to degree programs, based solely on those credits.

Standardized Tests

Many families worry about college entrance examinations—the Scholastic Assessment Test (SAT) and the test of the American College Testing Program (ACT)—and preparatory tests like the Preliminary Scholastic Assessment Test (PSAT). Obtain registration materials for these general abilities tests from any high school counseling office or via mail or online (see Resources section for contact information). These general abilities tests help admissions officers assess applicants.

Homeschoolers seeking admission to very selective colleges like Harvard and Stanford will also take one to three SAT II Subject Tests. Subject tests assess specific areas, such as writing, biology, and American history. A few college-bound homeschoolers also take Advanced Placement (AP) and College Level Examination Program (CLEP) tests. Why bother with these extra tests? Some colleges convert good AP and CLEP scores directly into college credit.

Call colleges of interest to learn which test results they require. Then head to the library or the study guide section of a large bookstore. Various publishers market books and software for all the standardized tests. If your teenage homeschoolers have no experience taking multiple-choice tests, do help them prepare. There are many workbooks, software programs, and classes to help your teen become comfortable with the format and learn the necessary skills.

QUICK & EASY

Does your teenager test poorly? Contact FairTest, http://www.fairtest.org, for a list of colleges and universities nationwide that no longer use the SAT or ACT to make admissions decisions.

Financial Aid

Homeschoolers apply for financial aid just like everyone else—primarily through the financial aid offices of colleges, but also through community groups. Aside from Reserve Officer Training Corps (ROTC) awards, financial aid offices disburse most of the big money. Applicants for admission should always request scholarship forms when they get application materials. Students interested in receiving military funding in return for service should contact recruiters and colleges with ROTC programs for more information. Of course, don't overlook community groups as a source of funding. Certainly apply for any scholarships awarded by groups with which you and your teens are associated—from employers and churches to service organizations like Rotary and Kiwanis.

> If your teenage home-
> schoolers have no
> experience taking
> multiple-choice tests,
> do help them prepare.

The Homeschool Advantage

Preparing for college is a big job no matter where our children are educated. Although homeschoolers have special circumstances, many of us have found our children better prepared than their schooled peers. Teenagers who matured in an institutionalized setting, in school, have always had someone there to tell them what to do, how to do it, and when to do it. Going to college and assuming responsibility for these things can be a big adjustment for many young people. Homeschoolers have a big advantage in this regard. Independent young adults who have taken charge of organizing their time and researching areas of interest without teacher support do well in most college settings.

OFF TO WORK!

PERHAPS YOUR HOMESCHOOLED graduate is ready and anxious to work. Many young adults explore job options during their teens and find exactly what they want to do, at least for the time being. Some enter satisfying and rewarding occupations without any formal training. Others find positions that offer on-the-job training, where they can learn as they work. Many home-schoolers say that entering the workforce after homeschooling seems the most natural thing in the world.

Finding Work They Love

Dennis, a homeschooler, had a typical teenage gig—employment at a fast-food restaurant. He reports, "When I turned eighteen, the owner of the store where I worked offered me a management training position. My parents and I had always planned on college, but after looking at the training and experience this job offered, I decided to accept the position and delay college. After working as a store manager for two years, many career opportunities opened up. I am now assistant manager for a large supermarket, and I love what I do. I never did go to college, but I have found work I really enjoy and plan to stay with for many years to come!" We often hear snide remarks about jobs flipping burgers, but for the motivated young person, even basic jobs like this can open doors to valuable opportunities.

Some homeschoolers explore careers through volunteer positions during their teenage years. Volunteering helps young adults determine their affinity for certain occupations and working conditions. Volunteering can also provide personal references, real job skills, and important connections with people working in the field of interest.

Mary fell into her dream job. As a home-schooler, she studied and researched several hours each week at her local library. Not surprisingly, the librarian came to know her well. Mary reports, "The library was very busy one day. One of the clerks was out with the flu, and it was a school holiday. I was trying to decide if I wanted to check out a book when the librarian approached me. She told me that there were

> Many young adults explore job options during their teens and find exactly what they want to do, at least for the time being.

five or six youngsters in the children's section and asked if I would help them. I had such a good time that I began volunteering two afternoons a week. I'm still at the library, but now they pay me. I get to see the new arrivals—books—before anyone else. What more could a person want in a job?"

Donna writes about her teenager's work. "He opted out of college because he already has an experience base. If he wanted to, he could probably teach a few college courses. He will work either in the entertainment industry or with computers. He found work he loves through passion, desire, and persistence—and a bit of luck, of course!"

Carolyn's children prefer employment to college. "Our son attended college one semester, got a 4.0, and quit to work. He decided he did not need college for his job. He is now a self-employed computer artist. Our daughter did not like college, even though she earned a 4.0 also. She quit and found employment as a full-time medical assistant. She now works in computers at another company. Her eventual goal is to go into the ministry."

Certainly many occupations beckon capable, ambitious young people. Two titles can help your teen decide between working and college. *The Question Is College* by Herbert Kohl helps teenagers correlate their talents and interests with various career fields. *What Color Is Your Parachute?* by Richard Bolles also helps young adults inventory their interests and also provides specific tips for that first full-time job search.

UNCLE SAM WANTS YOU!

OF COURSE, ENLISTMENT in the army, navy, marines, or air force is not for everyone. Some young adults, however, find the training, educational, and travel opportunities irresistible. As they serve their country in uniform, they garner valuable experience along the way.

Military enlistment has been a problem for some homeschoolers because the Department of Defense uses a three-tier enlistment eligibility system. Tier I, the highest level, includes graduates of accredited high schools and those who have completed at least fifteen credit hours of college. Tier II includes correspondence school graduates, GED recipients, and homeschoolers. Tier III is reserved for high school dropouts.

Although Tier II and III individuals do enlist, Tier I people receive preference. Tier I positions comprise about 90 percent of all military positions available, leaving little for Tiers II and III. Recently, the Department of Defense has initiated a pilot program regarding homeschoolers. Each year, up to 1,250 homeschool graduates will be allowed to enlist under Tier I.

If your teenager finds military enlistment appealing, do contact local recruiters. Interview more than one, if possible. Training of recruiters is uneven, and one may give you very different information than another.

TECHNICAL TRAINING AND APPRENTICESHIPS

> Homeschoolers can begin technical training at age fifteen or sixteen and learn a self-supporting skill before most adolescents have their high school diplomas.

MIRA IN OHIO says her homeschooler thinks ahead. "Our son plans to work as an electrician beginning at age sixteen. He figures if he starts then, he will be a journeyman at age eighteen. If he attends college for electrical engineering, he will have a good base to start with and a way to earn money working part-time while in college."

Kate reports that her son thinks along similar lines. She writes, "He is taking a two-year networking course right now, but he still wants to go on and get a four-year degree in computer programming. He is hoping to use his networking skills to get a good-paying part-time job while in college."

Homeschoolers have a tremendous advantage over teens who attend school full time. They can begin technical training at age fifteen
or sixteen and learn a self-supporting skill before most adolescents
have their high school diplomas. Still other homeschoolers wait and
start technical training and apprenticeship programs after completing high school at home. Either way, homeschooling proves to be no
bar to entry into most programs. In a few instances, you may have to
document high school just as you would for college entrance. In
most cases, however, a genuine interest and willingness to work hard
will qualify your teenager for admission to programs. To research
training and apprenticeship opportunities, begin with your Yellow
Pages, the reference section of your library, and the Internet.

SIMPLE STARTING POINTS

✦   *Stop, look, and listen!* In order to help our teens explore their
options, take every opportunity to listen to what they have to say.

✦   *Discuss how you will define graduation and grant a diploma.* Are
you most comfortable with a wait-and-see approach or would you
and your teenager prefer working toward a series of stated goals?

✦   *Explore career options with your teenager, and then decide
whether college is necessary.*

RESOURCES

Books

Barron's Profiles of American Colleges. Barron's Educational Series,
    2000.
Bear, John and Mariah Bear. *Bear's Guide to Earning College Degrees
    Nontraditionally,* 13th Edition. Ten Speed Press, 1999. *Also
    College Degrees by Mail and Modem 2000.*

Bolles, Richard. *What Color Is Your Parachute?* Ten Speed Press, updated annually.

Buffer, Elizabeth, et al. *Cracking the SAT II: English Subject Tests 1999–2000.* The Princeton Review, 1999. See similar titles for other subjects.

Chany, Kalman et al. *Paying for College Without Going Broke,* 2000 Edition. Princeton Review, 1999.

Claman, Cathy. *10 Real SATs,* edited by Cathy Claman. College Entrance Examination Board, 1997.

Cohen, Cafi. *And What About College? How Homeschooling Leads to Admissions to the Best Colleges and Universities,* Second Edition. Holt Associates, 2000.

Custard, Edward T. *The Best 311 Colleges: 2000 Edition.* Princeton Review, 1999.

Davis, Helm and Joyce Lain Kennedy. *College Financial Aid for Dummies.* IDG Books, 1999.

Ehrencraft, George, et al. *Barron's How to Prepare for the ACT: American College Testing Assessment Program,* 10th Edition. Barron's, 1998.

Farenga, Patrick. *Teenage Homeschoolers: College Or Not?* Holt Associates, 1995.

Fiske, Edward. *The Fiske Guide to Colleges 2000.* Times Books, 1999.

Gurvis, Sandra. *The Off-the-Beaten-Path Job Book: You CAN Make a Living AND Have a Life!* Citadel Press, 1995.

Kohl, Herbert. *The Question Is College: On Finding and Doing Work You Love.* Heinemann, 1998.

Latimer, Jon. *Peterson's Vocational and Technical Schools and Programs.* Peterson's Guides, 1997.

McKee, Alison. *From Homeschool to College and Work: Turning Your Homeschooled Experiences into College and Job Portfolios.* Bittersweet House, P.O. Box 5211, Madison, WI 53705, 1998.

Montross, David H. *Real People, Real Jobs: Reflecting Your Interests in the World of Work.* Consulting Psychologists Press, 1995.

Peterson's Guide to Distance Learning Programs, 2000. Peterson's Guides, 1999.

Robinson, Adam and John Katzman. *Cracking the SAT and PSAT 2000* (Annual). The Princeton Review, 1999. See also the CD-ROM version.

Rockowitz, Murray, Editor. *Barron's How to Prepare for the GED: High School Equivalency Exam.* Barron's Educational Series, 1998.

Unger, Harlow G. *But What If I Don't Want to Go to College? A Guide to Success Through Alternative Education.* Checkmark Books, 1998.

Wadsworth, Gordon. *Debt-Free College.* Financial Aid Information Services, 1999.

College Admissions Testing

ACT: ACT Registration, P.O. Box 414, Iowa City, IA 52243, 319-337-1270, http://www.act.org

The Advanced Placement Program (AP), The College Board, 45 Columbus Avenue, New York, NY 10023, http://www.collegeboard.org

College Level Examination Program (CLEP): The Official Handbook for the CLEP Examinations published by The College Board, P.O. Box 6601, Princeton, NJ 08541, http://www.collegeboard.org

FairTest: National Center for Fair and Open Testing, 342 Broadway, Cambridge, MA 02139, 617-864-4810, http://www.fairtest.org

Online Advanced Placement Courses, available to home educators nationwide from the Pennsylvania Homeschoolers' Association, Pennsylvania Homeschoolers, RR2, Box 117, Kittanning, PA, http://www.pahomeschoolers.com/courses

PSAT: Given only in October through private and public high schools; contact a high school counselor's office in August or

early September for registration information; for general information, call 609-771-7300

SAT I and SAT II: College Board SAT, Princeton, NJ 08541,
609-771-7600, http://www.collegeboard.org

Web Sites

College and University Homepages,
http://www.mit.edu:8001/people/cdemello/univ.html

Colleges for Homeschoolers,
http://www.learninfreedom.org/colleges_4_hmsc.html

Financial Aid Information Page, http://www.cs.cmu.edu/afs.cs/user
/mkant/Public/FinAid/finaid.html

Princeton Review College Search & Test Information,
http://www.review.com

U.S. Department of Education Student Guide,
http://www.ed.gov/prog_info/SFA/StudentGuide

16

LOOKING BACK

$\mathcal{L}$IFELONG HOME EDUCATORS hear their children's first words and see their first steps. Later they listen to that first sentence, read aloud, rejoice when their children can multiply and divide, and proudly plaster the refrigerator with elementary artwork. As the teen years approach, homeschooling seems like a natural continuation of a learning lifestyle. For others, the journey begins during their children's adolescence. Most new homeschooling families find that the trip provides opportunities for learning and living never previously imagined. As we say in chapter 1, it doesn't matter where you begin so long as you grasp the opportunity in front of you today.

"Okay," you say, "I am ready for the trip. I will grasp the opportunity. But I still have two questions. The first concerns results: How do homeschoolers do in the Real World? Second, I need the best single recommendation you can make: If you could tell new home educators just one thing, what would it be?"

Let's begin with the second concern.

ADVICE FROM THE SURVEY RESPONDENTS

OF COURSE, WE have incorporated valuable guidance from the survey respondents throughout this book. Nevertheless, we decided to ask a subset of those respondents, parents with grown homeschoolers, to offer a few parting comments. "If you could give one piece of advice to new home educators, what would it be?" To successfully homeschool teenagers, our veteran homeschooling parents recommend organization, persistence, communication, negotiation, and—above all—getting out of the way.

> To successfully homeschool teenagers, our veteran homeschooling parents recommend organization, persistence, communication, negotiation, and—above all—getting out of the way.

Ron touts organization and keeping priorities in mind. He writes, "Structure your life in a way that frees up the most time with your children that you can. This is *not* at all easy. The expectations of others have been very difficult to reduce. They don't see this as a full-time job and often do not respect what you are trying to do. Develop a tough outer skin."

Several respondents talk about persistence. Carolyn says, "Don't quit before high school. Those were the years that our children developed their skills and interests into paying jobs or valuable learning experiences. It's easier for parents, too!" Doreen agrees, commenting, "Hang in there. We sent our boys to private school for one semester, and they begged to come back home. Listen to their needs, and don't hold on too tight. Be willing to let them go to school or wherever if need be."

Tess emphasizes the importance of communication, telling beginners, "Make sure you and your teen are on the same page. Butting heads only gives you a headache."

Donna also urges you to listen to your teenagers, writing, "Back off, don't push. Let them get 'bored.' Allow them to find themselves and their own passions. By all means, facilitate and guide. Just let them do the driving. Trust in your child. When they realize that you do trust them, they will respect you and move forward."

Annette concurs with Donna, saying to newcomers, "Take it slow and easy the first few months. Don't jump in with lots of demanding academics. If possible, allow time for decompression from the school peer-pressure-oriented mindset."

Carolyn, who has watched her grown children negotiate life on their own, says, "Don't assume you can make the horse drink just because you take them to the river. You do everything you can to lead them the way they should go, but they finally decide what to do with their lives. You may have to watch them go through tough times before they get where they are going."

RESULTS OF HOME EDUCATION

JOURNALISTS, COLLEGE ADMISSIONS officers, graduate students, and even government experts have all tried to study homeschoolers. They want to categorize us. Maybe if they could characterize families who educate their children in home-based programs, they could find a way to regulate us or sell us something or even bring us back to school. Who knows?

Despite many efforts, home educators resist neat classification. As described in the first chapter, we come from varied walks of life and many segments of society. Our backgrounds are also highly varied. In contrast to one-size-fits-all mentality of too many public schools, each homeschooling family operates differently.

For those reasons, we offer no statistics here about the results of homeschooling. What would averages, which describe no single family, mean anyway? Instead we add to the constantly accumulating anecdotal literature on the results of homeschooling. Here we provide two essays written by homeschool graduates, one from a relatively structured environment, the second a definite unschooler. Both were chosen because they exhibit the wide range of opportunities that await all homeschoolers in their communities and the larger world. After each essay, meet the parents behind the writers as they answer a few interview questions about the results of home education.

Strings and Gardens

Breana Mock lives at home. Having graduated last spring, she majors in music education at the University of North Florida. She also assists with a choir of twenty-five four-year-olds at church and teaches a Suzuki violin group class. Here is her essay for a National Merit Scholarship, in which she recounts some of her experiences.

NATIONAL MERIT SCHOLARSHIP ESSAY

Music has always been an important part of my life. During high school I have developed areas of service and leadership through interests in children and gardening, which will continue to be major parts of my life.

I began taking violin lessons at the age of four and have since shared my music with others in many ways. I have been in the community orchestra at Jacksonville University and am in the first violin section of the University of North Florida's string ensemble. When I performed on violin for 4-H's Share the Fun event, I placed first at the county and district levels and second at the state level, and was later asked to play at the 4-H

Foundation Dinner and two Volunteer Recognition Dinners. The most unusual playing job I have had was when I played for a sale at Rhode's Furniture!

I have had several wonderful opportunities to work with children. At my school I enjoyed helping teach a young children's music class by playing songs for them, telling them about the violin, and helping them develop a love of beautiful music. I would enjoy continuing this as an adult. Last year I helped a kindergarten teacher in an underprivileged school, stapling papers, and supervising children. I most enjoyed helping small groups learn the alphabet, supervising two children at a time as they tried to match the capital and lowercase letters and identify each letter.

My interest in plants came through watching and helping my grandmother in her gardens. Last summer, Jacksonville's historic Cummer Gardens needed workers, so I began volunteering for several hours each week, planting new flowers, removing old ones, mulching, and weeding. My work there has inspired me to volunteer in other public gardens, such as those in libraries and nursing homes, in the future.

Several years ago I became involved in 4-H and entered their Horticulture Identification and Judging Competition. This program helped me learn how to identify many plants by their leaves, flowers, and other distinctive parts. I placed high in both county and district events, leading my team to the state level competition two years in succession.

Last year I put my expertise to practical use when I organized a 4-H community service project and volunteered in the Cummer Gardens in Jacksonville. In my community service project I taught two 4-H clubs how to plant and take care of potted pothos vines. When the vines were large enough, we took them to local nursing homes.

I have been a leader in many areas. In 4-H I have held four different offices. I have been very active in my church youth group, and this year was elected to the Senior Senate, a committee that helps plan the group's activities. I have also been involved in Sunday School leadership. I edited my school's newsletter for two years and was editor of our yearbook for four years. I was chosen to represent my school at A Summit for Jacksonville's Future, an all-day workshop dedicated to helping young people volunteer. This opened my eyes to many new ways of giving my time to help my community.

Two years ago I won both a school-wide essay contest and a national essay contest, and, as winner of the national contest, received a scholarship to a WorldView Academy Leadership Camp. When I went to this camp, I knew no one, but was soon able to form friendships with the other campers, cooperate with them in teams, and lead others in several activities. I learned a lot, including how to be confident and friendly, even in completely foreign situations.

My career plans include music therapy and music education. Through music therapy I will be able to work with children who have learning disabilities and emotional problems. When I become certified in music education, I will be able to teach children how to make beautiful music a part of their lives. Through hard work in these areas I will make my mark on the future while helping others.

Mom Writes

Breana's mother, Kristen Mock, tells about their experience in the following interview.

Q: How many years have you homeschooled?
A: We are in our fourteenth year of homeschooling.

Q: How would you describe your relationship with your grown homeschooler today?
A: Breana and I have an excellent relationship. It continues to grow as she matures. She is separating herself from us naturally as her opportunities away from home expand, but we still enjoy spend-

ing time together and talking with each other. I believe homeschooling is a major reason why we avoided the fights and rebellion that so many families go through.

Q: What approach did you use for high school?

A: We were involved in a co-op, meeting with a group of about twenty homeschool families one day per week. A mom who loved math taught the advanced math classes, a homeschooling nurse taught the advanced science classes, a dad taught drama and art, and so on. Every child had a parent involved in some way. The classes had a cap of ten students to allow for lots of individual attention and lively discussions. I didn't have to try to learn all the subjects that Breana studied, and she was taught by people who knew and loved their subjects. She learned the discipline of deadlines and being prepared for class (having the assignment done and bringing it with her, having pencil and paper or other needed supplies, studied up and ready to take a test or discuss the material). She also learned the art of bringing up and supporting ideas in group discussions, an especially important skill for a bright but shy student. Co-op was an excellent preparation for college.

Q: What were the best parts of homeschooling your teenage children?

A: There were so many advantages. Here they are, in no particular order.

As a high school homeschooler, Breana didn't have to waste time in class and between classes, something she particularly dislikes about college.

Because she was homeschooled, Breana had the opportunity to teach some of her violin teacher's students for one month while her teacher recovered from surgery. That month of teaching solidified her choice of music education as a college major and teaching violin as her career.

She was also able to spend a year where her math consisted only of PSAT/SAT preparation. Because of that year's study, she got a National Merit scholarship from her college worth over $11,000.

Instead of being in a biology lab group with five students taking turns at dissection, she got to do all the messy work herself, sealing details in her memory that would otherwise be erased by the smell!

Individual attention is always a plus, especially in writing. I was able to read Breana's work immediately or even work with her as she wrote. Therefore, she was able to do not only a lot of writing, but a lot of good writing.

Most importantly, homeschooling during the teen years has benefited our relationship. My children are not and never have been peer-dependent. We never went through the fighting and rebellion that seems so often to be a part of growing up. We have always had peace in our home and our whole family has enjoyed being together at all the ages and stages of our children. My daughters at ages sixteen and eighteen are mature while maintaining an appropriate level of innocence.

Q: As the parent of a grown homeschooler, with the knowledge you now have, what would you do differently if you had it to do over again?

A: I would spend less time on transitive and intransitive verb grammar exercises and more time correcting the grammar in her writing and that of others. Newspapers edited by machine provide much fodder for humorous moments.

In addition, I would spend more time on American history in the elementary and middle school years learning the stories that make up history. High school textbooks run superficially through so much material that I wonder if any of it will still be with them in a few years. We used the Greenleaf series for world history. It was interesting and memorable. If we had done the same sort of study for American history our textbook work would have been greatly enriched.

I would keep using math manipulatives all the way up into the middle-school years. Math is the weak area for both of my daughters. I think longer use of hands-on math materials would have built a better foundation than textbooks alone.

Finally, I would take more time off at Christmas.

Q: What recommendations do you have for new home educators?

A: I encourage new homeschoolers to learn about homeschool choices, but not to worry about finding the one right curriculum or method. There is no one size fits all when it comes to homeschooling.

Q: What recommendations do you have for families homeschooling teenagers?

A: If your child is college bound, start preparing now. Look into school and scholarship requirements and plan accordingly. If a scholarship requires three math courses, algebra I and above, you cannot wait until the junior year to teach algebra.

Museums, Writing, and Web-Page Design

Ariel Simmons is now a third-year student at Hampshire College in Massachusetts. She is studying history and education to further her interest in designing and developing museum exhibits for young children. She began her museum career as a teenage homeschooler when she interned at the Fort Worth Museum of Science and History. Here is one of her college application essays.

Autobiographical Statement

My education began formally, with lunch boxes and purple ditto sheets. I was set free when I was seven—not just from the school building, but from the notion that I could learn only what was given me to learn, when the powers-that-were deemed I should learn it. Since then, I have been the power-that-is, designing my schooling around my own interests. (The audience is much more receptive this way.) That's not to say I've avoided subjects crucial to a well-rounded education, but if I wanted to spend six months studying the Arthurian cycle, I did; and if I wanted to race through algebra as fast as my calculator could compute, I did that, too. I did not take tests, I did not receive grades, I did not whittle down what I was studying until it fit into a traditional subject offered in high school.

Most colleges use high school transcripts to see what prospective students have been doing the last four years of their lives. Here is what I've been doing:

As a volunteer for the Fort Worth Museum of Science and History, I worked initially in areas normally staffed by teens, but quickly moved to temporary-exhibit galleries, where touring exhibits from across the nation are featured. I've been involved in several special projects, including building exhibits for area libraries. I co-chaired the advisory committee, which oversees and guides the teen volunteer program. I also served on the activity committee, where I helped put together museum tours (Fort Worth has a unique concentration of museums, with four in a one-mile radius), lock-ins, and trips to Shakespeare in the Park. Though I am now a graduate of the program, I still attend meetings as an advisor, and am a member of an alumni group that mentors younger volunteers and works to produce special programs.

> I was set free when I was seven—not just from the school building, but from the notion that I could learn only what was given me to learn, when the powers-that-were deemed I should learn it.
>
> —Ariel Simmons

I interned in the museum's history department for over two years, primarily in the archives. It's hard to describe my duties there, as they changed from week to week. During my internship, I did everything from identifying and cataloging ancient human remains to restoring a robe with a fourteen-foot train worn by the Fort Worth Rodeo Queen in 1926.

In April 1995, I joined the Science Club, one of the oldest programs at the museum. Though I was interested in science, I was probably more interested in evening the sexes. (The club was almost exclusively male when I joined. Now the male to female ratio is about 1:1, though sometimes heavy on the female side.) Science Club has been a wild, wacky experience, and I doubt I could make a short list that would describe my activities there with any accuracy. In brief, we've adventured all over

Texas, done endless projects for the preschool (the museum has the largest museum-run preschool in the country), and collected a whole lot of road kill. I am currently trip coordinator and vice president.

Which nearly sums up my work at the museum, but not quite. I am now employed there, working in KidSpace (learning through creative play) and DinoDig (a reproduction of a local dinosaur excavation where children can "discover" fossilized bones).

My second internship has been with the *Fort Worth Star-Telegram,* working for the online paper, *Star-Text.* Though one of the oldest online newspapers in the nation, it was only last year that we moved from a text-based system to a graphic one with Internet access. Since then, my primary job has been web page design and creation. When we first launched our Internet service, we offered free Web sites for every local non-profit, as a community service. Obviously we had no idea how many organizations would fit the bill. A year later we're still working hard to get everyone online. I've contributed to, or built, many high-profile Web sites for local institutions, including the Van Cliburn Foundation and several of our art museums.

It was through *Star-Text* that I began working with New Directions for News, a think-tank based in Columbia, Missouri, that organizes workshops for newspaper editors and journalists nationwide. In November 1995, I was invited to speak at one of their conferences about the future of information and technology. I was asked back in 1996, and served on an NDN panel for the American Association of Sunday and Feature Editors, speaking again about the direction news is taking and the role technology will play. The opportunity to attend these events was priceless. Attending the lectures and participating in the workshops was much more valuable than the contacts I made, though they, too, are sure to serve me throughout my life.

Meanwhile, I took theater classes (Shakespeare, Commedia dell'Arte, and Greek tragedy studies) and performed in several productions, including *A Midsummer Night's Dream* and *The*

Best Christmas Pageant Ever. My behind-the-scenes work includes properties management and soundboard operation.

I also worked with my father this summer in his furniture shop. Though I'd collaborated with him often on furniture designs and drawn many of the projected finished pieces for customers, I'd never been a part of the actual production before. My months with him were mind-expanding and helped me develop a concept of art in multiple dimensions.

. . . And everyone said I'd be missing so much if I didn't attend high school.

Mom's Turn

Ariel's mother Cerelle Woods Simmons answers questions about their homeschooling.

Q: How would describe your relationship with your grown homeschooler today?

A: I think we have an enormous degree of mutual respect, and I count Ariel as one of my dearest and closest friends. Although she attends a school that is 1,500 miles away, we stay in frequent contact through e-mail and phone calls. So far, we haven't experienced any of the expected generational rifts. Sometimes I'm tempted to take pride in a good job well done, but the truth is that she did most of the job herself.

Q: What approach did you use for high school?

A: I call ours the "ad hoc" approach to homeschooling. We do whatever we need to do to satisfy the needs of the moment. Even in our early years, we never used a packaged curriculum or gave our children grades or standardized tests. As Ariel got older, I felt comfortable with giving her even more academic freedom, so we were actually more relaxed than ever during her high school years. As always, we relied heavily on the public library. Ariel's internships and volunteer positions took her out of the house more and more during those years. By the time her "senior" year rolled around, she was too busy doing things in the real word to be spending much time on typical school activities.

Q: What were the best parts of homeschooling your teenage children?

A: I think I was always the most thrilled when our house crack-led with the electricity of the "learning field" and everyone got caught up in a contagion of enthusiasm. This is something that's hard to explain to someone who has never experienced it, but those who have will know exactly what I'm talking about. I loved it when Ariel and I could bond over some new passion—there was a feeling of kinship and togetherness and sheer joy, really. Sometimes the passion was not something we shared, but it still brought me a world of happiness to see my teenager absorbing knowledge and practicing skills without being coerced or pushed. To me, this meant we had managed to preserve in Ariel the pure drive she'd had as a toddler. I judged it a success that her urge to grow and learn hadn't been stran-gled or shut down as a result of years of academic drudgery. To me, those "crackling times" were the moments of real victory.

One such moment stands out. It was the week she reread through a bunch of Shakespeare's comedies, hunting for similarities between his comedic characters and the stock characters in Italian Commedia dell'Arte. She ended up writing a short paper on the sub-ject, even though I never assigned papers of that sort. It was just a spontaneous thing that happened.

Q: As the parent of a grown homeschooler, with the knowledge you now have, what would you do differently if you had it to do over again?

A: Believe it or not, there's not much I would change, but I do think that if I could have known then what I know now, I wouldn't have worried nearly as much as I did.

Q: What recommendations do you have for new home educators?

A: My belief is that the most essential ingredient for a happy homeschooling experience is trust. I had to learn to trust my chil-dren, and I had to earn their trust, as well. Trust is a volatile thing, hard-won and easily lost, but everything else hinges on it, in my opinion. It was only mutual trust and respect that made my relation-ship with Ariel one that could support learning.

I also found it essential for me to learn to question long-held assumptions. I had grown up with beliefs about education that I had never thought to stop and examine. Eventually, many of those beliefs had to be abandoned—or at least modified—before I could grow as a parent and teacher.

And because the relationship between parent and child is so vital, I can't overemphasize the importance of kindness. This sounds almost too obvious to make a big deal about, but I've witnessed exceptions too often to take kindness for granted. Please be kind to your children, and please insist that they be kind to you and to one another.

Q: What recommendations do you have for families homeschooling teenagers?

A: All of the above and then some. Teenagers are not a separate species. They deserve to be a part of the fabric of society, and I suspect they become alienated only when they sense rejection by family and friends. The challenge is to integrate teens into as many facets of everyday life as possible. I know it sounds like I'm ignoring the academic side of homeschooling a teen, but academics have meaning after a child's emotional needs have been met.

Few are as lucky as Cerelle. Certainly, there are things we would change if we homeschooled our teenagers again. You also may have a few regrets at the end of your journey. For most travelers, that is part of the trip. Many good memories. A few disquieting memories. But memories, any way you look at it. Too many teenagers in our society never have sufficient experiences with parents and family to generate a large memory bank. Homeschooling families create thousands of mental snapshots of a journey that their children remember forever.

What a gift.

INDEX

Latin and SAT scores, 154
of learning strengths, 61
public school emphasis
on, 68
resources, 302–303
Atlases, 197–198
Atrium Center for Classical
Studies Web site, 216
Attention Deficit Disorder
(ADD)
benefits of home-
schooling, 58
dealing with, 180–182
resources, 187–188
Attitude, homeschooling
benefits for, 61
Audiocassette tape player, 204
Auditory learners, 48,
49–50. *See also*
Learning styles
Austen, Jane, 91, 95
Autobiographical statement
(Ariel Simmons),
313–316
AWANA youth group, 241

B

Backler, Alan, 138
Bany-Winters, Lisa, 161
Barnes and Noble, 200
Barron's The Easy Way
series, 114

*Bartlett's Familiar
Quotations,* 197
Beckett, Sister Wendy, 160
Beginning homeschooling.
See Simple starting
points; Starting to
homeschool
Bible concordances and
commentaries, 199
Bible, The, 91, 95, 199
*Big Book of Home Learning,
The,* 201, 281
Big Idea Web site, 216
Biography Channel,
224–225
Biology. *See* Science
Bittinger-Keedy math
program, 114
Blame for poor grades, 275
Blindness, 182–183
Bob Jones University, 114
Bolles, Richard, 298
Book discussion groups, 57
*Book of Positive Quotations,
The,* 197
Books. *See also* Libraries;
Reading
on academically talented
teens, 186–187
accessibility of, 195
almanacs, 198
amazon.com Web site,
199, 278

atlases, 197–198
bargains, 200–201
character-building, 40, 41
college information,
301–302
on communicating with
teenagers, 41
curriculum guides, 84
dictionaries, 196, 198, 199
encouragement/
support, 83
encyclopedias, 196, 197,
199, 219
with enrichment sugges-
tions, 283
essential references,
196–198
on family heritage,
62–63
general resources, 21–23
on health and safety, 63
history textbooks,
133–135
homeschool resource
guides, 201, 206–207
on independent-living
skills, 41
on the Internet, 226–229
island resources,
192–194
on learning styles, 62
on living within a
budget, 185

Kinesthetic learners, 48, 49–50. *See also* Learning styles
Kistler, Mark, 160
Kohl, Herbert, 298
Kung Fu, 50, 163

L

Lambert, Juline, 218
Language arts, 88–109. *See also* Reading; Writing
afterschooling, 277–278
importance of, 89–90
listening, 103–104, 105, 107
reading, 90–94, 106, 277–278
references, 196–197
resources, 105–109
simple starting points, 105
speaking, 103, 105, 107, 197
writing, 94–102, 106–107, 108, 278
Large families, 183–185, 188
Latin, 154–156. *See also* Foreign languages
Latter-Day Saints Church Family History Centers, 240
Learnables, 157
Learning Channel, 224

Learning difficulties. *See* Special-needs teens
Learning styles
auditory learners, 48
building on strengths, 50, 61
fitting education to, 49–50
kinesthetic learners, 48
pointers, 48
resources, 61, 62
school-phobic learners, 48
shoring up weaknesses, 50–52
types of intelligences, 47
visual learners, 48
Learningware Reviews Web site, 218
Leaving public schooling. *See* Simple starting points; Starting to homeschool
Lee, Harper, 95
Legal issues, 71–73
changes in last twenty years, 4
dealing with obstructions, 72–73
for diplomas, 291
drivers licenses, 165–166
Home School Legal Defense Association (HSLDA), 71–72, 232, 236, 292

learning about, 71
part-time homeschooling, 270–271
resources, 84
Lewis, C. S., 80, 91, 95
Libraries, 238–240
cautions, 240
computers at, 126
historical videos from, 141
interim homeschooling activity, 20
Inter-Library Loan program, 238
local history collections, 240
as money-saving resources, 79
popularity of, 231
recommended reading lists from, 105
sales at, 200
specialized libraries and collections, 240
as starting point for homeschooling, 21
uses for homeschoolers, 239
volunteering at, 243
Lifestyle, homeschooling as, 5
Link farms (Internet) for homeschoolers, 215–216, 227

VCR. *See* Television; Videos
Video games, restricting, 32
Videos. *See also* Television
  dance and exercise, 163
  foreign language versions,
    166–167
  free, 222
  historical, 138, 140
  instructional materials,
    225–226
  as island resources,
    192–193
  literary, 94
  resources, 228–229
  science, 127
  simple starting points, 226
Visual arts, 159–161,
  168, 246
Visual learners, 48,
  49–50. *See also*
    Learning styles
Visual performing arts,
  160–161, 168
Vocabulary
  building, 97
  resources, 106–107
Volunteering. *See also*
    Community-based ac-
    tivities
  counting as "school," 243
  as hands-on civics,
    143–144
  overview, 242–243
  resources, 249

Simmons's experience, 314
  sites from survey, 242

W, X

War and Peace, 91
Weaknesses in learning,
  shoring up, 50–52
Weather, planning accord-
  ing to, 262
Web sites. *See also*
    Computers and com-
    puter skills; Internet;
    Resources
  amazon.com,
    200, 278
  college admissions
    testing, 302–303
  college information, 303
  courses online, 228
  curriculum guides, 85
  driver education, 169
  enrichment goodies,
    283–284
  Federal Resources for
    Educational Excellence
    (FREE), 188
  filtering content,
    215–216, 220–221
  foreign languages,
    166–167
  general, 23
  grammar resources, 108
  homeschooling
    catalogs, 23

  homeschooling
    periodicals, 23
  homeschool resource
    guides, 207
  independent study pro-
    grams (ISPs), 85–86
  international organiza-
    tions, 248–249
  math, 129
  message boards, 84
  military families, 188
  music education, 167
  national organiza-
    tions, 248
  PBS, 224
  physical fitness, 168
  portals for home educa-
    tion, 215–216, 227
  reading lists, 108–109
  record-keeping
    resources, 85
  religion, 169
  science, 129
  search engines, 227–228
  social studies, 149
  software, free, 228
  software reviews, 227
  stay-at-home dads, 188
  support groups, 248–249
  teens' favorites, 216
  used books and
    curriculum, 186
  visual performing arts, 168
  for volunteering, 243

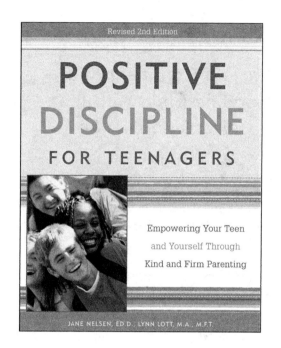

A Positive, Proven Approach to Single Parenting!

In this completely revised and updated edition of *Positive Discipline for Single Parents,* you'll learn how to succeed as a single parent in the most important job of your life: raising a child who is responsible, respectful, and resourceful.

Inside this reassuring book, you'll discover how to:

· Identify potential problems and develop skills to prevent and solve them

· Create a respectful co-parenting relationship with your former spouse

· Use non-punitive methods to help your children make wise decisions about their behavior

· How to do a job alone that was meant for two people

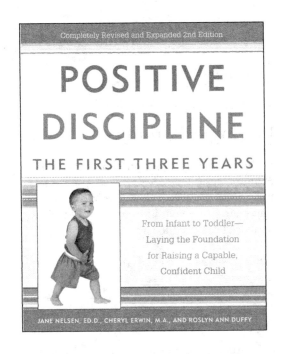